THE
OLD TESTAMENT
CASE FOR
NONVIOLENCE

Matthew Curtis Fleischer

Epic Octavius the Triumphant, LLC
Oklahoma City, OK

CONTENTS

For my God, whose will I seek.

1

VIOLENCE IN THE OLD TESTAMENT

At first glance, the situation isn't pretty. In fact, it's downright ugly.

Sometimes God himself committed mass murder, once drowning to death "every living thing on the face of the earth" except for a handful of humans (Noah and his family) and a few hundred animals (Gen. 7:21-23). Later he "struck down all the firstborn in Egypt" and produced citywide "wailing … for there was not a house without someone dead" (Exod. 12:29-30). On one occasion, he sent an angel to kill 185,000 people while they slept.[1] On another, he "rained down burning sulfur" on two whole cities (Sodom and Gomorrah), killing everyone who lived in them (Gen. 19:24-26).

At other times God helped or commanded his followers to commit mass murder. In fact, the instances in which Israel destroyed a city and all its inhabitants in direct obedience to God's instructions are too numerous to detail. The tenth chapter in the book of Joshua alone contains more than a dozen such examples.[2] Any time Israel attacked cities within the land God promised them (the "Promised Land"), they were under standing orders to "not leave alive anything that breathes. Completely destroy them … as the Lord your God has commanded you" (Deut. 20:16-17).[3] Similarly, whenever his followers conquered a city outside of the Promised Land and it tempted them to worship other gods, they were to "put to the sword all who live in that town. You must destroy it completely, both its people and its livestock" (Deut. 13:12-15). On one occasion when the Israelites themselves created an idol, God commanded each Levite man to "strap a sword to his side. Go back and forth through the camp from one end to the other, each killing his brother and friend and neighbor," which they did, executing about three thousand people (Exod. 32:27-28). On another occasion when many Israelites rebelled against him, he handed them over to his faithful followers, who slaughtered 500,000 of them.[4]

God spared no one from his violence,[5] not even women and children. In fact, on a few occasions, he explicitly commanded his followers to kill them. "Now go and attack Amalek, and utterly destroy all that they have; do not spare them, but kill both man and woman, child and infant, ox and

1

sheep, camel and donkey" (1 Sam. 15:3 NRSV). God was so jealous of his followers worshipping other gods that he commanded them to publicly stone to death any individual who merely tempted them to do so, even if it was their own wife or child.[6] In one fit of rage, God promised to grab those who disobeyed him and "smash them one against the other, parents and children alike.... I will allow no pity or mercy or compassion to keep me from destroying them" (Jer. 13:14). His prophet Hosea warned his own people of the same punishment for disobedience: "Even if they rear children, I will bereave them of every one.... Ephraim is blighted, their root is withered, they yield no fruit. Even if they bear children, I will slay their cherished offspring" (Hos. 9:12, 16). Likewise, when the people of Samaria had rebelled against him, he warned, "They will fall by the sword; their little ones will be dashed to the ground, their pregnant women ripped open" (Hos. 13:16). In a similar scene, God's prophet Isaiah announced that the "infants" of their enemy Babylon "will be dashed to pieces before their eyes; their houses will be looted and their wives violated" (Isa. 13:16). Their attackers "will have no mercy on infants, nor will they look with compassion on children" (Isa. 13:18).

God even promised he would cause his enemies, which broadly included anyone who disobeyed him, to cannibalize their own children. "I will make them eat the flesh of their sons and daughters, and they will eat one another's flesh because their enemies will press the siege so hard against them to destroy them" (Jer. 19:9). "Therefore in your midst parents will eat their children, and children will eat their parents" (Ezek. 5:10). "They will be drunk on their own blood, as with wine" (Isa. 49:26). "You will eat the flesh of your sons and the flesh of your daughters" (Lev. 26:29).

Mothers cannibalizing their own children? Seriously? Indeed, such abominations occurred. At least the prophet Jeremiah later lamented their occurrence.[7]

On the other hand, unlike Jeremiah, other Old Testament ("OT") writers rejoiced at the thought of such brutalities being inflicted upon their enemies: "Daughter Babylon, doomed to destruction, happy is the one who repays you according to what you have done to us. Happy is the one who seizes your infants and dashes them against the rocks" (Ps. 137:8-9).

Furthermore, God's violence often seemed arbitrary, petty, disproportionate, and vindictive. He killed seventy people merely for looking inside a box (the Ark of the Covenant) he had commanded them not to.[8] Later he killed a man (Uzzah) for disobediently touching it while trying to prevent it from falling to the ground.[9] He sent a bear to maul forty-two boys who had taunted the baldness of one of his prophets (Elisha).[10] He burned 102 men alive just to prove he was God.[11] After he killed a man named Er, he killed Er's brother for refusing to impregnate Er's widow.[12] After one of God's followers (Samson) picked a fight with the Philistines, God gave him the power to strike down 1,000 men with a donkey's jawbone and later the strength to collapse a building onto 3,000 people, crushing them to death.[13] On another occasion, God helped Samson satisfy a gambling debt by giving him the strength to kill and rob thirty men.[14] As one of Israel's enemies was retreating, God hurled "huge stones from heaven on them," killing more of them than the Israelites had killed by the sword (Josh. 10:9-11 NRSV). When God destroyed Sodom and Gomorrah, he also killed a good man's wife simply for disobeying his command to refrain from watching it.[15] Ever heard of Job? God allowed Satan to torture him and kill his children as part of a divine bet. Do you know why childbirth is so painful? Because one woman (Eve) disobeyed God one time thousands of years ago in the Garden of Eden.[16]

God also frequently demanded that his followers enthusiastically take part in his vengeance. He proclaimed, "A curse on anyone who is lax in doing the Lord's work! A curse on anyone who keeps their sword from bloodshed!" (Jer. 48:10). When one of his priests, Phinehas, drove a spear right through an idolater and into the stomach of another, God praised him for being "zealous for the honor of his God" (Num. 25:7-13). When the Israelites complained to their leaders that God was killing his own people, God sent a plague to kill 14,700 more.[17] After receiving direct instructions from God to inflict vengeance on the Midianites, Moses became angry when a group of army officers killed all the men but spared the women and children, taking them as plunder instead of putting them to death. In fact, he was so outraged he ordered them to fix it by killing everyone who remained except for the virgin girls, who they could save for themselves.[18]

If you doubt the strictness with which God demanded Israel's obedience, read Leviticus 26:14-39. He promises the disobedient will experience sudden terror, wasting diseases and fever, barren ground, wild animals who will rob them of their children and destroy their cattle, plagues, hunger, cannibalism, paranoid fear, defeat at the hands of their enemies, destruction of their cities, rule by those who hate them, and ultimately death. God wasn't messing around.

In addition to shedding appalling amounts of blood, God also instituted civil laws so strict and comprehensive even a control-obsessed tyrant like Stalin would have been jealous. He regulated every aspect of ancient Israelite life (e.g. work, family, health, food, drink, religion, politics, etc.) and often in excruciating detail, right down to the type and location of the fringes (called tzitzits) on their clothing. Worst of all, the punishments for violating such laws were often shockingly harsh. For example, he prescribed the death penalty for adultery, sex before marriage, homosexual intercourse between men, prostitution, incest, bestiality, rape, kidnapping, sorcery, false prophecy, idol worship, blasphemy, merely approaching the tabernacle (if you weren't a Levite), touching the foot of Mount Sinai, showing contempt for a judge or priest, laboring on the Sabbath, taking advantage of the widow or fatherless, and even attacking, cursing, or disobeying your parents.[19] Lest you think it was all empty threats, the Bible records many examples of such punishments actually being imposed, often by the humiliating and tortuous means of public stoning.

Speaking of intolerance, God also demonstrated bias against the physically disfigured and handicapped. In a passage worthy of Hitler's *Mein Kampf*, he told Moses to tell Aaron:

> For the generations to come none of your descendants who has a defect may come near to offer the food of his God. No man who has any defect may come near: no man who is blind or lame, disfigured or deformed; no man with a crippled foot or hand, or who is a hunchback or a dwarf, or who has any eye defect, or who has festering or running sores or damaged testicles.... because of his defect, he must not go near the curtain or approach the altar, and so desecrate my sanctuary. (Lev. 21:17-19, 23)

Likewise, "No one whose testicles are crushed or whose penis is cut off shall be admitted to the assembly of the Lord" (Deut. 23:1 NRSV).

To top it all off, the violence and bloodshed committed by God and those under his direction doesn't merely appear in a few atypical passages. It is pervasive. Preeminent Christian pacifist John Howard Yoder observed that "holy war is undeniable in the foundational experience of the Hebrew people."[20] He admitted that "the entire impression left with the modern reader by the narrative of the Hebrew Bible is one of violence being not merely tolerated but fostered and glorified."[21] Likewise, Catholic priest and pacifist John Dear acknowledged that "the Hebrew scriptures are replete with portrayals of a warmaking God," one "who wipes out the enemies of Israel and who is tempted to destroy Israel as well."[22] Pastor and peace theologian Jean Lasserre concurred: "Everywhere in the Old Testament human life is cheap, and the best believers have scarcely felt any scruples about shedding blood."[23] Here's how OT professor Eric Seibert describes it:

Violence appears early and often in the Old Testament. Stories of killing and kidnapping, rape and murder, war and genocide line its pages. Virtually every book of the Old Testament contains some mention of violence, and violence features very prominently in several of them. It is an integral part of many of the most well-known and beloved Bible stories: Noah and the ark, Joshua and the Battle of Jericho, David and Goliath, Daniel and the lions' den—to name just a few![24]

Summarizing biblical scholar Raymund Schwager's analysis, theologian and nonviolent activist Walter Wink writes,

> There are six hundred passages of explicit violence in the Hebrew Bible, one thousand verses where God's own violent actions of punishment are described, a hundred passages where Yahweh expressly commands others to kill people, and several stories where God irrationally kills or tries to kill for no apparent reason (for example, Exod. 4:24-26). Violence, Schwager concludes, is easily the most often mentioned activity and central theme of the Hebrew Bible.[25]

And then there's the OT's legacy of violence. Throughout modern history, people have cited the OT to justify slavery, war, colonialism, and even genocide, not to mention all the other evils associated with such endeavors, like theft, rape, and kidnapping. It played a role in rationalizing the Christian Crusades, the Catholic Inquisition, the Thirty Years' War, the Western world's enslavement of Africans, the slaughter of American Indians, apartheid in South Africa, and many other historical atrocities. In fact, both sides in every major war fought between "Christian" nations during the last few centuries invoked the OT to sanction their violence, including the American Revolution, the American Civil War, WWI, and WWII.

That may be the worst aspect of the OT's appalling legacy. Christians themselves have contributed to it as much as anyone. As clergyman and OT scholar Christopher J. H. Wright observes, "The centuries of Christendom have witnessed professing Christian leaders right up to modern times using the methods of conquest, torture, execution, horrifying punishments, and racist genocide—and claiming theological justification from their reading of the Old Testament."[26] Even many of the church's greatest theologians, like Augustine and Calvin, cited it to justify Christian violence.

Ironically, and unfortunately, the OT's violence isn't limited to the OT. Why would a good and wise God allow such widespread violence to be included in the Bible knowing it would inevitably be co-opted by fallen humans to justify further violence? After all, no one inclined towards violence or looking to justify his violence will read the OT and conclude that violence is unacceptable.

All of this has caused non-Christians to be even less gracious in their OT analyses. Atheist, scientist, and philosopher Richard Dawkins describes the God of the OT as "arguably the most unpleasant character in all fiction: jealous and proud of it; a petty, unjust, unforgiving control-freak; a vindictive, bloodthirsty ethnic cleanser; a misogynistic, homophobic, racist, infanticidal, genocidal, filicidal, pestilential, megalomaniacal, sadomasochistic, capriciously malevolent bully."[27] He adds, "And the Bible story of Joshua's destruction of Jericho and the invasion of the Promised Land in general, is morally indistinguishable from Hitler's invasion of Poland, or Saddam Hussein's massacres of the Kurds and the Marsh Arabs."[28] Similarly, Brendan Powell Smith claims Israel's God "exhibits all the worst attributes of man" and calls him "power-mad, belligerent, masochistic, petty, woefully insecure, extremely dangerous and unpredictable (and seemingly not too bright)."[29] Even American Founding Father and deist Thomas Paine weighed in:

> Whenever we read the obscene stories, the voluptuous debaucheries, the cruel and torturous executions, the unrelenting vindictiveness, with which more than half the Bible is filled, it would be more consistent that we called it the word of a demon, than the word of God. It is a history of wickedness, that has served to corrupt and brutalize mankind; and, for my part, I sincerely detest it, as I detest everything that is cruel.[30]

I could go on. We haven't even mentioned the countless number of animal sacrifices God demanded from Israel. But you get the point. The OT is full of all kinds of God-driven atrocities—holy warfare, genocide, infanticide, capital punishment, cannibalism, rape, plagues, famines, etc.—and portrays God as a dictator, torturer, executioner, and mass murderer. There's no getting around it. The God of the OT seems like a moral monster, to put it mildly.

So what are we supposed to do with all of this OT violence? There are three primary, and intertwined, issues. First, can we reconcile the violence of the OT with the nonviolence of the New Testament ("NT")? Can we honestly and rationally square God's violent OT actions and commands with Jesus' nonviolent actions and commands? Second, who are we to imitate and obey? Are we to ruthlessly and mercilessly slaughter our enemies like the OT God or are we to self-sacrificially love our enemies like Jesus? What is the Christian moral standard today—the OT, the NT, or a bit of both? Third, what is God really like? Is he more like the angry, jealous, jihadist God revealed in the OT or the patient, merciful, nonviolent God revealed in Jesus?

In the following chapters, I will answer all of those questions and more. I will explain not only how the OT's violence can be reconciled with the NT's nonviolence but also how it *supports* the NT's case for nonviolence and how the OT *itself* advocates for nonviolence. And along the way, I will vindicate God's character.

---

[1] Isa. 37:36-37; 2 Kings 19:35.

[2] See also Josh. 6:21; 8:24-29; 11:6-23; Judg. 1:17; Deut. 2:32-35; 3:3-6.

[3] See also 7:1-2.

[4] 2 Chron. 13:1-18.

[5] Whenever I refer to *violence* in this book, I mean the use of physical force against a person or his property. In other words, I mean it in the relatively narrow, traditional sense, not in the broader, more modern sense of any action that causes any type of physical or nonphysical (verbal, psychological, spiritual, structural, cultural, etc.) harm. Actions that cause the latter types of harm are often as destructive as those that cause physical harm, but they are not our concern here. We have our hands full with the former type.

[6] Deut. 13:6-15.

[7] Lam. 2:11; 2:20; 4:10.

[8] 1 Sam. 6:19.

[9] 2 Sam. 6:6-7.

[10] 2 Kings 2:23-24.

[11] 2 Kings 1:9-12.

[12] Gen. 38:6-10.

[13] Judg. 15:1-15; 16:27-30.

[14] Judg. 14:11-19.

[15] Gen. 19:24-26.

[16] Gen. 3:16.

[17] Num. 16:41-49.

[18] Num. 31:1-18.

[19] Exod. 19:12; 21:15-17; 22:18-24; 31:14-15; 35:2; Lev. 20:9-21; 21:9; 24:10-16; Num. 1:48-51; Deut. 17:12; 18:20-22; 21:18-21; 22:20-27.

[20] John Howard Yoder, *Christian Attitudes to War, Peace, and Revolution*, ed. Theodore J. Koontz and Andy Alexis-Baker (Brazos Press, 2009), 5974, Kindle.

[21] John Howard Yoder, *The Original Revolution: Essays on Christian Pacifism*, Revised Edition (Herald Press, 2012), 1129, Kindle.

[22] John Dear, *The God of Peace: Toward a Theology of Nonviolence* (Eugene, OR: Wipf and Stock Publishers, 2005), 34.

[23] Jean Lasserre, *War and the Gospel* (Eugene, OR: Wipf and Stock Publishers, 1998), 60.

[24] Eric A. Seibert, T*he Violence of Scripture: Overcoming the Old Testament's Troubling Legacy* (Fortress Press, 2012), 616, Kindle.

[25] Walter Wink, *The Powers That Be: Theology for a New Millennium* (New York: Galilee Doubleday, 1998), 84.

[26] Christopher J. H. Wright, *The God I Don't Understand: Reflections on Tough Questions of Faith* (Zondervan, 2009), 1267, Kindle.

[27] Richard Dawkins, *The God Delusion* Reprint Edition (Mariner Books, 2008), 581, Kindle.

[28] Ibid., 3884.

[29] Brendan Powell Smith, "Interview: The Brick Testament's Reverend Brendan Powell Smith!" posted June 6, 2008 at https://nexuszine.wordpress.com/2008/06/06/interview-the-brick-testaments-reverend-brendan-powell-smith/.

[30] Thomas Paine, *The Age of Reason*.

2

INCREMENTAL ETHICAL REVELATION

The key to resolving the apparent moral contradictions between the Old and New Testaments is understanding the incremental manner in which God revealed his ethical ideal to humankind. He unveiled it within a developing story, not in standalone rules meted out one verse, paragraph, or incident at a time. That's why the Bible is a narrative, not an encyclopedia or constitution. Its ethical storyline goes like this: (1) God chose a specific group of people, (2) set them apart from the rest of the world, (3) gave them a list of rules that improved their ethics beyond anything the world had ever known, (4) gradually continued revealing ethical improvements to them, and (5) then completed his ethical revelation in Jesus. God didn't just fly by earth one day and drop off a list of finalized rules. He first established a relationship with his chosen people and then progressively taught ethics to all of humanity through them.

Of course, because of our sinful nature and God's respect for free will, the ride has been anything but smooth. We've spent most of our time veering off course, sometimes even traveling backward. But with Jesus' example as our guide and the help of the Holy Spirit, we've also inched forward.

In this chapter and the following two, we will inspect a few aspects of God's incremental ethical revelation. Then in Chapter 5, we will explore why he might have chosen such a method.

Initial Improvements

To properly interpret and correctly understand the moral significance of God's OT actions, we must place them in their cultural and historical contexts. We must analyze them within the moral climate in which he acted, not the moral climate of today. We must view them from the ethical perspective of humans back then, not from our modern post-Jesus perspective, which is the product of centuries of moral progress built upon God's OT actions. Yoder explains:

The right way to read the first chapter of Genesis is not to compare it to the accounts that the geologist or the biologist gives of the origin of the earth or the species, but rather to contrast it with the other ancient Near Eastern cosmogonies in order to understand its distinctive message about God as Creator and Provider. In a similar way, the right reading of the accounts of the wars of Yahweh is not to seek in them a comparison to the wars of our time or of the Roman Empire, but to contrast them with the other religious justifications of domination in their own epoch. It is those elements of originality that will progressively define for us a specifically Israelite understanding of Yahweh as different from the gods of the nations.[1]

When we view the OT this way, we see that God's guidelines for Israel, although barbaric by our current standards, were actually an ethical improvement by the ancient world's standards. Consider the following examples, many of which ethics professor Paul Copan discusses in more detail in his excellent book *Is God a Moral Monster?: Making Sense of the Old Testament God.*

Criminal penalties. Compared to its ancient Near Eastern ("ANE") contemporaries, the Mosaic Law's punishments were notably humane. For many offenses, the Code of Hammurabi, Egyptian law, Assyrian law, and Babylonian law all required that the tongue, breast, hand, nose, or ear be cut off, while the Mosaic Law never imposed mutilation as a punishment. The penalty for perjury or libel in Egyptian law was a minimum of one hundred and a maximum of two hundred strokes while Mosaic laws never allowed over forty strokes for any crime.[2] According to Hammurabi, a negligent homebuilder whose construction collapsed and killed a child was to have his child put to death, while Israel forbade killing children for their parents' offenses—and vice versa.[3] Hammurabi also put thieves to death, while the Mosaic Law only required paying double compensation.[4] In general, the ANE legal codes required physical mutilation or even death for property crimes, while Israel emphasized monetary compensation. As Copan writes, "People mattered more than property in Israel...."[5] Likewise, although the Mosaic Law applied the death penalty liberally by our standards, it applied it much less liberally than its pagan neighbors. And in almost every situation where the death penalty was sanctioned, lesser penalties, like fines, were allowed. Maybe most impressively, Israel attempted to punish only actual wrongdoers, while its neighbors exercised no such restraint.

Even Israel's notorious "eye for an eye" legal principle was a moral advancement.[6] In an era in which punishments were often more harmful than their crimes, it functioned as a *limitation* on legal vengeance. It introduced proportionality, the notion that the punishment should fit the crime *but be no worse*. Two thousand years after Jesus, it's easy to view such a principle as promoting harsh legal retaliation, but at the time it actually limited it.

There were also other factors at play in the ANE that prevented God from being any more lenient on crime than he was in the Mosaic Law. For example, from a practical standpoint, Israel didn't have a justice system like we do today. There was no network of police officers, courts, judges, prosecutors, defense lawyers, appeals processes, and prisons. In fact, Israel didn't even have a homeland for the first few decades of its national existence. Consequently, as OT professor David T. Lamb notes, justice "needed to be simple, swift and straightforward."[7]

Likewise, from a cultural standpoint, humanity's conception of what constituted a "just" punishment was much more severe in the ANE than today. Therefore, had God been any more lenient than he was at that time, the Israelites would have likely questioned his justness. Biblical studies professor Alden L. Thompson explains:

> Thus by recognizing how much the customs of the day permeate the biblical account, we no longer need to "blame" God for perpetrating such harsh, cruel, and unjust punishments. Judged by Israel's standards, Joshua had lived by both the letter and the spirit of justice when he commanded in the name of Yahweh that Achan and his family be destroyed. For Yahweh to have commanded anything different at that point in time would have been seen as grossly unjust, and would have raised the question in the minds of thoughtful Israelites as to whether or not Yahweh really knew what justice was all about, and hence if he were really worthy to be God in Israel. But Yahweh knew his people and acted accordingly.[8]

So although many of the God-ordered legal punishments in the OT were harsh and barbaric by current standards, they were less harsh and less barbaric than anything else the world had ever seen. And, they were likely as lenient as the historical circumstances allowed.

Legal protections for the disadvantaged. OT Israel also introduced new, revolutionary legal protections for the weak and defenseless— particularly widows, orphans, and foreigners. For starters, they were not to be mistreated, taken advantage of, or otherwise oppressed.[9] But that wasn't all. They were also to be proactively defended, given justice, provided with food and clothing, and loved.[10] Foreigners were even treated as native-born and given equal treatment before the law.[11] Such respect for the lower classes was unheard-of anywhere else in the known world at that time—and is still missing from most of the world today.

The Mosaic Law also revolutionized the institution of slavery, which was practiced in every ANE culture and was an integral part of economic, political, and religious life.

Israel's slavery laws were particularly accommodating to native Israelites. Selling them into slavery was forbidden.[12] In fact, kidnapping an Israelite to treat or sell as a slave was punishable by death.[13] However, poor Israelites could sell themselves into debt slavery and convicted Israelites could be sold to make restitution for their crimes.[14] Nonetheless, all such people were to be treated as hired workers, not slaves.[15] They were much more like indentured servants than slaves. Copan compares them to modern-day employees, claiming their "servanthood wasn't much different *experientially* from paid employment in a cash economy like ours."[16] Regardless of how you label them, the Mosaic Law repeatedly declares they were not to be treated harshly.[17] They were even given a day of rest each week and allowed to celebrate certain festivals.[18] They could also be redeemed out of their debt bondage at any time.[19] And if not redeemed early, they and their families were freed after six years and sent off with a healthy supply of provisions.[20] Once redeemed or freed, they regained the full standing of free citizens.

Foreign slaves, on the other hand, were treated more like property and less like hired servants. The Israelites were allowed to buy foreigners as slaves and to enslave those they had conquered, whom they could keep for life and then bequeath to their children.[21] However, contrary to their neighbors' policies, the Israelites did not have absolute ownership of their foreign slaves. They could not do with them whatever they pleased. For example, they couldn't kill them or permanently injure them.[22] If they blinded a slave or even merely knocked out one of his teeth, they had to free the slave as compensation.[23] Before marrying a captured woman, the man had to provide her with food and shelter for a month while she mourned her parents. If she later fell out of favor with him, he was forbidden from turning her into his slave or selling her to someone else. Instead, he was required to free her.[24] Furthermore, in contrast to Hammurabi's imposition of the death penalty on those who helped runaway slaves, the Mosaic Law required that such slaves (at least those fleeing from neighboring nations) be given safe harbor and allowed to live wherever they wanted, instead of being returned to their masters.[25]

Although these slavery restrictions seem inadequate by modern standards, to say the least, they were revolutionary in their day. That any limitations were placed on the treatment of foreign slaves at all was a radical moral advancement. As Copan reports, "No other ancient near Eastern law has been found that holds a master to account for the treatment of his own slaves...."[26] So yes, under the Mosaic Law foreign slaves were callously considered property, but if you had to be a slave in the ANE, you were much better off as a slave in Israel than anywhere else.

It's true God did not immediately abolish slavery, but it's equally true he did immediately institute unprecedented legal protections for slaves, ones that ensured they were treated as more than mere property. In doing so, he humanized them. For the first time, slaves were viewed as human beings with dignity and worth, albeit as less than fully equal. Thus, the key moral lesson here is not that God is a monster for failing to immediately abolish slavery but that he is a moral hero for promptly introducing the notion that slaves are humans too, a notion that placed humankind on a trajectory that would eventually result in the abolition of slavery, even throughout the wider secular world. Contrary to Christopher Hitchens's claim that the OT is "a warrant for trafficking in humans" and "for slavery," it was actually a license for abolishing both.[27]

In every area of legislation, God introduced a new respect for human life. OT scholar and theologian Walther Eichrodt explains:

> The norms given in the Book of the Covenant (Exod. 20–23) reveal, when compared with related law-books of the ancient Near East, radical alterations in legal practice. In the evaluation of offences against property, in the treatment of slaves, in the fixing of punishment for indirect offences, and in the rejection of punishment by mutilation, the value of human life is recognized as incomparably greater than all material values. The dominant feature throughout is respect for the rights of everything that has a human face; and this means that views which predominate universally elsewhere have been abandoned, and new principles introduced into legal practice. Ultimately this is possible only because of the profundity of insight hitherto undreamt of into *the nobility of Man,* which is now recognized as a binding consideration for moral conduct.[28]

Or as Copan succinctly puts it, "persons mattered more in Israel's legislation than in other cultures in the ancient Near East."[29] Thompson concurs: "Judged by the cultures around ancient Israel, the laws given to Israel show remarkable signs of 'humanization.'"[30]

Most impressively, this unprecedented respect for human life didn't just apply to the social elite. It applied to *all* human life. Accordingly, God's laws were also groundbreaking in their treatment of women.

Women's rights. As Lamb notes, the book of Genesis paints "a highly favorable image of women—one that would have been shockingly progressive within its ancient Near Eastern context."[31] It tells us God created women in his image just as he did men.[32] Yes, he created men first, but being created first doesn't imply superiority. After all, God created animals before men but that doesn't signify their superiority. Precisely the opposite. God also gave women the same tasks, responsibilities, and dominion over creation as men.[33] And when God told Eve that her husband would rule over her, he wasn't proclaiming how he wanted life to be but instead how it would be because of the Fall (i.e. because of human sin).[34] He was acknowledging that the fallen world will generally be ruled by physical might and violence, abilities that tend to favor men, especially in the ANE.

God also instituted severe punishments for rape. Anyone who raped an engaged woman was to be put to death.[35] Anyone who raped a non-engaged virgin was to pay her father fifty shekels, marry her, and never divorce her.[36] That seems like an oppressive and sexist punishment to us today, but it wasn't back then. It actually protected women. In the ANE, unengaged and unmarried rape victims suffered a social stigma that often prevented anyone else from marrying them, thereby condemning them to a life of poverty in their patriarchal and sexist culture. Forcing the rapist to marry his victim ensured her financial security. The OT even provides us with one such example. When a woman named Tamar was about to be raped by her half-brother Amnon, she begged him not to do it, and after he had, she begged him not to send her away, telling him that doing so would be more unjust than the rape itself.[37]

God led the charge for women's rights in the ANE in other ways too. For example, Israel had many female leaders. Deborah was a political and spiritual leader,[38] Esther was a heroine who became queen of Persia and prevented the murder of her people, and Miriam, Abigail, Hannah, Sarah, and Huldah were all prophets.

Egalitarianism. God shaped Israel into the most egalitarian society the ANE, and arguably the world, had ever seen. In contrast to the socioeconomic orders present in the rest of the ANE, he structured Israel around the principle that all people are equal. It was uniquely non-hierarchical and lacked the typical social classes based on power or privilege. As biblical professor Joshua A. Berman explains it, "the Pentateuch articulates a new social, political, and religious order, the first to be founded on egalitarian ideals and the notion of a society whose core is a single, uniformly empowered, homogeneous class."[39]

God designed the economic system to advance the financial interests of the common man, not a powerful elite. He gave ownership of most of the land, which was the primary means of prosperity, to the people, not the king or some ruling class.[40] He created a society in which "all families were entitled to own land" and "everyone had equal access to gain wealth," to use theologian Preston Sprinkle's words.[41] He curbed wealth accumulation by prohibiting the sale of land in perpetuity, thereby ensuring land stayed within the family to which it was originally allotted.[42] He prohibited charging interest to fellow Israelites, which prevented members of the community from profiting from each other's misfortunes.[43] And if a debtor became insolvent, neither they nor their family could be imprisoned. As Berman notes, "The creditor's right to repayment in all of these laws is subordinated to the economic survival and the personal dignity of the debtor."[44] He also imposed predefined, reoccurring periods of debt forgiveness, land redemption, and liberation of debt slaves.[45] He even eliminated paying tributes to a political elite. Everyone was required to pay a small tithe, but the proceeds were used to help the poor and provide a meager standard of living for the priests, not enrich the king or his cronies.[46] Tithe revenue wasn't even used to fund homeland defense, let alone expand the empire. In all these ways, OT Israel's economic laws minimized exploitation and wealth disparities. Berman summarizes:

> The biblical law collections sought to erect an economic order that was not centrally controlled, and indeed recognized the legitimacy of acquiring wealth. At the same time, they sought to ensure a modicum of social equality by placing a premium on the strengthening of relationships within the covenantal community and minimizing extreme advantage. These laws sought to ensure that all would have a chance to live honorably, mitigating against the establishment of a wealthy elite, while at the same time allowing the market to operate freely otherwise.[47]

He adds, "While not seeking equality of outcome in terms of distribution of wealth as in socialist schemes, the economic laws of the Pentateuch strive to ensure that all members of the polity remain landed and economically secure...."[48]

God also prohibited the centralization of political power. He split Israel into twelve separate tribes and then dispersed political power among them, essentially implementing a system of checks and balances. For example, he divested Israel's king of most typical kingship powers and duties. The king did not control the army. God did. God determined when, how, and who to fight. The king didn't even head the pre-battle rituals. God's priests did.[49] In fact, God didn't even grant the Israelites a king until after Israel had completed its primary military campaign, the conquest of Canaan.[50] And then after allowing a king, God specifically prohibited him from accumulating military power.[51]

In reality, Israel's king had little power over any aspect of national life. He was not the head of the state religion. The priests were. He was not the source of laws. God was. He didn't adjudicate legal disputes. Independent judges appointed by the people did.[52] Nor was the king above the law. He was subject to it like everyone else.[53] As we saw earlier, he also didn't have much control over the economy. He didn't even have the discretion to cancel debts or free slaves. God's preordained timeframes governed the timing and circumstances of such things.[54] And to top it all off, the king was also explicitly prohibited from accumulating wealth.[55] All such kingship restrictions were, according to Berman and many others, "without parallel in the ancient Near East."[56]

God imposed limitations on the powers of other national leaders too. As noted earlier, judges were appointed by and answered to the people. Similarly, the priests, who possessed the immense power associated with running the state's religion, were not given any land or inheritance and instead were forced to live off the tithes offered to God, just like the powerless orphans and widows.[57] Furthermore, the prophets, who possessed no official authority, acted as a check on everyone's power by proclaiming God's truth to them.[58]

God instituted a political system of widely shared and severely restricted powers. The result was a small, limited government. As Berman puts it, "Israel defined itself, according to the Pentateuch, in opposition to the empire of oppression, Egypt, but also in opposition to the centralized, bureaucratic states that populated the land of Israel."[59]

Notice the underlying principles at work, all of which were revolutionary at the time. First, God introduced the idea that government is subject to a moral law higher than itself. He subordinated every person (the king, judges, priests, prophets, commoners, etc.) and every public institution (the monarchy, judiciary, priesthood, etc.) to his supreme law. For example, anticipating the day when Israel would request an earthly king like all other nations had, God ordered that their king write a copy of God's law for himself, study it closely every day, and learn to obey it fully.[60] In other words, he insisted on a nation of laws, not men.

Second, and maybe most radically, God introduced the idea of equality before the law. In contrast to its ANE contemporaries whose legal sanctions often varied according to social rank, the Mosaic Law held all legal citizens to the same standards.[61] Not only was everybody subject to a higher law, all citizens were subject to the *same* higher law. For example, all offenders received the same punishment regardless of their social rank and all landowners paid the same tithe regardless of their political connections. Likewise, when God instructed the king to study and obey the law, he also ordered him to refrain from thinking he was better than his fellow citizens.[62]

Third, to protect individual rights, God introduced the legal notion of due process. Before putting someone to death, the Israelites were required to thoroughly investigate the incident and obtain the testimony of at least two witnesses, who were themselves required to impose the death penalty.[63] Bearing false witness violated one of the Ten Commandments and was punishable by the same penalty the witness was trying to falsely impose.[64] Parents were not to be punished for the crimes of their children, and vice versa.[65] As discussed earlier, the disadvantaged were to be treated with dignity and given justice. Even the death penalty was rooted in respect for human dignity: "Whoever sheds the blood of a human, by a human shall that person's blood be shed; for in his own image God made humankind" (Gen. 9:6 NRSV).

These three underlying principles, unprecedented in their time, are so common now they are largely taken for granted, at least in the western world. As Berman notes, we largely have the God of the OT to thank for this. "While ancient Greece is often considered the cradle of modern political thought, the patrimony of modern political thought rests no less squarely in the texts of the Bible, particularly the Pentateuch."[66]

Of course, OT Israel wasn't perfectly egalitarian. It didn't perfectly level the economic playground, perfectly enforce equality before the law, or perfectly protect everyone's due process rights. But it did a much better job than anyone else in the biblical world ever had. All of its egalitarian-oriented laws were either entirely unprecedented in the ANE or unprecedented in the degree to which they benefited the average citizen.[67] It's not going too far to conclude that God, by how he structured OT Israel's society, introduced the notion of an egalitarian society to humanity.

Warfare policy. Even God's OT warfare policies constituted a notable ethical improvement. Here are his primary instructions regarding conduct in battle:

> When you draw near to a town to fight against it, offer it terms of peace. If it accepts your terms of peace and surrenders to you, then all the people in it shall serve you at forced labor. If it does not submit to you peacefully, but makes war against you, then you shall besiege it; and when the Lord your God gives it into your hand, you shall put all its

males to the sword. You may, however, take as your booty the women, the children, livestock, and everything else in the town, all its spoil. You may enjoy the spoil of your enemies, which the Lord your God has given you. Thus you shall treat all the towns that are very far from you, which are not towns of the nations here. But as for the towns of these peoples that the Lord your God is giving you as an inheritance, you must not let anything that breathes remain alive. You shall annihilate them—the Hittites and the Amorites, the Canaanites and the Perizzites, the Hivites and the Jebusites—just as the Lord your God has commanded.... (Deut. 20:10-17 NRSV)

At first glance, those instructions look anything but morally commendable. From our post-Jesus, twenty-first-century perspective, we read them and are shocked that God ordered (not merely allowed) fighting battles (including offensive ones of conquest) during which he *required* that all males be killed and also allowed women and children to be taken as plunder, when he didn't also demand their death.

But none of those things would have stood out as morally offensive to the inhabitants of the ANE. Instead, they would have noticed the *restrictions* on their war conduct. Instead of noticing God had ordered the extermination of enemy combatants and the occasional killing of civilians, they would have noticed the *limitations* he placed on such behavior. They would have noticed that the cities outside of the Promised Land now had to be given a reasonable opportunity to peacefully surrender. If they did, their inhabitants were to be kept alive as forced laborers, *not slaughtered.* If they did not, *only* the males were to be killed, not the women and children. In short, they would have noticed they were no longer free to do whatever they pleased in war. That was a new ethical development. And that's the moral of the story.

And those weren't the only historically unique warfare restrictions God imposed on OT Israel. He also prohibited militarism. Israel was not to stockpile weapons, develop foreign alliances, or accumulate a war chest.[68] It wasn't even allowed to keep a standing army, let alone institute ongoing professional military training. It had no war college. And when it gathered troops, anyone who had recently built a new house, planted a new vineyard, gotten engaged, or feared combat was exempted from service without condemnation.[69]

Furthermore, Israel could only wage war when God said so, and compared to the surrounding nations, he didn't say so often. He instructed them to conquer and defend the territory he had promised them and nothing more. All other warfare—imperialism, colonialism, border expansion, etc.—was forbidden.[70] They were to be content with the land he had given them. Sprinkle elaborates:

We could look at many other examples of such God-centered wars, but suffice it to say that the Israelites aren't given a green light to go out and kill whomever they want whenever they feel threatened. Nor are they ever allowed to invade a country to dismantle an unjust government or preemptively strike a nation building chariots of mass destruction. Warfare comes with stringently limited objectives. In some cases Israel never swings a sword. Such vengeance left in God's hands is one incremental step toward His ethical ideal, where all forms of violence and war would be banned.[71]

As Sprinkle notes, God also usually did most of the fighting himself, sometimes all of it. Israel was never to take matters into its own hands or rely on its own strength for victory. Whenever it did, it failed or God rebuked it, or both, as we will explore in greater detail later.

Even the OT's descriptions of Israel's military victories were unusually mild. Most of them are summed up in a single, matter-of-fact declaration that Israel took the city and "utterly destroyed every person in it," "utterly destroyed all that breathed," or "left no one remaining" (Josh. 10:28-42 NRSV). There's almost no evidence of bloodlust and almost no glorification or celebration of violence. The OT writers don't revel in the carnage by providing gory descriptions of Israel's killing. As public theologian Brian D. McLaren notes, "those who are smitten are simply smitten and buried, and that's it. They are not shamed and tortured for a while by the 'godly' before death and then shamed and tortured by God after death...."[72]

In contrast, the gruesome detail with which Israel's contemporaries jubilantly recounted their victories exuded a sadistic enjoyment of killing and torture.[73] OT professor Lawson Stone explains:

> Finally, the world of Moses, Joshua, Gideon and David was a world of unspeakable violence perpetrated by massive, well-armed professional armies. The kings of Egypt, Asia Minor and Mesopotamia gloried in their brutality and savagery. In countless inscriptions throughout the history of the ancient Near East, the great kings boasted of boring through their enemies' bodies, ripping their entrails out, galloping their horses and chariots through the gore of enemy bodies, splashing through enemy blood as if crossing a river, impaling thousands of "rebels" on stakes around conquered cities, flaying the skin off of their defeated enemies in full view of their families, and hideously mutilating the dead. And you know, almost nobody in the ancient Near East found this shocking. Rather, most thought it glorious proof that the gods had favored the king. Compared to the graphic detail, intensity, and sheer mass of these ancient descriptions, the Old Testament looks rather tame, even modest.[74]

As Sprinkle concludes, "All wars are brutal. But there's a difference between documenting that a war happened, as the Old Testament usually does, and reveling in the gruesome details to reinforce one's military might."[75]

Similarly, outside of a few exceptions, the OT never praised violence as the ideal. It never considered the mastery of violence a virtue. It never displayed those who registered the most kills as the nation's greatest heroes. Little Israelite boys did not grow up wanting to emulate their culture's great warriors.

Even the God-performed and God-commanded mass killings in the OT were comparatively restrained. They were not done in arbitrary, hasty, vengeful, or bloodthirsty ways. They were all exceptional cases that contained three moderating elements. First, they were *responses* to extreme immorality and wrongdoing. Second, they were all preceded by plenty of time and opportunity to repent. And third, God always spared everyone who did repent.

For example, God destroyed the earth with a flood (1) because of human wickedness (2) but only after giving humankind plenty of time to repent in response to Noah's preaching during the ark-building process, and (3) he spared those who repented, which ended up being only Noah and his family.[76] We find the same pattern in the destruction of Sodom and Gomorrah, the killing of the Egyptian firstborn, the conquest of the Promised Land, and the destruction of the Amalekites.[77] As such, even the violent mass killings were a step in the right ethical direction.

So yes, God's OT warfare policies violate our modern moral sensibilities and seem grossly inadequate by today's standards, but they represented a radical moral advancement in their day. For the first time in human history, God ordered the demilitarization of a society, limited warfare to specific circumstances and objectives, imposed restrictions on conduct during battle and after victory, and refused to glorify killing. When God met Israel, it was entangled in the unending cycle of violence, but by the time he was done with it, it was on the path towards nonviolence and peace, albeit a long winding one.

In summary, although God's OT laws and actions were imperfect, incomplete, fell far short of creation ideals, and left much to be desired by current standards, they constituted a significant ethical improvement at the time. They were, of course, not entirely different from those of the surrounding pagan cultures. "But at key points," Copan observes, "whopping differences exist between the Mosaic law and other ancient Near Eastern codes. The Sinai legislation presents genuinely remarkable, previously unheard-of legal and moral advances."[78] When God directly intervened, he immediately dialed back Israel's violence and killing, pointed it in a different direction, and built humanity a bridge to a nonviolent future. Therefore, although OT Israel doesn't represent the ethical ideal, it represents the necessary first step toward it. As the author of Hebrews later observed, its laws were "a shadow of the good things to come" (Heb. 10:1 NRSV).

Early Moral Concessions

The moral concessions God made in the OT and later revoked in the NT are another example of God's incremental revelation. Because of humanity's moral immaturity, he temporarily allowed some less-than-ideal ethical practices. Because of primitive human hardheartedness, he permitted behavior in the early stages of his ethical revelation that he no longer tolerates. As Paul wrote in the NT, "In the past God overlooked such ignorance, but now he commands all people everywhere to repent" (Acts 17:30).[79] Nonetheless, the accommodations he made were still ethical improvements. Let's take a look at a few examples.

Divorce is the most obvious. Throughout the entire Bible, God praises marriage as a sacred covenant meant to last a lifetime. Consequently, he despises divorce. In fact, in the last book of the OT, he proclaimed, "I hate divorce" (Mal. 2:16 NRSV). Nonetheless, he permitted it under the Law of Moses, but only with groundbreaking protections for women, who were particularly vulnerable to poverty and shaming in ancient Israel's patriarchal society.[80] Then, in the NT, Jesus proclaimed:

> It has been said, "Anyone who divorces his wife must give her a certificate of divorce." But I tell you that anyone who divorces his wife, except for sexual immorality, makes her the victim of adultery, and anyone who marries a divorced woman commits adultery. (Matt. 5:31-32)

Shortly thereafter, the Pharisees, who legalistically observed the OT law, confronted Jesus about the inconsistency between his and Moses' divorce policies. The entire interaction is worth quoting:

> Some Pharisees came to him, and to test him they asked, "Is it lawful for a man to divorce his wife for any cause?" He answered, "Have you not read that the one who made them at the beginning 'made them male and female,' and said, 'For this reason a man shall leave his father and mother and be joined to his wife, and the two shall become one flesh'? So they are no longer two, but one flesh. Therefore what God has joined together, let no one separate." They said to him, "Why then did Moses

command us to give a certificate of dismissal and to divorce her?" He said to them, "It was *because you were so hard-hearted* that Moses allowed you to divorce your wives, but from the beginning it was not so. And I say to you, whoever divorces his wife, except for unchastity, and marries another commits adultery." (Matt. 19:3-9 NRSV)[81]

In other words, Jesus revoked God's earlier ethical concession (divorce on demand), which he explained was only permitted because of human hardheartedness, and then instituted God's ideal ethical standard (no divorce except in cases of adultery).

Polygamy is another good example. Since creation, God's ethical ideal has been monogamy.[82] Nonetheless, in the OT, he tolerated the already-widespread practice, while also placing new ethical restrictions on it.[83] But Jesus reiterated the creation ideal of monogamy, which his early followers carried forward, turning it into what has been official church policy for the last two thousand years.[84]

We can also view many of the initial ethical improvements we discussed earlier through a concession lens. Consider slavery. Because it was a commonly accepted part of ANE life by the time God began directly intervening in human history, he didn't immediately abolish it but did immediately improve it, primarily by requiring a more humane treatment of slaves. Then, in the NT, Jesus began his public ministry by announcing that God had sent him "to proclaim freedom for the prisoners and … to set the oppressed free" (Luke 4:18). Now, that's not an explicit condemnation of slavery per se, but it is an implicit one. Plus, Jesus introduced additional anti-slavery principles (e.g. the equality of all humans before God, the golden rule, the command not to "lord it over" others, etc.) that would eventually lead his followers to eradicate it from the Western World.

In fact, Jesus' disciples immediately began that process. They rejected the inferiority of slaves by declaring one's status (slave or free) irrelevant because all are equal before God.[85] They instructed slave masters to "not threaten them," to provide them "with what is right and fair," and to generally treat them like they wanted to be treated by their master (God) (Eph. 6:5-9; Col. 4:1). After announcing he would not *order* his friend Philemon to do what he ought to do in Christ, Paul *asked* him to treat his slave Onesimus as a brother, not a slave.[86] That insinuates Paul believed Christ was antislavery. Paul also indirectly condemned slavery in a letter to Timothy when he included "slave traders" in a list of the "godless and sinful" (1 Tim. 1:9-10 NRSV).

Furthermore, instead of treating slaves as mere helpless victims who had nothing to contribute to the kingdom movement, the apostles encouraged them to use their circumstances to glorify God as best they could by performing their duties with sincerity, honesty, and diligence, which is the same thing we are all called to do.[87] The apostles had so much respect for the equal dignity of slaves they treated them as equally responsible humans with an equally respectable and important role to play in doing God's work. That's why Paul, who encouraged slaves to gain their freedom whenever possible, also warned them not to turn the pursuit of such freedom into a false idol.[88] All of us, even slaves, have a higher calling than merely improving our lot in life. Contrary to what some biblical interpreters have concluded, such instructions didn't condone slavery. They highlighted that all of us, even slaves, are responsible for advancing God's kingdom on earth by sacrificially loving our enemies and returning good for evil, regardless of the circumstances in which we find ourselves.

It's true there is no explicit call for abolishment of slavery in the NT, as biblical opponents like to note, but it's equally true there is palpable progress in that direction. Enough anti-slavery ideas are communicated to lead attentive readers to that logical conclusion. We must never forget that before Jesus no group had seriously questioned the institution of slavery and that after Jesus his followers eventually abolished it.

We must also not forget the historical context within which the NT actors were operating. At that point in the kingdom movement, Jesus and the apostles had more on their minds than simply abolishing one of secular society's many evil institutions. They believed abolishment needed to occur, but they knew they first had to get the church off the ground. They had to get it up and running in the right direction so it could begin moving society towards eradicating evils such as slavery. They also knew they needed to abolish slavery by God's means (i.e. by nonviolence), which required social capital they did not yet possess. Any violent attempt at abolition would have been a rejection of the essence of the kingdom Jesus came to establish and would have certainly become just another historically insignificant, zealot-like rebellion. Under the circumstances, Jesus and the apostles did the most effective thing they could have for the abolition movement: sow the ideological principles necessary to effectuate it. In doing so, they revoked God's earlier slavery concession.

Similarly, we can also view much of the violence and war in the OT as a concession. "As with polygamy, slavery, and divorce," Sprinkle explains, "the law of Moses *accommodates to* and offers *moral improvements upon* ancient Near Eastern warfare policy and violence."[89]

God temporarily permitted (and occasionally even commanded) such immorality but only in limited circumstances and for limited purposes, as detailed earlier. Then Jesus later revoked all such concessions by doing things like refusing to use violence himself, instructing his disciples to turn the other cheek, and proclaiming that God's followers do not fight.

In light of everything just discussed, we must not lose sight of OT professor Bruce Birch's insightful warning:

> Any treatment of the Hebrew Bible with regard to ethics, especially as an ethical resource to contemporary communities, must acknowledge the impediment created by the simple fact that these texts are rooted in a cultural context utterly unlike our own, with moral presuppositions and categories that are alien and in some cases repugnant to our modern sensibilities.[90]

Preparing the Way for Jesus

Although all of God's initial moral improvements and temporary concessions were good in their own right, as we have just seen, they weren't the end goal. They pointed humanity in the proper direction, but they didn't specify the journey's end. They advanced humanity down the right road, but they didn't drop it off at the final destination. They were only the beginning of God's ethical revelation, not its completion. Simply put, their role was to lay the ethical groundwork for the life and teachings of Jesus. Or to paraphrase Paul, the OT law was but a tutor to prepare Israel and the wider world for Jesus' arrival.[91]

At least that's how Jesus himself saw things. He referred to the OT as "Scriptures that testify about me" (John 5:39), proclaimed that Moses "wrote about me" (John 5:46 NRSV), and explained to his disciples "what was said in all the Scriptures concerning himself" (Luke 24:27), including what was written about him "in the law of Moses, the prophets, and the psalms" (Luke 24:44 NRSV).

---

[1] John Howard Yoder, *The War of the Lamb: The Ethics of Nonviolence and Peacemaking*, ed. Glen Stassen, Mark Thiessen Nation, and Matt Hamsher (Brazos Press, 2009), 1358, Kindle.

[2] Deut. 25:1-3.

[3] Deut. 24:16.

[4] Exod. 22:4.

[5] Paul Copan, *Is God a Moral Monster?: Making Sense of the Old Testament God* (Baker Books, 2011), 1797, Kindle.

[6] Exod. 21:24; Lev. 24:19-20; Deut. 19:21.

[7] David T. Lamb, *God Behaving Badly: Is the God of the Old Testament Angry, Sexist and Racist?* (IVP Books, 2011), 1011, Kindle.

[8] Alden L. Thompson, *Who's Afraid of the Old Testament God?*, 5th Edition (Energion Publications, 2011), 1671, Kindle.

[9] Exod. 22:21-22; 23:9; Deut. 24:14-17; Jer. 7:5-7; 22:3; Isa. 10:1-2; Ezek. 22:7, 29; Zech. 7:10; Mal. 3:5.

[10] Deut. 10:18-19; 14:28-29; 24:19-21; 26:12-13; 27:19; Lev. 19:9-10; 23:22; Isa. 1:17; Ps. 146:7-9.

[11] Lev. 19:33-34; 24:22; Num. 9:14; 15:15-16.

[12] Lev. 25:42.

[13] Deut. 24:7; Exod. 21:16.

[14] Lev. 25:39; Exod. 22:3.

[15] Lev. 25:40, 53.

[16] Copan, *Is God a Moral Monster?*, 2572.

[17] Lev. 25:43, 46, 53.

[18] Exod. 20:8-10; Deut. 16:13-14.

[19] Lev. 25:47-55.

[20] Deut. 15:12-18; Exod. 21:2-11; Jer. 34:12-14; Lev. 25:40-41, 54.

[21] Lev. 25:44-46; Deut. 20:10-14; Lev. 25:44-46.

[22] Exod. 21:20-21.

[23] Exod. 21:26-27.

[24] Deut. 21:10-14.

[25] Deut. 23:15-16.

[26] Copan, *Is God a Moral Monster?*, 2782.

[27] Christopher Hitchens, *God is Not Great: How Religion Poisons Everything* (New York: Twelve, 2007), 102.

[28] Walther Eichrodt, *Theology of the Old Testament* (Philadelphia: Westminster John Knox Press, 1967), 321.

[29] Copan, *Is God a Moral Monster?*, 1784.

[30] Thompson, *Who's Afraid of the Old Testament God?*, 413.

[31] Lamb, *God Behaving Badly*, 497.

[32] Gen. 1:27.

[33] Gen. 1:28-31.

[34] Gen. 3:16.

[35] Deut. 22:25-27.

[36] Deut. 22:28-29.

[37] 2 Sam. 13:1-20.

[38] Judg. 4:4.

[39] Joshua A. Berman, *Created Equal: How the Bible Broke with Ancient Political Thought* (Oxford University Press, 2008), 182, Kindle.

[40] Lev. 25:32-34.

[41] Preston Sprinkle, *Fight: A Christian Case for Non-Violence* (David C. Cook, 2013), 645, Kindle.

[42] Lev. 25:25-28.

[43] Exod. 22:25; Lev. 25:35-37; Deut. 23:19-20. Of course, we must bear in mind that people in the ANE borrowed money to survive, to obtain life's basic necessities, not to buy nonessential consumer goods like most of us do today.

[44] Berman, *Created Equal*, 2084.
[45] Deut. 15:1-18; Lev. 25:8-54; Exod. 21:1-6.
[46] Deut. 14:22-29; 26:12; Num. 18:8-32.
[47] Berman, *Created Equal*, 2310.
[48] Ibid., 3501.
[49] Deut. 20:2-4.
[50] Deut. 17:14-15.
[51] Deut. 17:16-17.
[52] Deut. 16:18-19; 17:8-13.
[53] Deut. 17:18-20.
[54] Deut. 15:1-18; Lev. 25:8-54; Exod. 21:1-6.
[55] Deut. 17:17.
[56] Berman, *Created Equal*, 1122.
[57] Deut. 12:12; 14:27-29; 18:1.
[58] Duet. 18:18.
[59] Berman, *Created Equal*, 1860.
[60] Deut. 17:14-20.
[61] Lev. 19:15; Deut. 17:18-20.
[62] Deut. 17:20.
[63] Deut. 13:12-15; 17:2-4, 6-7; 19:15.
[64] Exod. 20:16; Deut. 19:16-19.
[65] Deut. 24:16.
[66] Berman, *Created Equal*, 108.
[67] See generally Berman, *Created Equal*.
[68] Deut. 17:16-20.
[69] Deut. 20:5-9.
[70] Deut. 2:2-6, 9, 19.
[71] Sprinkle, *Fight*, 747.
[72] Brian D. McLaren, *A New Kind of Christianity: Ten Questions That Are Transforming the Faith*, Reprint Edition (HarperCollins, 2010), 1713, Kindle.
[73] See generally Fight and Is God a Moral Monster?
[74] Lawson Stone, "7 Keys to Understanding Violence in the Old Testament" posted July 22, 2013 at http://www.seedbed.com/violence-in-the-old-testament-starting-points/.
[75] Sprinkle, *Fight*, 809.
[76] Gen. 6 and 7; 1 Pet. 3:20.
[77] Gen. 18 and 19; 1 Pet. 3:9; 2 Pet. 2:7; Exod. 7-12; Deut. 9 and 18; Lev. 18:24-25; Josh. 2; 1 Sam. 15:2-3; Exod. 17.
[78] Copan, *Is God a Moral Monster?*, 1690.
[79] See also Rom. 3:25.
[80] Deut. 24:1-4; 22:13-19.
[81] See also Mark 10:2-12.
[82] Gen. 2:18-24.
[83] Exod. 21:10; Deut. 17:17, 21:15-17.
[84] Matt. 19:3-6; Mark 10:7-8; 1 Tim. 3:2, 12; Tit. 1:6; Eph. 5:22-33; 1 Cor. 6:16.
[85] Gal. 3:28; Col. 3:11.

[86] Philem. 1:12-16.

[87] Col. 3:22-25; Tit. 2:9-10; 1 Tim. 6:2; 1 Pet. 2:18-21; Eph. 6:5-9; 1 Cor. 7:20-24.

[88] 1 Cor. 7:20-24.

[89] Sprinkle, *Fight*, 547.

[90] Bruce Birch, "Old Testament Ethics," in *The Blackwell Companion to the Hebrew Bible*, ed. Leo G. Purdue (Oxford: Blackwell, 2001), 297.

[91] Gal. 3:23-25.

3

FULFILLMENT IN JESUS

God's incremental ethical revelation reached its climax in the life and teachings of Jesus. In the Sermon on the Mount, he proclaimed:

> [17]"Do not think that I have come to abolish the Law or the Prophets; I have not come to abolish them but to fulfill them. [18]For truly I tell you, until heaven and earth disappear, not the smallest letter, not the least stroke of a pen, will by any means disappear from the Law until everything is accomplished. [19]Therefore anyone who sets aside one of the least of these commands and teaches others accordingly will be called least in the kingdom of heaven, but whoever practices and teaches these commands will be called great in the kingdom of heaven. [20]For I tell you that unless your righteousness surpasses that of the Pharisees and the teachers of the law, you will certainly not enter the kingdom of heaven. (Matt. 5:17-20)

What Jesus meant by "fulfill" is key. He did not mean he came to discard the law or to render it obsolete. He did not mean he came to meet its requirements or to satisfy its demands so we no longer have to. He did not mean he came to appease God's need for perfect obedience, thereby releasing us from the need to obey. Fulfillment in those senses would have essentially been abolishment, which Jesus explicitly rejected.

The next two sentences out of Jesus' mouth (vv. 18-19) confirm this. In them, he (1) declared that not even "the smallest letter" of the law will cease to apply until Jesus returns to earth to complete God's kingdom (i.e. until "everything is accomplished") and (2) then warned everyone against setting aside even just "one of the least of these commands."[1]

Likewise, Jesus sprinkled the rest of the sermon with similar admonitions to obey everything he taught. "Be perfect, therefore, as your heavenly Father is perfect" (Matt. 5:48 NRSV). "Not everyone who says to me, 'Lord, Lord,' will enter the kingdom of heaven, but only the one who does the will of my Father in heaven" (Matt. 7:21 NRSV). Jesus even concluded the sermon with one: "And everyone who hears these words of mine and does not act on them will be like a foolish man who built his house on sand" (Matt. 7:26 NRSV).

So what did Jesus mean when he said he came to fulfill the law? He meant he came to finalize God's ethical revelation. He came to complete it, to bring it into full bloom. He came to provide us with God's perfect, eternal, and universally applicable moral code. He came to reveal God's ethical ideal, to show us exactly what God wants from every human. He came to demonstrate how to perfectly do God's will, how to flawlessly advance his kingdom. Instead of coming to excuse us from obedience, he came to show us how to perfectly obey. As the writer of Hebrews later described him, Jesus was the "perfecter of faith" (Heb. 12:2). Or as Paul put it, "Christ is the culmination of the law" (Rom. 10:4). For as both of them explained, the law was only "a shadow of the good things" to come, "not the realities themselves" (Heb. 10:1). "The reality … is found in Christ" (Col. 2:17). No more concessions. No more accommodations. No more gradual steps forward. This is it. The OT introduced biblical ethics and then Jesus perfected them.

Everything Jesus proceeded to preach made this clear. First, in verse 20 (quoted earlier), he told his followers to be more moral than the Pharisees. The Pharisees were righteous according to the OT law. They followed it meticulously. But Jesus said we must do better. In doing so, he wasn't saying we should follow the OT law better than the Pharisees did. That's impossible. They followed it to the letter, sometimes beyond. Instead, he was saying that following the OT law, even perfectly, isn't good enough. He was taking Christian ethics to the next level. He was proclaiming that we must follower a higher, more complete, more perfect law—his law.

Jesus then explained how to be more righteous than the Pharisees when six times he repeated the formula, "You have heard that it was said … But I tell you …":

1. You have heard that it was said to the people long ago, "You shall not murder, and anyone who murders will be subject to judgment." But I tell you that anyone who is angry with a brother or sister will be subject to judgment. (Matt. 5:21-22)

2. You have heard that it was said, "You shall not commit adultery." But I tell you that anyone who looks at a woman lustfully has already committed adultery with her in his heart. (Matt. 5:27-28)

3. It has been said, "Anyone who divorces his wife must give her a certificate of divorce." But I tell you that anyone who divorces his wife, except for sexual immorality, makes her the victim of adultery, and anyone who marries a divorced woman commits adultery. (Matt. 5:31-32)

4. Again, you have heard that it was said to the people long ago, "Do not break your oath, but fulfill to the Lord the vows you have made." But I tell you, do not swear an oath at all. (Matt. 5:33-34)

5. You have heard that it was said, "Eye for eye, and tooth for tooth." But I tell you, do not resist an evil person. (Matt. 5:38-39)

6. You have heard that it was said, "Love your neighbor and hate your enemy." But I tell you, love your enemies and pray for those who persecute you, that you may be children of your Father in heaven. (Matt. 5:43-45)

In these six antitheses, Jesus compared his teaching to that of the OT and highlighted the difference. But he wasn't transgressing the OT law. He was transcending it. He wasn't abolishing it. He was elevating it. He wasn't diminishing it. He was bringing it to its fullest expression. He wasn't violating the letter of the law. He was going beyond it. As NT professor Richard B. Hays puts it, "the teaching of Jesus constitutes an intensification—rather than an abrogation—of the requirements of the Law. The Law prohibits murder, but Jesus forbids even anger; the Law prohibits adultery, but Jesus forbids even lust."[2] He elaborates:

Matthew is concerned to affirm that this countercultural *polis* must be understood as a fulfillment rather than a negation of the Torah (5:17–20). The righteousness to which Jesus' followers are called intensifies and exceeds the most rigorous standards of Israel's most scrupulous interpreters of the Law. Thus, the six antitheses (5:21–48) raise the ante by radicalizing the demands of the Law. They sketch the identity of the new community that Jesus is bringing into being. That sketch can hardly be mistaken for a comprehensive new legal code; rather, it suggests by way of a few examples the character of this new community in which anger is overcome through reconciliation (5:21–26), lust is kept under discipline (5:27–30), marriage is honored through lifelong fidelity (5:31–32), language is simple and honest (5:33–37), retaliation is renounced (5:38–42), and enemy-love replaces hate (5:43–48). Even though this portrayal of the community of disciples is new and revelatory, it is at the same time a fulfillment of the deepest truth of the Law and the prophets (cf. also Matt. 22:34–40).[3]

Let's see how this played out by taking a closer look at the last two antitheses. The fifth antithesis may be the most radical. Here's the full text:

You have heard that it was said, "Eye for eye, and tooth for tooth." But I tell you, do not resist an evil person. If anyone slaps you on the right cheek, turn to them the other cheek also. And if anyone wants to sue you and take your shirt, hand over your coat as well. If anyone forces you to go one mile, go with them two miles. Give to the one who asks you, and do not turn away from the one who wants to borrow from you. (Matt. 5:38-42)

Here, Jesus took a fundamental component of the OT law (an eye for an eye), which was a moral advancement in its time, and moved far beyond it. He took retributive justice, which was already a step above vengeance, and transformed it into restorative justice. He took a good civil law, one that promoted peace by limiting retribution, and turned it into one that promoted even greater peace by self-sacrificially eschewing retribution. Whereas the Mosaic Law restricted retaliation, Jesus forbade it and demanded self-sacrifice. Whereas the *lex talionis* said, "Show no pity: life for life, eye for eye, tooth for tooth, hand for hand, foot for foot" (Deut. 19:21), Jesus said, "Do not resist an evil person" and instead turn the cheek, give more than is demanded, and lend without expecting repayment. Jesus essentially said, "Instead of pursuing justice for yourself, just love."

In the sixth antithesis, Jesus declared that all of his teachings (including the five prior antitheses) apply to everyone, even our enemies. Here's the full text:

> You have heard that it was said, "Love your neighbor and hate your enemy." But I tell you, love your enemies and pray for those who persecute you, that you may be children of your Father in heaven. He causes his sun to rise on the evil and the good, and sends rain on the righteous and the unrighteous. If you love those who love you, what reward will you get? Are not even the tax collectors doing that? And if you greet only your own people, what are you doing more than others? Do not even pagans do that? Be perfect, therefore, as your heavenly Father is perfect. (Matt. 5:43-48)

There was no OT law that commanded God's followers to hate their enemies, but there was also no OT law that prohibited them from doing so. On the other hand, there was an explicit OT command to love your neighbor, but the context implied that "your neighbor" was your fellow Israelites.[4] Therefore, before Jesus' arrival, the prevailing sentiment was that it was okay to hate your enemy as long as you loved your fellow countrymen. In fact, there was even a sense in which hating non-Israelites was an aspect of loving your fellow Israelites.[5] We feel the same pressure today. To hate another person's enemies is seen as loving loyalty, while refusing to hate them is seen as unloving betrayal.

Nevertheless, in the midst of that prevailing attitude, Jesus proclaimed that his followers are (1) to hate no one, not even their enemies, and (2) to love everyone, not only their fellow countrymen or those on "their side." After all, anybody can love their own kind and hate those who are different. Even the Hitlers of the world do that. God calls Christians to a higher, more perfect ethic: enemy love.

In a later encounter with the Pharisees, Jesus summarized his fulfillment of the law in one word: love. Here's the interaction as recorded in Matthew 22:35-40:

> One of them, an expert in the law, tested him with this question: "Teacher, which is the greatest commandment in the Law?"
>
> Jesus replied: "'Love the Lord your God with all your heart and with all your soul and with all your mind.' This is the first and greatest commandment. And the second is like it: 'Love your neighbor as yourself.' *All the Law and the Prophets hang on these two commandments.*"[6]

In other words, Jesus' perfection of the law boils down to a single command: to love.[7] That's it. All of Jesus' other commands simply clarified how to do so. And all the OT laws and prophecies simply paved the way for that perfect, complete, eternal, universally applicable law.

Paul reiterated this point throughout his NT writings. To the church in Galatia, he wrote: "For the entire law is fulfilled in keeping this one command: 'Love your neighbor as yourself'" (Gal. 5:14). To the church in Rome, he wrote:

> Let no debt remain outstanding, except the continuing debt to love one another, for whoever loves others has fulfilled the law. The commandments, "You shall not commit adultery," "You shall not murder," "You shall not steal," "You shall not covet," and whatever other command there may be, are summed up in this one command: "Love your neighbor as yourself." Love does no harm to a neighbor. Therefore love is the fulfillment of the law. (Rom. 13:8-10)

To the church in Colossae, he wrote:

> Therefore, as God's chosen people, holy and dearly loved, clothe yourselves with compassion, kindness, humility, gentleness and patience. Bear with each other and forgive one another if any of you has a grievance against someone. Forgive as the Lord forgave you. And over all these virtues put on love, which binds them all together in perfect unity. (Col. 3:12-14)

James gave his Jewish Christian readers a similar instruction: "If you really fulfill the royal law according to the Scripture, 'You shall love your neighbor as yourself,' you are doing well" (Jas. 2:8).

Nationalism

Jesus' perfection of the OT law wasn't limited to the Sermon on the Mount or his commands to love. It pervaded all of his teachings, although not always so explicitly. For now, we need only explore one more example, an often overlooked but highly significant one: Jesus' reorganization of God's followers from a nation into a church.

Since creation, God has always wanted his followers to be distinct from all other earthly organizations. Initially, he formed them into the uniquely theocratic, demilitarized, morally advanced nation of Israel. Unfortunately, they couldn't maintain their distinctiveness for long. They got tired of being "different" and asked God for a king "such as all the other nations have" (1 Sam. 8:5). In their sin, they wanted a typical earthly kingdom led by a typical warrior-king. God interpreted their request as a rejection of his leadership and warned that a king would exploit them for his own purposes, particularly his own militaristic ones. Nonetheless, they persisted, reiterating their request to have a king so they could "be like all the other nations, with a king to lead us and to go out before us and fight our battles" (8:20). So God, fully aware that nationalism did not coincide with his will and would only get his people into trouble, accommodated them.

God also allowed their nationalism to run its naturally destructive course and eventually Israel's enemies overcame it. For the next seven centuries, they found themselves entangled in typical nationalistic struggles—political exile, a return home, rebuilding efforts, struggles for independence, and additional defeats. When Jesus arrived, Israel was under Roman occupation and struggling to keep its national identity alive. It was this nationalistic context that shaped the Israelites' expectations for God's promised Messiah. Most expected him to restore their national sovereignty and elevate it to previously unseen levels of political domination.

But when the Messiah arrived, he would have none of it. Jesus didn't gather God's followers and take back territory, militarily or otherwise. Instead, he repeatedly declined to adopt the agenda of Jewish nationalism. He unequivocally rejected typical kingship, declining the devil's offer of control over all the kingdoms of the world, refusing to use his supernatural powers for political gain, running from a crowd that wanted to enthrone him, waiting to announce his messiahship until he could redefine it to exclude nationalism, choosing to ride on a donkey instead of a war horse during his inauguration parade, and eventually declaring himself king of all people and all nations, not just Israel.[8] Likewise, he shunned all political power and commanded his followers to do the same, instructing them not to "lord it over" others, sending them into the world as sheep among wolves (not as a well-organized army or political brigade), scattering them across the globe as foreigners, exiles, and sojourners whose primary citizenship is in heaven, and ordering them to put their swords away instead of defend him (let alone a nation), while also definitively proclaiming to the Romans that his followers do not fight.[9]

Jesus' anti-nationalism may have been most obvious in his open inclusion of Gentiles (i.e. all non-Israeli/non-Jewish people). Since the beginning of God's intervention into human history, membership in his kingdom had always been tied to Israelite ethnicity/citizenship. Israel alone was God's chosen people. Then Jesus changed everything. He welcomed anyone who believed in God and sought to do his will. Membership in God's kingdom was now available to *everyone*, even Gentiles. In fact, Jesus not only welcomed gentile believers, he actively sought them out, specifically calling them to follow him.[10]

This shift to inclusion was unmistakable. After Jesus' death, Peter acknowledged, "I now realize how true it is that God does not show favoritism but accepts from every nation the one who fears him and does what is right" (Acts 10:34-35). God doesn't want "anyone to perish, but everyone to come to repentance" (2 Pet. 3:9). Paul concurred: "God … desires everyone to be saved and to come to the knowledge of the truth" (1 Tim. 2:3-4 NRSV). "For I tell you that Christ has become a servant of the circumcised on behalf of the truth of God in order that he might confirm the promises given to the patriarchs, and in order that the Gentiles might glorify God for his mercy" (Rom. 15:8-9 NRSV). With his blood, John noted, Jesus "ransomed for God saints from every tribe and language and people and nation" (Rev. 5:9 NRSV). Jesus died for everyone, not just Jews.[11] "For God so loved the *world* that he gave his one and only Son, that *whoever* believes in him shall not perish but have eternal life" (John 3:16). Jesus even brought salvation to Israel's gentile enemies, including their archenemies, the Canaanites.[12] As Copan observes, "God's ultimate concern to save even his own (people's) enemies comes full circle with the redemption of the Canaanites."[13] Instead of waving Israel's national flag over the corpses of its vanquished enemies, Jesus died on the cross to save them.

Jesus also commanded his followers to incorporate Gentiles into God's kingdom. He instructed them to preach the gospel to all peoples and all creation[14] and ordered them to "go therefore and make disciples of all nations," which they did (Matt. 28:19 NRSV). Paul recognized he had "received grace and apostleship to bring about the obedience of faith among all the Gentiles for the sake of his name" (Rom. 1:5 NRSV).[15] He told the Gentiles, although you were previously "excluded from citizenship in Israel and foreigners to the covenants of the promise," because of Jesus you are now included among God's people and "are no longer foreigners and strangers, but fellow citizens with God's people and also members of his household" (Eph. 2:11-13, 19). Jesus even gave his disciples the power of the Holy Spirit to help them be his "witnesses in Jerusalem, in all Judea and Samaria, and to the ends of the earth" (Acts 1:8 NRSV).

Of course, none of this made the Jewish leaders happy. In fact, they believed Jesus was such a threat to Jewish nationalism they colluded to have him murdered. John's gospel records the scene:

> So the chief priests and the Pharisees called a meeting of the council, and said, "What are we to do? This man is performing many signs. If we let him go on like this, everyone will believe in him, and the Romans will come and destroy both our holy place *and our nation*." But one of them, Caiaphas, who was high priest that year, said to them, "You know nothing at all! You do not understand that it is better for you to have one man die for the people than to have the whole nation destroyed." He did not say this on his own, but being high priest that year he prophesied that Jesus was about to die for the nation, and not for the nation only, but to gather into one the dispersed children of God. So from that day on they planned to put him to death. (John 11:47-53 NRSV)

Ultimately, they succeeded. "What surely sealed the fate of Jesus," professor Donald B. Kraybill notes, "was his bold challenge to the symbols of Jewish identity. His words and action scorched the flag of Jewish nationalism."[16]

The Jewish nationalists were right to be afraid. In doing all this (rejecting national kingship, eschewing political power, welcoming Gentiles, etc.), Jesus denationalized God's followers. He turned them from a nation into the church, from a typical earthly kingdom into the transnational, interethnic, nongovernmental, nonviolent, geographically dispersed organization we call the universal church. He revoked God's earlier nationalistic concession and declared statehood to be inappropriate for his followers. He revealed God's institutional ideal to be the nationless body of Christ. In short, he perfected the organizational structure of God's followers.

That's good news. Jesus freed us from the concerns and constraints of maintaining an earthly nation. Because God's interests are no longer tethered to any particular nation's interests, obedience to him no longer involves political power struggles. Instead, doing his will today requires transcending such nationalistic entanglements. It means engaging in transnational disciple-making, not nation building. God doesn't want us to make America into a Christian nation. He wants us to be the church.

By denationalizing his followers, Jesus dissolved the political barriers that typically divide people. He did away with the morally arbitrary lines we call national borders. In Paul's words, Jesus united Jew and Gentile. He "made the two groups one and has destroyed the barrier, the dividing wall of hostility … to create in himself one new humanity out of the two … and in one body to reconcile both of them to God through the cross" (Eph. 2:14-16). He "came and preached peace to you who were far away and peace to those who were near. For through him we both have access to the Father by one Spirit" (Eph. 2:17-18). In God's fellowship, "there is no Gentile or Jew, circumcised or uncircumcised, barbarian, Scythian, slave or free, but Christ is all, and is in all" (Col. 3:11).[17] As pastor and theologian Gregory A. Boyd puts it, "A central aspect of [God's] Kingdom revolution, therefore, is manifesting the beauty of what it looks like for a people to be freed from the idol of nationalism and to be reunited under the God who is Lord of all nations."[18]

Jesus' command to love our enemies further supports this thesis.[19] It is the ultimate border destroyer. Because of it, there are no longer neighbors and non-neighbors. There are only neighbors. There are no longer natives and foreigners. There are only natives. There are no longer insiders and outsiders. There are only insiders. There is no longer an "us" and a "them." There is only "us." Yoder explains:

> The Christian reason for rejecting the arms race is not that it may escalate or lash back and endanger us. It is not that a Soviet missile pointed at Bangor or Chicago will spread its destruction where you or I live. It is that we have institutionalized the competition of world systems by placing millions of people "over there" in the category of "enemy." We are in bondage to the institutional commitment to call them enemies. That is wrong even if we do not plan to kill them. It was wrong to see them that way when they had no way to strike back and there was no danger of backlash or fallout. It was wrong in the European takeover of America when the original inhabitants of the continent were denied human dignity. It was wrong in the "good old days" when wars could be "won." It was wrong most fundamentally not because war gets out of hand, not because the other side is catching up with us, and not because of the waste or the risk of error. It is wrong religiously as a denial of the cross of Christ. Who is our neighbor? The God of Abraham, the God of all three Abrahamic faiths, calls believers into a wider vision and to a righteous compassion that reaches beyond themselves and for which they will sacrifice themselves. God calls them to recognize that they belong to a human community wider than clan or nation.[20]

To explain it another way, Jesus perfected the ethical ideal of inclusion. In the OT, God introduced the notion of inclusivity through Israel by instituting laws that welcomed and protected outsiders, like immigrants. In the NT, Jesus took it a step farther by abolishing the exclusivity of nationalism. In the OT, God created a covenant with Israel alone. In the NT, Jesus expanded God's covenant to include all humanity. In the OT, God limited membership in his kingdom to Israelites. In the NT, Jesus offered membership to everyone, regardless of their race, ethnicity, or nationality.

As it turns out, inclusivity was always God's intent, always his ethical goal. He simply used one group of people (Israel) to forge a path to all people. From the beginning, the Bible repeatedly tells us God chose Israel and set it apart not as an end in itself but as a means of blessing all people and all nations.[21] Over and over again, both Testaments proclaim God used Israel to make himself known to all people on earth,[22] so that all would eventually come to follow him and abide in truth.[23] He established a relationship with the Israelites so that all peoples would eventually have an opportunity to do the same. Paul called God's use of Israel for such a purpose "the gospel in advance" (Gal. 3:8). And that is why, in Boyd's words, Jesus would not "let himself be co-opted by any nationalistic agenda—not even on behalf of God's 'chosen nation.' For the kingdom that Jesus came to establish is about fulfilling God's dream of reuniting all the nations."[24]

Simply put, there was nothing nationalistic about Jesus. He refused typical earthly kingship, refused political power, and refused to let national boundaries limit his ministry. In fact, he wasn't merely non-nationalistic. He was anti-nationalistic. He didn't merely fail to meet Israel's nationalistic expectations. He theologically terminated them. He made a conscious, concerted, blatant effort to forever erase nationalistic divisions from among God's followers.

Furthermore, Jesus didn't merely reorganize God's followers. He reconfigured their entire identity. Before Jesus, they were identifiable primarily by their unique *nationalistic* characteristics—the worship of only one God, a slightly advanced moral code, unusual ceremonial laws, different religious rituals, a restrained warfare policy, etc. After Jesus, they were set apart by their uniquely *non-nationalistic* characteristics—their border/race/ethnicity-transcending inclusiveness and self-sacrificial love of everyone, even enemies.

Any type of Christian nationalism today is ethical backsliding. It reverses what Jesus accomplished by reintroducing ethnic and political membership criteria, by resurrecting the dividing line between Jew and Gentile, and by turning neighbors back into enemies. There's a reason why "the concept of a Christian nation is completely absent from the gospel or its proclamation by the apostles and the early church," as author John D. Roth observes.[25] Just as Israel rebelled against God in the OT by demanding a king "like the other nations" have, we rebel against God today by prioritizing national interests above universal love "like the other nations" do.

One important caveat: Although Jesus denationalized God's followers, he didn't depoliticize them. The church isn't an apolitical entity. It's an alternative political entity. In fact, the Greek word for church, *ekklesia*, is a political word, not a religious one. Historically, it meant "the political assembly of citizens of an ancient Greek state."[26] Yoder translated it as a "town hall, gathering, or assembly ... where people come together to make decisions and to do business."[27] The church deals with the same issues as all traditional political communities, just in a nontraditional way. It is absolutely political. It just does politics differently—lovingly.

God gave Jesus the final word on Christian ethics. His life and teachings represent the culmination of God's incremental ethical revelation. He fulfilled the law by revealing God's perfect, eternal, and universally applicable moral code. And, as we are about to see, his fulfillment has far-reaching implications for our use of violence.

---

[1] See also Luke 16:17.

[2] Richard Hays, *The Moral Vision of the New Testament: Community, Cross, New Creation; A Contemporary Introduction to New Testament Ethic* (HarperOne, 2013), 9085, Kindle.

[3] Ibid., 9004.

[4] Lev. 19:16-18.

[5] Ps. 139:19-24.

[6] See also Matt. 7:12 and Mark 12:28-31.

[7] See also John 13:34; 15:12-13, 17; 1 John 4:21.

[8] Matt. 4:8-10; 16:13-25; 21:1-11; 26:52-53; Luke 4:5-8; 9:18-24; 19:28-38; John 6:1-15; 12:12-16; Mark 8:27-35.

[9] Matt. 10:16-18; 20:25-28; 26:50-52; Mark 10:35-45; Luke 22:24-30; John 18:36; Phil. 3:20; 2 Cor. 5:20; 1 Pet. 1:17; 2:9-11; Heb. 11:13-16.

[10] Rom. 1:6.

[11] 1 John 2:2; 1 Tim. 2:6.

[12] Ps. 87:4-6; Mark 7:25–30; Matt. 15:22.

[13] Copan, *Is God a Moral Monster?*, 4051.

[14] Mark 13:10; 16:15; Matt. 24:14; Luke 24:45-47; Rev. 14:6.

15 See also Rom. 15:7-22.

16 Donald B. Kraybill, *The Upside-Down Kingdom* Updated Edition (Herald Press, 2012), 2169, Kindle.

17 See also Gal. 3:28.

18 Gregory A. Boyd, *The Myth of a Christian Religion: Losing Your Religion for the Beauty of a Revolution* (Zondervan, 2009), 1187, Kindle.

19 Matt. 5:43-44; Luke 6:27-28; 10:25-37; Rom. 12:20-21.

20 John Howard Yoder, *Revolutionary Christian Citizenship* (Yoder for Everyone), ed. John C. Nugent, Branson Parler, and Andy Alexis-Baker (Harrisonburg, VA: Herald Press, 2013), 147.

21 Gen. 12:3; 18:18; 22:18; 26:4; 28:14; Ps. 72:17; Acts 3:25; Gal. 3:8.

22 Exod. 9:16; Josh. 4:24; 1 Kings 8:43, 60; 1 Chron. 16:24; 2 Chron. 6:33; Ps. 67:2, 3; 96:3; 98:3; 102:15; 145:10-12; Isa. 12:4-5; 42:10; 45:6; 49:6; 52:10; Jer. 33:9; Matt. 24:14; 28:19; Luke 3:6.

23 Ps. 22:27; 33:8; 48:10; 64:9; 67:7; 72:11; 86:9; 97:6; 138:4-5; Isa. 2:1-4; 45:22; 56:3-8; 60:3; 66:18, 23; Dan. 7:14; Zeph. 2:11; Hag. 2:7; Mal. 3:12; Rom. 14:11; 16:26; Phil. 2:10, 11; Rev. 15:4.

24 Boyd, *The Myth of a Christian Religion*, 1183.

25 John D. Roth, *Choosing Against War: A Christian View* (Intercourse, PA: Good Books, 2002), 137.

26 http://www.thefreedictionary.com/ekklesia.

27 Yoder, *Revolutionary Christian Citizenship*, 31.

4

NONVIOLENCE AS FULFILLMENT

Notice the antiviolence theme running through the heart of Jesus' fulfillment of the law. He always directed the law towards less violence. In fact, he removed *all* remaining violence from the law, thereby completing the process God began in the Mosaic Law.

For example, Jesus undermined all of the violence inherent in the OT's retributive laws by replacing "eye for an eye" with "do not resist," "turn the other cheek," and "give more than is demanded." Then he repudiated all remaining violence by commanding us to love our enemies, for if we are not to use violence (as the biblical definition of love demands) against our enemies then against whom can we use it? Likewise, he also renounced all violence when he condensed all of his ethical instructions into the golden rule, for we don't want others using violence against us so we shouldn't use it against them.[1]

Even Jesus' denationalization of God's followers has significant antiviolence implications. At first glance, it may not even look like an ethical revelation, but it has profound and far-reaching moral consequences. Allow me to explain.

The only violence God sanctioned in the OT was for nationalistic purposes. That's because nations require violence. To exist, they need criminal laws, warfare policies, and armed men to enforce them. By their nature, they have order to maintain, territory to defend, national sovereignty to preserve, and history to control. But transnational, interethnic, nongovernmental, geographically dispersed organizations (like the church) do not. People living as exiles and sojourners and foreigners on earth—people whose primary citizenship is in heaven, who can exist within any and all nations simultaneously, and whose supreme loyalty is to a different type of king and kingdom—do not. Therefore, by denationalizing God's followers, by reorganizing them from a nation into a church, Jesus eliminated the one thing for which God has ever allowed violence and warfare—the nation. OT professor John C. Nugent elaborates:

> God must creatively solve the problem of forging a people of peace in a world of war. The Yahweh wars are part of his solution. God delivers

41

and sustains the Israelites with his own sword so they will not grow too accustomed to swords of their own. Such protection will only be required for a time. God will eventually scatter his people throughout the world so they can take his peace to the nations. The sword will then become superfluous for God's people since their identity will be rooted in faith, mission, and Spirit—not geography, biology, and personal prosperity. This will be a significant shift. It will grate against their sense of self-preservation. God will therefore have to show his people the way of peace firsthand. He will send his Messiah to teach them the disarmed life and to demonstrate its superior power. He will show them how to struggle against the sword without being seduced by it. He will conquer sin and death—not with a superior show of force, but with the superior force of love.[2]

The core logic goes like this: To exist as a theocratic nation, Israel needed land. To gain and control land, Israel needed to use violence. Today, however, God calls us to exist as a church, not a theocratic nation. Therefore, because we don't need to acquire or control land, we don't need to use (and no longer have an excuse for using) violence.

In fact, God calls us to live as a set-apart people whose existence bears witness to a wholly different kind of kingdom, an inclusive, transnational, non-forceful one that by definition cannot be embodied while engaging in violent nationalistic endeavors. Thus, what was once productive is now counterproductive. The limited violence that previously played a role in advancing God's kingdom on earth when it was encapsulated in a nation is self-defeating now that God's kingdom has taken the form of the body of Christ. The nationalistic violence that previously contributed to the distinctiveness of God's followers now negates that distinctiveness. In this sense, Jesus perfected Christian distinctiveness.

To use a biblical phrase, God now calls us to be a nation of priests.[3] He calls us to play the same role the priests played within the nation of Israel. Like them, he hasn't given us an allotment of land and consequently calls us to act in ways that those with land to control and protect cannot. He has freed us from running a nation and controlling history so we can serve the world in ways others can't. Or as the Jesus and the NT writers repeatedly stated, we are to focus on loving, forgiving, returning good for evil, and living at peace with everyone[4] and leave vengeance, justice, and judgment to God, for *he* will use government for such things,[5] just like he did throughout the OT.[6]

Furthermore, once we realize that (1) God loves and pursues every person of every nationality equally, (2) all people everywhere are potential partakers of his covenant, and (3) he no longer cares about any nation's existence, then using violence against others for nationalistic purposes no longer makes sense, for any reason. Yoder hammers the point home:

> What is the human community that we want to defend and for which we are ready to run risks? Is it the nation? What are the moral claims of that unity today? Is it the political and military elite within a nation? It is that for many of us. But from a Christian perspective our neighbor must include the whole world. As David Brouwer puts it, "them is us over there." There is no moral ground for placing national identity above the rest of the world. There may be moral grounds for a constructive patriotism, but not at the cost of the others.[7]

It's tragic when Christians kill others on behalf of their nation and allow their national allegiances to resurrect the wall between believers and nonbelievers, the wall that Jesus tore down for the purpose of "making peace" and ending "hostility" (Eph. 2:14-16 NRSV). And it's the epitome of tragic when Christians kill *other Christians* on behalf of their nation.

Jesus' institutional reorganization of God's followers was also, to a large extent, an ethical reorganization—away from temporarily sanctioned limited violence and toward total nonviolence. By denationalizing them, Jesus completed the demilitarization God began in the OT and effectively transformed all nationalistic violence into a sin. And in the process, he definitively revealed Israel's national existence to be an ethical accommodation, not part of God's original intent. To quote Boyd, "God's very decision to further his purposes through a particular nation that would be established in a particular land, that would be governed by violently enforced laws and defended with violence, was itself a huge accommodation on God's part," one that "was from the start destined to come to an end once God's true character and will were revealed in the crucified Christ."[8]

Similarly, just as Jesus perfected the organizational structure of God's followers by removing all violence, he also perfected Christian warfare by removing all violence. Notice he didn't abolish it. He didn't proclaim that God's followers no longer have enemies or that they should no longer oppose their enemies. Instead, he redefined their enemies and reconfigured their means of opposition. In the OT, God's enemies were other humans and were to be overcome with violence. In the NT, Jesus declared that the enemy is evil itself and is to be overcome with love.[9] We are still to wage war on our enemy (evil), but we are to wage a different type of war (spiritual, not physical) with a different type of weapon (love, not violence).[10] Instead of injuring and killing other humans, we are to pray for, bless, forgive, and serve them. Instead of responding to violence with violence, we are to self-sacrificially absorb the violence others use against us, just like Jesus did. Evil wins when we do the former. God wins when we do the latter. And as biblical scholar Peter C. Craigie points out, "therein lies the new principle of the Kingdom established by Jesus; its strength lies not in the exercise of violence, but in the humble act of submission to violence."[11] Unfortunately, he adds, "It is in the light of this fundamental change of principle that the tragedy of so much of Christian history may be seen. Over and over again, Christians have forgotten that God the Warrior became the Crucified God."[12]

Of course, a full explanation of all the ways in which Jesus advocated nonviolence is outside the scope of this book—although I do provide a few more examples in Chapter 10. For now I will leave you with one more thought: The only reason the violence in the OT is a problem is because the NT is so obviously antiviolence. The OT's violence only demands an explanation, it only presents an ethical quandary for Christians today, because it so clearly and completely contradicts Jesus' call to nonviolence. In this sense, the "problem" of violence in the OT is further proof of how thoroughly opposed to violence the NT is.

Nonviolence Was Always the Goal

As it turns out, nonviolence was always God's intent, always his ethical ideal. In God's original creation, the Garden of Eden, there was no violence. Man, woman, and beast all lived together in harmony. It was a place of perfect peace, and in God's words, "it was very good" (Gen. 1:31).

In fact, in God's original creation, even the food chain was entirely free of violence. He designed both man and beast to be vegetarians. Immediately after giving man dominion over all the earth and animals, God said, "I give you every seed-bearing plant on the face of the whole earth and every tree that has fruit with seed in it. They will be yours for food" (Gen. 1:28-30). Then he told the animals the same thing.[13] Shortly thereafter, "God made all kinds of trees grow out of the ground—trees that were pleasing to the eye and good for food," "took the man and put him in the Garden of Eden to work it and take care of it," told him he was "free to eat from any tree in the garden" except one, and tasked him with naming the animals (Gen. 2:9, 15-17, 19-20). It wasn't until *after* the fall of man and the flood that God told man he could start eating animals.[14]

Moreover, many OT prophets later confirmed God's desire for a world without violence of any kind when they foretold of the reestablishment of his kingdom on earth as a time when "the wolf will live with the lamb, the leopard will lie down with the goat, the calf and the lion and the yearling together; and a little child will lead them. The cow will feed with the bear, their young will lie down together, and the lion will eat straw like the ox. The infant will play near the cobra's den, and the young child will put its hand into the viper's nest" (Isa. 11:6-8).[15]

In the world as God originally created it and intended it to be, there was no violence between God and man, between man and man, between man and beast, or between beast and beast. It doesn't get any more nonviolent than that.

Furthermore, not only did God create a nonviolent world, he created it in a uniquely nonviolent manner. "In contrast to the creation stories of many other Middle Eastern peoples," Roth notes, "there is no hint in Genesis of a grand cosmic battle in which God needed to defeat other rivals in order for creation to come into being. The biblical account of creation does not rest on a primal, violent struggle for power."[16] Instead, God simply spoke the world into being. He said, "'Let there be light;' and there was light" (Gen. 1:3 NRSV).

Violence doesn't appear in the Bible until after the fall of man. After being evicted from the Garden of Eden for eating the forbidden fruit, Adam and Eve had two sons, Cain and Abel. Eventually, Cain became jealous of Abel and killed him. God reacted by decrying, "What have you done? Listen … now you are cursed from the ground…. When you till the ground, it will no longer yield to you its strength; you will be a fugitive and a wanderer on the earth" (Gen. 4:10-12 NRSV).

There are three facts worth noting here. First, humans, not God, introduced violence to the world. Violence is the result of humanity's rebellion against God, not the product of God's original design. Or as OT professor Jerome F. D. Creach puts it, violence is a man-made "intrusion" that represents "a major disruption of the order God intended."[17] Second, God immediately responded to such violence with condemnation. The first time violence appeared in the Bible, God swiftly denounced it. Third, God didn't respond to such violence with violence, or even force. Instead, he responded by limiting Cain's ability to grow and harvest food, which turned him into a vagabond. In addition, after Cain said he was afraid of violent retaliation *by other humans*, God marked. him as a warning to others not to inflict the same violence on him that he had used against

Abel.[18] In other words, God responded to humankind's first act of violence not with violence (or force) but with natural consequences and an act of mercy—an oddly self-restrained initial reaction for a God who some claim is a raging, genocidal, bloodthirsty baby murderer.

Unfortunately, within a few generations, man's wickedness had escalated to the point of enveloping the entire earth.[19] It got so bad God regretted creating humans and decided to wipe the world clean with a flood.[20] However, although "all the people on earth had corrupted their ways," one man "found favor in the eyes of the Lord" (Gen. 6:8, 12). That man was Noah, and God instructed him to build an ark to save himself, his family, and every type of animal.[21]

For our purposes, the Flood story contains three important violence-related insights. First, although the Bible implies that some of the wickedness that deeply troubled God was sexual in nature, the only specific evil mentioned is violence: "Now the earth was corrupt in God's sight and was full of violence" (Gen. 6:1-11). Second, God declared the earth was filled with violence *because of humans*: "So God said to Noah, 'I am going to put an end to all people, for the earth is filled with violence because of them'" (Gen. 6:13). Third, after the flood waters receded and Noah and his family exited the ark to repopulate the world, God issued the following instruction: "And from each human being, too, I will demand an accounting for the life of another human being. Whoever sheds human blood, by humans shall their blood be shed; for in the image of God has God made mankind" (Gen. 9:5-6). In other words, as Nugent describes it, "God reins in human violence by declaring all blood sacred."[22]

Therefore, God flooded the earth and instituted the death penalty for murder in response to man's violence and to end such violence, not because he is inherently violent or prone to savagery. Precisely the opposite. Shedding human blood offends God because humans are made in his image.

The pro violence crowd doesn't get off to a good start in the Bible. The beginning of human history is all about God's nonviolence and humankind's conflicting, rebellious, corrupt, disobedient violence. God created a nonviolent world, humans introduced violence into it, God immediately condemned such violence, tried to restrain it, and then humans proceeded to spread violence over the entire earth until God's heart was so troubled by it he regretted creating them and found it necessary to essentially start over.

God was not the first to employ violence. He was the first to condemn violence. He was not the first to kill. He was the first to outlaw killing. To put it another way, God didn't initiate the use of force against humans. He responded to humankind's initiation of force (i.e. violence) with reactive force designed to suppress such violence. So the next time someone asks you why God couldn't have designed a world in which violence wasn't necessary, you can say he did, but humans introduced it anyway.

These first few chapters of the OT set the framework through which the rest of the OT's violence must be viewed. They demand that we view the God of the OT as the creator of a nonviolent world who despises and combats the corrupting influence of human violence—and who sometimes even uses violence himself (or at least strong reactive force) to counteract it.

The Antiviolence of the OT Prophets

As the OT story progressed, the prophets played a crucial role in keeping God's antiviolence intentions alive while ancient Israel wavered in its obedience, often lost its way, and frequently backslid. French theologian Jacques Ellul explains their function:

> In addition, the same texts and all the prophetic books bring to light a politically very odd phenomenon, namely, that for every king there was a prophet. The prophet (e.g., in the case of David) was most often a severe critic of royal acts. He claimed to come from God and to carry a word from God. This Word was always in opposition to royal power. Naturally, the prophets were often expelled; they were obliged to flee; they were put in prison; they were threatened with death, etc. But this did not make any difference. Their judgment was regarded as the truth. And again their writings, usually in opposition to power, were preserved, were regarded as a revelation of God, and were listened to by the people. None of them came to the aid of a king; none was a royal counselor; none was "integrated." The prophets were a counterforce, as we might put it today. This counterforce did not represent the people— it represented God.[23]

Pope Benedict XVI articulated it this way: "In the Old Testament, the preaching of the prophets vigorously challenged every kind of injustice and violence, whether collective or individual, and thus became God's way of training his people in preparation for the Gospel."[24]

To that end, the prophets repeatedly and consistently made two main points. First, they condemned Israel's decline into militaristic nationalism. The OT contains a tug of war between God's anti-nationalistic and anti-militaristic intentions for Israel and Israel's own conflicting, fallen preferences. Remember, God intended for Israel to be a uniquely theocratic, demilitarized, non-nationalistic nation, and that's how he originally organized them. But almost immediately after entering the Promised Land, the Israelites began backsliding. They started losing their distinctiveness and mirroring the wicked ways of the surrounding nations. Then, as Sprinkle puts it, "Israel's descent into secular militarism hits rock bottom in 1 Samuel 8" when it "explicitly demands a king, 'that we also may be like all the nations' (v. 20)."[25] Essentially, they asked to become like the very nations from which God had worked so hard to distinguish them. Although God viewed their request as a rejection of his kingship and his plan for them, he conceded to their request (another one of his moral concessions). Thereafter, Sprinkle continues, "What began as a God-ordained war against the Canaanites turned into a pattern of unsanctioned and arbitrary violence. Israel's lust for power cultivated a grisly warfare policy gleaned from their Canaanite and Assyrian neighbors."[26]

The most obvious aspect of Israel's post-conquest backsliding was a shift to militarism. During this time, it greatly expanded its military. Saul began by creating a class of professional soldiers and then Solomon expanded it, adding heavy weaponry like horses and chariots.[27] In fact, "By the time of Solomon," writes Nugent, "Israel had acquired its own king, its own standing army, a standard approach to diplomacy, and a socioeconomic system with a wealthy class that could impress neighboring nations."[28]

Not surprisingly, at the same time, Israel slowly began trusting in its own military might instead of God's provision. Its military development was, at its heart, a rejection of its originally designed God-run and God-protected government. Looking back on Israel's shift to earthly kingship as exemplified in the reign of King Solomon, OT professor Walter Brueggemann observes, "The entire program of Solomon now appears to have been a self-serving achievement with its sole purpose the self-securing of the king and dynasty. It consists of … the steady abandonment of the radicalness of the Mosaic vision."[29] Borrowing a phrase from George Mendenhall, he refers to Solomon's reign as "the paganization of Israel."[30] Or as I once heard someone say of Israel's shift to traditional kingship, it was the institutionalization of rebellion.

Unfortunately, as Nugent notes, Israel "came out from Babylon and Egypt only to become a smaller and weaker version of them. There was nothing impressive about that. They were not shining a distinctive light."[31] Instead of serving as a blessing to the surrounding nations by reflecting God's sovereignty, "they conducted international business as usual."[32]

Much, if not most, of the violence in the OT occurs within this rebellious, militaristic period. As such, it was not God commanded or even God sanctioned. In fact, it was in direct conflict with God's clearly articulated intentions. And he never let the Israelites forget that. That's why he sent in the prophets, and that's why the prophets started consistently appearing in the OT texts at that time. In Yoder's words, "As soon as Israel got a king 'like the other nations' ... God called forth prophets, starting with Samuel in Saul's time, who saw in these political transactions by Israel's kings the embodiment of disobedience."[33]

For example, according to almost all OT prophets, a good king was a non-militaristic, God-trusting king (regardless of whether Israel was conquered under his leadership) while a bad king was a militaristic, violence-trusting one (regardless of how much he expanded Israel's territory or power). Ellul explains:

> We can say that in the biblical accounts "good" kings are always defeated by Israel's enemies, and the "great" kings who win victories and extend their borders are always "bad." "Good" means that they are just, that they do not abuse their power, and that they worship the true God of Israel. "Bad" means that they promote idolatry, reject God, and are also unjust and wicked. The presentation is so systematic that some modern historians suggest that the accounts were written by antimonarchists and partisans.[34]

To be more specific, the prophets repetitively condemned Israel for two *militaristic* mistakes: (1) investing in their own military strength by stockpiling weapons and building fortifications and (2) forming military alliances with other nations. For example, Isaiah declared:

> Alas for those who go down to Egypt for help
>   and who rely on horses,
> who trust in chariots because they are many
>   and in horsemen because they are very strong,
> but do not look to the Holy One of Israel
>   or consult the Lord!
> Yet he too is wise and brings disaster;
>   he does not call back his words,
> but will rise against the house of the evildoers,
>   and against the helpers of those who work iniquity.
> The Egyptians are human, and not God;
>   their horses are flesh, and not spirit. (Isa. 31:1-3 NRSV)

Oh, rebellious children, says the Lord,
who carry out a plan, but not mine;
who make an alliance, but against my will,
  adding sin to sin;
who set out to go down to Egypt
  without asking for my counsel,
to take refuge in the protection of Pharaoh,
  and to seek shelter in the shadow of Egypt;
Therefore the protection of Pharaoh shall become your shame,
  and the shelter in the shadow of Egypt your humiliation. (Isa. 30:1-3
NRSV)[35]

Occasionally, God bypassed the middleman and did the condemning himself. King David's reign is illustrative. In fact, his story is essentially a microcosm of Israel's. He began his kingship by humbly submitting to God and leaving all military strategy and initiation of warfare to him. But then success and power corrupted him. He began taking more control of the army—enlarging it, choosing who to fight, when to fight, and how to fight, taking credit for victories, etc. He started using it to expand the empire instead of merely defend it. And eventually, he strayed so far from God's anti-militaristic plan that God prohibited him from building his temple: "You shall not build a house to my name, because you have shed so much blood in my sight on the earth" (1 Chron. 22:8 NRSV).[36]

Unfortunately, almost all of Israel's kings over the next few centuries continued down the same militaristic path, and all were similarly condemned.[37] In fact, as Yoder notes, the prophetic criticism of militaristic nationalism increased as time went on:

The critique underlying the stories of Judges and Samuel and Kings becomes increasingly clear as the prophets go on. By the time of Isaiah it called for formal renunciation of politics and diplomacy as usual, of alliances with Egypt, and of modernized military technology. By the time of Jeremiah, trusting God had come to entail renouncing statehood and accepting Diaspora as the fitting way for the people of God to live. Jeremiah's letter to the exiles (Jer. 29) called them to take their being scattered among the nations as normal—i.e., as mission. Promises of early restoration are denounced as lying dreams. The prophets who make such promises were not sent by Yahweh.[38]

Yoder's last sentence raises a point worth addressing: Not every single OT prophet supported the antiviolence cause. Just like rulers today seek out and promote experts who already agree with them, as opposed to those who are truly objective, so did many of Israel's kings. Thus, OT Israel was not immune to false prophets. Nevertheless, the great majority of OT prophets, particularly those the Bible puts forth as God's true representatives, communicated an antiviolence, antimilitarism, anti-warfare message.

The fate of Israel's militaristic monarchy proves the point. It was a short-lived, human-led experiment that ended in complete disaster. Far from being a blessing, it played into God's negative warnings about it.[39] Nugent explains:

> As he predicted through Moses (Deut. 31–32), the whole project began to crumble under the weight of its own inadequacies. The commoners revolted against oppressive nobles, and the kingdom split in two. Though each kingdom lasted for a time, a few centuries later, larger nations came along and conquered them one after the other.[40]

In other words, when the Israelites insisted on becoming a militaristic society, God relented, withdrew his divine protection, and gave them over to the natural, self-destructive consequences of their choice. As a result, the antiviolence prophets were proven correct and the pro-violence prophets were unmasked as false prophets.

Jesus' life also proves the point. In fact, the key to distinguishing between the false prophets and those who carried God's message is to uncover which ones came true in Jesus. He fulfilled the antimilitaristic, antinationalistic, nonviolent prophecies, not the wrathful, bloodthirsty, vengeful ones. For example, he began his ministry by pronouncing he was the fulfillment of Isaiah's type of messiah, one who came to offer hope to the poor and oppressed, not seek vengeance on God's enemies.[41] Thereafter, he proceeded to fulfill Isaiah's "Suffering Servant" prophecies, including being "despised and rejected by mankind, a man of suffering, and familiar with pain," "pierced for our transgressions," "crushed by our iniquities," "oppressed and afflicted," "led like a lamb to the slaughter," and buried "with the wicked … *though he had done no violence*" (Isa. 53:1-12).[42] Likewise, he fulfilled Zechariah's prophecy that the Messiah would come "lowly and riding on a donkey" and would "take away the chariots from Ephraim and the warhorses from Jerusalem" and would "proclaim peace to the nations" (Zech. 9:9-10).[43] In short, Jesus was the sacrificial lamb and suffering servant that the nonviolent prophets had predicted, not the militaristic conqueror the violent ones had hoped for. As Jesus himself would later say, "For even the Son of Man did not come to be served, but to serve, and to give his life as a ransom for many" (Mark 10:45).[44]

And remember, as previously discussed, Jesus unequivocally rejected the type of kingship Israel tried to embody. He wanted nothing to do with typical earthly kingship. As Brueggemann notes, "In both his teaching and his very presence, Jesus of Nazareth presented the ultimate criticism of the royal consciousness."[45] Jesus unmasked Israel's kinship as just another moral concession and not God's ideal. That alone is enough to prove the antiviolence prophets right and the militaristic prophets wrong.

Additionally, Ellul argues that the preservation of the anti-militarism prophecies over the pro militarism ones is itself evidence of their superior truth:

> The astounding thing to me is that the [anti militarism] texts were edited, published, and authorized by rabbis and representatives of the people (if one can say that) at a time when the kings in question were reigning. There must have been censorship and controls, and yet these did not prevent the writings from being circulated. Furthermore, the accounts were not merely preserved but were also regarded as divinely inspired. They were treated as a revelation of the God of Israel, who is thus presented as himself an enemy of royal power and the state. They were sacred texts. They were included in the body of inspired texts (there was as yet no canon). They were read in the synagogues (even though they must have seemed like antiroyalist propaganda to rulers like Ahab). They were commented upon as the Word of God in the presence of all the people.[46]

> None of the false prophecies that were favorable to the kings has been preserved in the holy scriptures. The struggles of the true prophets have been preserved, however, and the fact that logically the royal authority ought to have suppressed them shows that we have in their declarations the Word of God. As I see it, these facts manifest in an astounding way the constancy of an antiroyalist if not an anti-statist sentiment.[47]

In addition to condemning militarism, the second thing the prophets did to keep God's antiviolence vision alive was to continually remind Israel that God would eventually reestablish his originally created nonviolent world. They prophesied about a future in which war would be no more, violence would be extinct, swords would be turned into plowshares, and all nations, humans, and animals would be at peace with one another, living together in complete harmony.[48] Likewise, they prophesied about a nonviolent, lamb-like, servant Messiah who would begin such a restoration and whose peace would eventually extend to the ends of the earth and last forever.[49] As Wright observes, the prophet Isaiah "links this hope of an end to war with his promise of the coming of God's messianic king, who will reign over an era of cosmic peace between nations and between humanity and nature."[50] Thus, "Peace, not war, is the mark of the reign of God."[51] Or as OT professor Stephen B. Chapman puts it, "warfare is an unnatural disruption within the created order and not a feature of 'the way things are supposed to be.'"[52]

In fact, this is how the OT ends–with a yearning for peace, a hunger for an end to all violence, and a hope for a Messiah who would achieve it all. "This longing," Sprinkle writes, "creates the seam that stitches together the seemingly contradictory portraits of violence in the Old Testament and nonviolence in the New. The stage is set. The journey is under way. It's time for the Messiah to bring us back to Eden."[53]

In all these ways, the prophets laid much of the groundwork for the ethical transition from the violence, warfare, and nationalism of the OT to the nonviolence and denationalization of the NT. The changeover wasn't a completely unexpected, instantaneous pivot orchestrated by Jesus alone. By the time Jesus arrived, war had already ceased to be the duty it had been when Israel was growing into nationhood and seizing territory. In fact, the later prophets had even begun to see war as punishment from God. Likewise, as Israel's national story progressed through internal division, invasion, and political exile, the reestablishment of national sovereignty had become increasingly less important, violent attempts to restore it had begun to be viewed as mistakes, and denationalization had begun to be accepted as God's will.[54]

Even the use and acceptability of violence in general had been trending down for decades, if not centuries, before Jesus arrived. The general wrongness of killing had been long-established, as evidenced by the Ten Commandments. The death penalty was being imposed less often. The Mosaic Law's retributive, eye-for-an-eye penalties were continually being relaxed. And the prophets were condemning violence more and more. At one point, the writer of Proverbs even blatantly declared that God hates "hands that shed innocent blood" (Prov. 6:17 NRSV), while King David proclaimed that God "hates the lover of violence" (Ps. 11:5 NRSV). As Yoder observed, "the violence of the Old Testament legislation was mitigated well before the time of Jesus."[55] He elaborates:

> Not only did Judaism, as defined since Jeremiah, forsake visions of kingship and sovereignty for its historical present. Judaism also forsook violence. The rabbinic literary corpus is by its nature complex and contradictory. Some passages reject violence completely, even in self-defense. Others retain the memory of a judicial system qualified to punish people, and of limited wars, since such were there in their ancient histories; but the rabbis' guidance about the moral life of the ongoing Jewish community calls for a fundamentally non-violent lifestyle, even under persecution. This guidance occurs on grounds not of tactics or weakness, but because that is now seen to be the will of God.[56]

Professor William Klassen summarizes the point: "There is, therefore, no conflict between the teaching of Judaism on this matter and what Jesus himself as a first-century Jew taught."[57] In Yoder's words, "Jesus's pacifism was not an innovation; it was an intensification of the nonviolence of Jeremiah, Ezekiel, and the singer of the Servant passages of the book of Isaiah."[58] Furthermore, Jews were essentially pacifistic from the second century until the twentieth, much more so than Christians were. Such a history implies they read the OT as I'm suggesting we read it—as pointing towards and promoting nonviolence.

Although by the end of the OT many Jews, led by the prophets, had mostly rejected violence, warfare, and nationalism as contrary to God's will and as an ineffective means of advancing his kingdom on earth, doubts remained, as did conflicting voices. That's where Jesus comes in. He definitively settled the matter in favor of nonviolence and denationalization.

To summarize the role of the OT prophets, God used them to keep his antiviolence intentions in the public eye. They did so primarily by reminding God's followers that he had never sanctioned militarism and only ever sanctioned warfare for a limited, temporary purpose. Anytime the Israelites stepped outside of those narrow bounds, the prophets were quick to condemn them. Furthermore, the prophets also carried a more positive antiviolence message. They foretold of a future nonviolent world, as God originally intended it to be, and reassured God's followers he was moving history in that direction.

Of course, all of this begs a vital question: If it's our purpose as God's church to presently embody his future, fully established kingdom (as a foretaste of it, as a sign pointing to it, as a means of making it a reality, etc.) and that kingdom is wholly nonviolent like the prophets proclaimed, shouldn't we be wholly nonviolent?

The Biblical Arc of Christian Ethics

To bring together everything we have discussed so far, the Bible contains an explicit ethical arc, one with a distinct pattern of progression. To see it, we simply need to analyze God's OT actions and commands chronologically within their cultural context and in light of what Jesus claimed in the NT. When we do, we realize that God began moving the human race forward as soon as he directly intervened. All of his ethical instructions, while not perfect, were improvements. And, most importantly, they all paved the way for the grand finale of his ethical revelation: Jesus Christ.

Furthermore, the Bible's ethical arc clearly bends toward total nonviolence. It heads in that direction the entire time, from creation all the way to the end of the NT. It's the story of God creating a nonviolent world, humans corrupting it with violence, and God beginning to work with humankind to return it to its originally intended nonviolent state. As such, nonviolence is God's ethical ideal, the perfection of his law.

Of course, I don't mean this in an all-inclusive sense. God's ethical ideal is more than mere nonviolence. It is love, and love goes beyond nonviolence by requiring proactive acts of kindness, forgiveness, and mercy. Nonetheless, nonviolence is an essential component of his ethical ideal. It's the necessary first step in loving others. It's a prerequisite to embodying God's kingdom. After all, love first does no harm.[59]

Therefore, our marching orders today are wholly nonviolent. The OT sowed the seeds of nonviolence, the NT fertilized them, and today God calls us to reap the nonviolence harvest. We only need to obey the plain meaning of Jesus' simple, straightforward commands.

We can already see how many of the popular views of the OT are wrong. The OT is not pro violence. Nor does the biblical case for nonviolence begin in the NT. It begins at creation, which means it begins in the OT. Similarly, the nonviolence of the NT doesn't contradict the violence of the OT. It is based in the OT and grows out of it. It is the climax of the OT's ethical storyline. Simply put, the OT is the foundation upon which the NT's nonviolence is built. In a fallen world, nonviolence needs such a foundation, as we are about to see.

---

[1] Matt. 7:12; 22:39-40; Luke 6:31; Mark 12:31; Rom. 13:8-9; Gal. 5:14.

[2] John C. Nugent, *The Politics of Yahweh: John Howard Yoder, the Old Testament, and the People of God*, Theopolitical Visions Book 12 (Cascade Books, 2011), 2211, Kindle.

[3] Exod. 19:5-6; 1 Pet. 2:9; Rom. 15:15-16; Rev. 1:6; 5:10.

[4] Matt. 5:9, 38-42; 18:21-22; Luke 6:37; 1 Pet. 2:21-23; 3:9; Eph. 4:31-32; Rom. 12:17-21; 13:8-10; 14:19; Heb. 12:14; 1 Thess. 5:13; 2 Cor. 13:11.

[5] Rom. 12:19; 13:1-7; 1 Pet. 2:13-14; Heb. 10:30; 2 Thess. 1:6-8; John 19:10-11; Rev. 14:7.

[6] Judg. 2:14-15, 20-21; 3:12-14; 6:1; Isa. 5:25-30; 10:5-19; 45:1; 46:11; Josh. 7:10-12; Num. 14:41-45; Jer. 5:19; 15:14; 20:4-5; 21:7; 25:8-11; 27:4-7; 34:21; Ezek. 21.

[7] Yoder, *Revolutionary Christian Citizenship*, 146.

[8] Gregory A. Boyd, *The Crucifixion of the Warrior God: Interpreting the Old Testament's Violent Portraits of God in Light of the Cross, Volumes 1 & 2* (Fortress Press, 2017), 16107, Kindle.

[9] Matt. 5:38-48; Rom. 12:17-21; 1 Pet. 2:18-23; 3:8-9.

[10] 2 Cor. 10:1-5; Eph. 6:10-17.

[11] Peter C. Craigie, *The Problem of War in the Old Testament* (Grand Rapids, MI: Wm. B. Eerdmans Publishing Co., 1979), 100.

[12] Ibid.

[13] Gen. 1:30.

[14] Gen. 9:3.

[15] See also Isa. 65:25, Hos. 2:18, and Ezek. 34:25.

[16] Roth, Choosing Against War, 65.

[17] Jerome F. D. Creach, *Violence in Scripture: Interpretation: Resources for the Use of Scripture in the Church* (Westminster John Knox Press, 2013), 455, Kindle.

[18] Gen. 4:13-16.

[19] Gen. 6:1-5.

[20] Gen. 6:6-7.

[21] Gen. 6:14-22.

[22] John C. Nugent, *Endangered Gospel: How Fixing the World is Killing the Church* (Cascade Books, 2016), 843, Kindle.

[23] Jacques Ellul, *Anarchy and Christianity* (Eugene, OR: Wipf and Stock Publishers, 2011), 51.

[24] Post-Synodal Apostolic Exhortation *Verbum Domini* http://w2.vatican.va/content/benedict-xvi/en/apost_exhortations/documents/hf_ben-xvi_exh_20100930_verbum-domini.html.

[25] Sprinkle, *Fight*, 1366.

[26] Ibid., 1363.

[27] Gerhard von Rad, *Holy War in Ancient Israel*, translators John H. Yoder and Marva J. Dawn (Grand Rapids, MI: Wm. B. Eerdmans Publishing Co., 1996), 75 and 77.

[28] Nugent, *Endangered Gospel*, 1006.

[29] Walter Brueggemann, *Prophetic Imagination: Revised Edition* (Fortress Press, 2012), 606, Kindle.

[30] Ibid., 627.

[31] Nugent, *Endangered Gospel*, 1018.

[32] Ibid., 1020.

[33] John Howard Yoder, *Discipleship as Political Responsibility*, translator Timothy J. Geddert (Scottdale, PA: Herald, 2003), 27–28.

[34] Ellul, *Anarchy and Christianity*, 50.

[35] See also Hos. 12:1.

[36] See also 28:3.

[37] 1 Kings 4:26; 10:26; 1 Kings 12 thru 2 Kings 25.

[38] Yoder, *The War of the Lamb*, 1447.

[39] 1 Sam. 8:6-18.

[40] Nugent, *Endangered Gospel*, 1008.

[41] Isa. 61:1-2; Luke 4:16-21; Matt 11:1-6.

[42] See also Isa. 7:14, 9:1-2, 40:3, 50:6; Luke 24:25-27, 44-48.

[43] Matt. 21:1-11; Luke 19:28-38; John 12:12-16.

[44] See also Matt. 20:28; John 13:1-17.

[45] Brueggemann, *Prophetic Imagination*, 1548.

[46] Ellul, *Anarchy and Christianity*, 50-51.

[47] Ibid., 51-52.

[48] Isa. 2:4; 11:6-9; 60:17-18; 65:25; Mic. 4:3; Ezek. 34:25; Hos. 2:18; Ps. 46:9.

[49] Zech. 9:9-10; Ezek. 37:26; Isa. 9:6-7; 53:2-12; Ps. 22:7-8, 16; 109:4.

[50] Wright, *The God I Don't Understand*, 1747.

[51] Ibid., 1755.

[52] Stephen B. Chapman, *Holy War in the Bible*, ed. Heath A. Thomas, Jeremy Evans, and Paul Copan (InterVarsity Press, 2014), 957, Kindle.

[53] Sprinkle, *Fight*, 1569.

[54] Yoder, *Christian Attitudes to War, Peace, and Revolution*, 2452.

[55] Ibid., 6088.

[56] Yoder, *The War of the Lamb*, 1473.

[57] William Klassen, *Love of Enemies: The Way to Peace* (Eugene, OR: Wipf and Stock Publishers, 2002), 66.

[58] Yoder, *The War of the Lamb*, 2084.

[59] Rom. 13:10.

5

WHY INCREMENTAL REVELATION?

Let's shift gears from exploring *how* God incrementally revealed his ethical ideal to analyzing *why* he did so. Why gradually instead of all at once? Obviously, we can't know precisely why God does everything he does. He possesses knowledge, wisdom, and abilities we can't even conceptualize, let alone understand. But we can speculate based on what we do know.

As always, the key here is context. This time, however, it's not so much historical or cultural as pedagogical. In other words, the key to comprehending why God used incremental revelation is to place his revelation not only in its historical and cultural context but more importantly in the context of how humans learn—and consequently, how God chose to teach them.

Great advances in human knowledge and understanding do not happen all at once. They only occur gradually by building upon the intellectual discoveries and lessons of earlier generations, one step at a time. Consider the long, winding path humanity traversed to arrive at the scientific revolution. It didn't pop up overnight. It was preceded by centuries of small steps in the right direction.

This makes sense. We are rational beings. We can't leap from Point A to Point E without first traversing Points B, C, and D, otherwise Point E gets dismissed as nonsensical. We reject what we don't understand, what doesn't have a proper foundation in human thought and experience. We are also emotional beings with free will. No matter how logical a new idea is, we can and often do initially reject it. Plus, the powerful among us usually have a vested interest in maintaining the status quo and resisting new advances, no matter how beneficial they are for humanity as a whole. For all these reasons, new ideas must often gestate for a generation or two before they take hold. Acceptance is never automatic nor instantaneous. Hence the need for incremental revelation.

To state it more plainly, God had to teach humanity proper behavior the same way parents have to teach their children. He had to bring us along gradually as our evolving maturity permitted. Yoder explains:

59

This conception of the pedagogical concession can perhaps be compared to the difference between a parent's commanding a child not to touch matches or electric plugs at the age of two and his instructing the child to use matches or an electric plug a few years later. The parent is not inconsistent, nor has the nature of fire or electricity changed; but there have been changes in the capacity of the child to understand and to use them. Actions may be permissible or even mandatory when he understands how to do them which were forbidden and harmful before.[1]

Sprinkle describes it this way:

One way to solve the tension is to recognize that the old and new covenants are different. Please note: I didn't say that the *God* of the old and the *God* of the new are different. God is the same yesterday, today, and forever. But sometimes His rules change because His relationship to humanity is taken to a new level. The same is true for us. I don't let my five-year-old drive my car, but when she's sixteen, I just might let her. And I don't let my nine-year-old daughter date boys, but when she turns … thirty-five, I might entertain the thought. You get the point. Just because something is commanded under the old covenant doesn't mean it'll be the same in the new.… God's rules in the Old Testament are different from those in the New. God's relationship with Israel was different from God's relationship with the church.[2]

Laying the Ethical Groundwork

All of this means God had to teach humanity certain moral fundamentals (or prerequisites) before he could effectively teach it any specifics. He had to explain and instill the introductory basics before he could explain and instill the more advanced particulars. He had to put humans through Morality 101 before sending them to Morality 410.

For example, God had to first prove he was the one and only true God. Prior to his interactions with Israel, humans had only known polytheism. He had to teach them monotheism. He had to separate himself from all other competitor gods and show them to be false. Similarly, he had to demonstrate he was worthy of supreme and sole obedience. He had to show he was trustworthy—that he knew what he was doing, was in control, and had humanity's best interests in mind. And, he had to reveal his desire for obedience, the importance of obedience, and the type of obedience he sought: complete, perfect, and wholly trusting.

That's what God was doing in the OT. He was not teaching a course on specific moral behaviors. He was laying the necessary groundwork for a future course on them. He was building the moral foundation upon which his future commands about how to behave could be received, understood, and accepted. He was teaching them about obedience in general before teaching them precisely what to obey. He was proving that morality exists and that it matters before demanding compliance with specific morals.

In this sense, the OT merely sets the stage for what we think of as Christian ethics. It tackles the bigger-picture moral issues. It addresses the issues that are more fundamental than whether specific actions (like violence) are wrong. It answers questions like: Who is God? What does he want? Why should I obey him? What's in it for me?

Furthermore, at each point along humanity's educational journey, God had to be careful not to give it more than it could handle. He had to continually respect its current level of moral development, otherwise his lessons would have been squandered. As Thompson explains, "He wished to show them a better way. But if human beings are to be treated as real human beings who possess the power of choice, then the 'better way' must come gradually. Otherwise, they will exercise their freedom of choice and turn away from that which they do not understand."[3]

This is why, as Copan writes, "Sinai legislation makes a number of moral improvements without completely overhauling ancient Near Eastern social structures and assumptions."[4] He elaborates:

> Given certain fixed assumptions in the ancient Near East, God didn't impose legislation that Israel wasn't ready for. He moved *incrementally*.... God didn't banish all fallen, flawed, ingrained social structures when Israel wasn't ready to handle the ideals. Taking into account the *actual*, God encoded more *feasible* laws, though he directed his people toward moral improvement.[5]

Not coincidentally, Jesus used this same strategy during his ministry. He too was careful not to give his pupils more than they could handle. At one point, he told his disciples, "I have much more to say to you, more than you can now bear" (John 16:12). Likewise, he used parables when speaking to crowds because it was "as much as they could understand," but "when he was alone with his own disciples, he explained everything" (Mark 4:33-34).[6]

Later, the apostles adopted the same approach. In his letter to the church at Corinth, Paul wrote, "I could not address you as people who live by the Spirit but as people who are still worldly—mere infants in Christ. I gave you milk, not solid food, for you were not yet ready for it" (1 Cor. 3:1-2). The writer of Hebrews made the same point to his audience:

> We have much to say about this, but it is hard to make it clear to you because you no longer try to understand. In fact, though by this time you ought to be teachers, you need someone to teach you the elementary truths of God's word all over again. You need milk, not solid food! Anyone who lives on milk, being still an infant, is not acquainted with the teaching about righteousness. But solid food is for the mature, who by constant use have trained themselves to distinguish good from evil. (Heb. 5:11-14)

This is why God wisely established common ground in the OT before breaking new ground in the NT. He taught the commonsensical basics before moving to the relatively unintuitive specifics. He employed methods they already knew and understood before introducing different, unfamiliar, countercultural methods. He intuitively proved his power, control, intentions, and trustworthiness before counterintuitively demanding self-sacrificial love. He restrained and redirected their violence before commanding nonviolence. And he did all of this in a manner that allowed him to always be improving their ethical behavior, always moving it toward his ideal.

Then, as soon as God judged humans morally mature enough to begin grappling with his ethical ideal, he sent Jesus. As soon as he deemed humanity ready to receive the full truth, he revealed it in human form.[7] In the words of Paul, "when the fullness of time had come, God sent his Son" (Gal. 4:4 NRSV). Theology professor William T. Cavanaugh explains it in terms of the six antitheses in Jesus' Sermon on the Mount:

> In each of these, Jesus takes an aspect of the Mosaic law ("You have heard it said") and extends it ("But I say to you"). Now that the Messiah has come, we are capable of more than merely refraining from murder; we are now directed to remove anger from our hearts. Now that the Messiah has come, we are capable of more than merely abstaining from sleeping with another's spouse; we are now directed to overcome lust as well..... Now that the Messiah has come, we are capable of more than merely limiting revenge to an eye for an eye or merely loving our neighbors; we are now instructed to renounce revenge entirely, and to love even our worst enemies and our persecutors.[8]

Prior to all the tutoring work God did with Israel in the OT, humanity was too morally immature to handle God's message of nonviolent, suffering love. Here's Yoder:

> Perhaps insight into the destructiveness of violence and the redemptiveness of love is a very refined kind of cultural understanding accessible only to cultures with a certain degree of advancement. It would have been too much to ask for the rough and illiterate tribesmen of the age of Moses and Joshua. For the age of Jesus, however, standing on the shoulders of the civilizing preparation of later prophets and the

experience of exile and Roman rule, the nature of such an imperative became much more readily conceivable.[9]

Not only did God have to work around humanity's evolving moral maturity, he had to do so while also respecting its free will. According to Boyd, "because God supremely values authentic *agape*-love relationships, and because he does not want to dehumanize people, he relies on influential rather than coercive power to accomplish his purposes."[10] He continues:

> For this reason, I submit, God had to accommodate his self-revelation to the spiritual state and cultural conditioning of his people in the ages leading up to Christ. Only gradually could God change people's hearts and minds so that they could receive more and more truth about his true character and about his ideal will for them.[11]

Sure, God could have waved a wand and turned everyone into perfectly mature and completely obedient robots, but that would have contradicted the whole point of creating humans in the first place. God desires a relationship with us, which means we must have free will and he must respect it.

This is God's great balancing act. He must give us enough reason to believe in him without giving us so much evidence that he effectively removes all possible doubt. He must demonstrate his existence and superiority without crushing our ability to freely choose. He must make the truth attractive but not irresistible, believable but not irrefutable. He must teach us the benefits of obedience and disadvantages of disobedience while allowing us enough freedom to reject such wisdom. We often want God to remove all need for us to have faith, but it doesn't work like that. As Nugent explains, "For God's Spirit to show itself continually in obvious ways that are immune to misinterpretation and rejection is to deny the possibility of human faith. Who could say 'no' to an ever-present flurry of undeniable miracles?"[12]

This is not only why God only selectively performs miracles, it's also partly why he only selectively reveals himself to us, only selectively explains things to us, and only requests our obedience instead of forcing it. Plus, it's also why he doesn't simply snap his fingers and rid the world of all evil, pain, and suffering. Human choice would disappear with them. God doesn't want robots. He wants us to freely choose him, to voluntarily obey him, and to willingly partner with him to redeem the world.

We see God leaving room for human free will throughout the OT. It's why he capitulated to the Israelites on certain moral issues, like divorce and polygamy. It's why he granted their rebellious request for a militaristic king in 1 Samuel 8. And, it's why he allowed them to disobey him over and over again without ever supernaturally forcing obedience.

But it's also why he allowed their disobedience to run its natural course. It's why he allowed their militaristic nationalism to self-destruct, as all militaristic nationalism eventually does. It's why he gave them over not only to their sinful desires but also to the natural consequences of such desires. He was teaching them (and us) that obedience is in humanity's best interest while simultaneously respecting their free will. After all, the only way to convince free beings to voluntarily choose path A over path B is to show them the negative consequences of choosing path B.

Similarly, God also needed to teach humans to think for themselves *from his perspective*. He hasn't given us a comprehensive list of exactly how to act in every possible moral scenario (only a list of general principles and a few examples of how to embody them). He had to impart a certain amount of understanding so we would be equipped to make moral choices in the gray areas of life. He had to teach us *why* we should obey, not merely to obey. He had to give us the wisdom necessary to effectively apply his general principles to everyday life then, now, and thousands of years in the future. Such wisdom takes time to develop. It takes incremental revelation.

All of this might make better sense if we look at it in the context of a hypothetical example. Imagine a man you have never met nor even heard of shows up at your front door and hands you a list of rules for how you should live the rest of your life. A little confused, you take a moment to read the rules and immediately notice (1) they differ significantly from how you and everyone else live and (2) they contradict commonly accepted wisdom about the best way to live a successful life. As soon as you finish reading them, the stranger then demands that you immediately obey all the rules perfectly or you will suffer drastic consequences.

What would be your reaction? Wouldn't you be thinking to yourself: Who is this guy? Who does he think he is? Why should I believe him? Where did he get this ridiculous list? These rules won't help me. How is it good for me to live more like a servant and less like a king? Why should I voluntarily have less sex, less wealth, and less power? Why should I obey rules that will only make me less comfortable and less safe? This guy is crazy. Plus, does he really think he can punish me if I don't obey him? What a joke. He and what army?

Wouldn't you dismiss the stranger as a nutcase? In fact, wouldn't you have to be a nutcase yourself to blindly start following him?

But what if the stranger got to know you first? What if he established a relationship with you and proved he had your best interests in mind? What if he also demonstrated a superhuman knowledge of all things and supernatural power over all things? What if he proved to you he was trustworthy and worthy of obedience? What if every time you listened to him good things happened and every time you didn't bad things happened? What if he did all of this before handing you a list of rules, rules that were no longer completely unfounded but instead were a logical extension of everything he had already been teaching you? Now what are the odds you would follow him? Wouldn't you now be a fool not to?

God's Introductory Ethical Lessons

Let's take a closer look at a few of the basic lessons God taught in the OT and how he did so.

Establishing his existence and superiority. The first thing God had to do upon entering human history was to establish his existence. After that, he had to establish his superiority. He had to establish himself as a god and not just any god, but the one and only true God. He had to conquer polytheism. And to convince humans of such realities, he had to engage in demonstrations of power. Or as NT professor Timothy G. Gombis puts it, "anyone claiming ultimate cosmic supremacy needs a list of triumphs to validate such a contention."[13] In fact, God himself often explained he had or would perform a certain miracle so humans would "know that I am the Lord."[14]

This makes sense. But why did God often use violence to perform such demonstrations? I see at least two reasons. First, God had to communicate to humans in the language that humans in the ANE thought the gods communicated in. He had to do the things that humans thought made a god a god. He had to showcase himself in the manner in which humans believed all gods showcased themselves. Because they believed violence was the ultimate power, he had to demonstrate his superior power through superior violence. To convince humanity to abandon its confidence in violence and place it in him instead, he had to prove he was more powerful than violence by miraculously intervening in their violent conflicts. He had to beat the false gods at their own game before he could convince humans to believe in a God who plays a different game.

Second, had God not first demonstrated his superior ability to use violence, no one would have believed Jesus when he preached nonviolence. They would have thought he advocated turning the other cheek because he was incapable of doing anything else. They would have attributed his suffering to mere weakness and an inability to avoid it, instead of to a voluntary, self-sacrificial love. Similarly, had God not first established his ability to forcefully administer justice, everyone would have thought his later refusal to punish sin was due to mere powerlessness, instead of mercy and grace. After all, a judge can't truly commute a sentence unless he possesses the ability to enforce it. In short, had God not demonstrated his violent power in the OT, everyone would have dismissed the embodiment of his ethical ideal, Jesus, as a powerless, foolish, failure of a man. Many did anyway.

Teaching the basics of obedience. God also spent much of the OT teaching humanity about obedience—his desire for it, its importance in his plan for redeeming all creation, the type of obedience he expects (perfect, trusting, childlike obedience), humanity's fallen inability to perfectly obey, the natural and severe consequences of disobedience, etc.

For example, consider the events in 1 Samuel 15. As a means of punishing the Amalekites for ambushing Israel as they fled Egypt, God commanded King Saul to "go and attack Amalek, and utterly destroy all that they have," including putting all of their men, women, children, infants, and animals to death (vv. 1-3 NRSV). King Saul did as God had commanded—mostly. He killed all the Amalekites and their animals *except for* their king, Agag, and the best livestock. Saul's failure to perfectly obey his instructions displeased God, to the point that he told Samuel, "I regret that I made Saul king, for he has turned back from following me, and has not carried out my commands" (vv. 10-11 NRSV).

What's the moral of the story? It has nothing to do with the morality of violence or killing. It's about obedience. It's about God establishing his desire for complete and perfect obedience, regardless of what we think of his commands. We must not let our modern moral sensibilities regarding violence and killing distract us from the real lesson here, or anywhere else in the OT. God hadn't got to those issues yet. He knew humans would not obey his seemingly counterproductive nonviolent commands unless he first taught them the need to fully obey his commands regardless of whether they understood them or thought they could improve upon them.

It's also worth noting that God reiterates this passage's lesson many times throughout the OT in the form of explicit, direct commands to completely and perfectly obey.[15]

Developing trust. One of the primary tasks God was performing in the OT, and the one we will focus on, was developing trust. He was teaching humanity to trust in him and him alone, instead of in other gods, themselves, or violence. In fact, God spent much of his time in the OT making promises to the Israelites, commanding them to trust his promises, faithfully fulfilling his promises, and then repetitively reminding them of his perfect record of doing so.[16]

Moreover, recognizing God's desire for complete trust is the key to understanding many of his otherwise puzzling actions. For example, it helps explain why immediately after rescuing the Israelites from slavery in Egypt he sent them into the barren wilderness for forty years where food and water were scarce. Because he wanted them to learn to trust in his material provision instead of in riches or their own economic self-sufficiency, he intentionally placed them in a situation where they had to rely on him for life's basic necessities. And then he provided. Each morning he miraculously sent enough bread from heaven (called manna) to sustain them for the day,[17] and when they ran out of water, he made it spring forth from a rock.[18] Here is Moses' description of what God was up to in the wilderness:

> You shall eat your fill and bless the Lord your God for the good land that he has given you. Take care that you do not forget the Lord your God, by failing to keep his commandments, his ordinances, and his statutes, which I am commanding you today. When you have eaten your fill and have built fine houses and live in them, and when your herds and flocks have multiplied, and your silver and gold is multiplied, and all that you have is multiplied, then do not exalt yourself, forgetting the Lord your God, who brought you out of the land of Egypt, out of the house of slavery, who led you through the great and terrible wilderness, an arid wasteland with poisonous snakes and scorpions. He made water flow for you from flint rock, and fed you in the wilderness with manna that your ancestors did not know, to humble you and to test you, and in the end to do you good. Do not say to yourself, "My power and the might of my own hand have gotten me this wealth." But remember the Lord your God, for it is he who gives you power to get wealth, so that he may confirm his covenant that he swore to your ancestors, as he is doing today. (Deut. 8:10-18 NRSV)

Similar reminders to trust in God instead of wealth are sprinkled throughout the rest of the OT, along with warnings about the negative consequences of failing to do so.[19]

God's desire to build trust also explains why he always used underdogs to accomplish his purposes. They are a necessary component of convincing humans to put their trust in him because they keep the focus on his providence. Had God used powerful humans to do his bidding, human power would have gotten the credit. Paul explains:

> Consider your own call, brothers and sisters: not many of you were wise by human standards, not many were powerful, not many were of noble birth. But God chose what is foolish in the world to shame the wise; God chose what is weak in the world to shame the strong; God chose what is low and despised in the world, things that are not, to reduce to nothing things that are, so that no one might boast in the presence of God. He is the source of your life in Christ Jesus, who became for us wisdom from God, and righteousness and sanctification and redemption, in order that, as it is written, "Let the one who boasts, boast in the Lord." (1 Cor. 1:26-31 NRSV)

Later Paul reminded the Ephesians that we have all been saved by grace through faith and not by works "so that no one may boast" (Eph. 2:8-9 NRSV). In other words, God glorified himself by using the weakest of men to triumph over the strongest because using the strongest of men to triumph over the weakest would have only made humans arrogant.

The Bible is full of such underdog stories. God chose a stutterer (Moses) to negotiate Israel's release from slavery in Egypt, a 500-year-old man (Noah) to build an ark big enough to save every kind of animal from the world's largest flood, and a 100-year-old man and his 90-year-old wife (Abraham and Sarah) to begin birthing the nation of Israel.[20] He helped one man (Samson) slay a thousand enemies with nothing but the "jawbone of a donkey," and deployed a small group of young male captives to humble the powerful Babylonian empire by, among other things, miraculously delivering three of them (Shadrach, Meshach, and Abednego) from a blazing furnace and another (Daniel) from a night in a lions' den.[21] Even Jesus himself, the Savior of the world, fits this underdog pattern. He was a poor, humble, ordinary-looking, carpenter from a tiny, politically unimportant village called Nazareth. He was weak in every earthly sense of the word, yet God used him to conquer evil itself.

In Pastor Joshua Ryan Butler's words, "God usually chooses the last kids picked on the playground when it's time for a revolution."[22] Israel itself qualified as such. "Out of all the mighty old empires," Butler continues, "God chooses to reveal himself to the ancient world not through Egypt, Babylon, or Rome, but through a ragtag nation of weak and outcast slaves. When God calls Israel out of Egypt, they are 'the last and the least,' getting their butts kicked on the outskirts of the empire."[23]

God even used the commonly accepted and seemingly prudent religious practice of polytheism to teach Israel trust. In the ANE, humans worshiped just about every god they could get their hands on. After all, why not cover all your bases and have as many deities on your side as possible? But God wanted Israel's sole trust (and needed to stand out among the gods, as we will soon explore), so he commanded them to worship no other gods and to destroy the idols of their conquered enemies. An equivalent command today might be to forgo buying insurance (health, auto, house, crop, life, disability, etc.) or refrain from taking similar commonsensical precautions.

This anti-false god theme permeates the OT. Over and over again, God ordered the Israelites to not worship other gods.[24] In fact, that's the first of the Ten Commandments.[25] God also repeatedly promised to bless those who trusted in him instead of false gods and to curse or destroy those who didn't, which he did.[26]

God was particularly concerned about Israel's encounters with the false gods of their conquered enemies. He ordered the Israelites to completely destroy them to avoid being ensnared by them.[27] He also commanded the Israelites to not make treaties with foreign nations for that same reason—because their allies would tempt them to worship their false gods.[28] And remember God's genocidal commands to kill all the inhabitants of the Promised Land we mentioned earlier: "Do not leave alive anything that breathes," "You must destroy all the peoples," "show them no mercy," etc.? Their purpose was to protect the Israelites from getting entangled with false gods: "for they will turn your children away from following me to serve other gods," "otherwise, they will teach you to follow all the detestable things they do in worshiping their gods," "do not serve their gods, for that will be a snare to you," etc.[29] God even commanded the Israelites to kill any of their fellow Israelites who enticed them to worship other gods, even if it was their own spouse, child, sibling, or closest friend.[30] When it came to worshipping (i.e. trusting in) other gods, God didn't mess around.[31] He saw it as a blatant, rebellious rejection of his sovereignty.[32]

Most importantly for our purposes, recognizing God's desire for complete trust explains his hatred for and prohibition of militarism. He wanted Israel to trust in his power, not their own military might. He wanted them to rely on his abilities, not their own. He wanted them to place their hope in him, not themselves. That's why he commanded them not to train for war, maintain a standing army, stockpile weapons, enter into foreign alliances, or amass a war chest, and it's why he was always quick to condemn their flirtations with developing a military.

Throughout the entire OT, trusting in military might and trusting in God are seen as mutually exclusive. Over and over, Israel faced the same choice: it could engage in militarism or trust in God, but not both. The two are simply incompatible. To build a strong military is to at least partially trust in it instead of God and thereby deny God the *complete* trust he desires (and is due). The prophet Ezekiel went so far as to describe Israel's military alliances with foreign nations as spiritual prostitution, accusing them of engaging "in prostitution with the Egyptians" and "with the Assyrians too" and even expanding their "promiscuity to include Babylonia" (Ezek. 16:23-29).

God's desire to build trust also explains why he repeatedly sent Israel into battle greatly outnumbered and outgunned. He was teaching them he was in control and would take care of them even when the odds were overwhelmingly stacked against them. That's why he repeatedly put them in situations where victory lay entirely outside of their control and could only come from him. He wanted to eliminate any doubt that success was due to his power and abilities, not theirs. Over and over again he thrust them into helpless circumstances where they had to trust in him, and then he faithfully rescued them.

To state it another way, military victory was to be a miracle, one performed by God. As Yoder wrote, "Yahweh himself gives the victory. It is not that the Israelites did a better job than their enemies of deploying their forces or that they had better weapons or stronger allies."[33] Israel's holy wars "were not calculating, strategic applications of violence in order to achieve stated political goals. They were strange events."[34] Its warfare was "not statecraft as usual. It had no standing army, no generals, no war colleges, and no horses or chariots. Holy war was a miracle when it happened."[35] Sprinkle concurs: "Victory comes from Yahweh, not swords and spears.... Israel was to remain militarily *weak*. They were never to assemble 'enough military power to defeat the enemies.' God does that."[36] "Israel's 'army'—if we can even call it an army—is a group of weekend warriors whose skills, or lack thereof, testify to the power of God, who alone ensures victory."[37] Or as Butler puts it, "Israel's battle strategies look ridiculous because they are designed to. They highlight that God is the one really doing the fighting."[38] "God gives Israel victory in spite of herself, not because of herself."[39] Let's take a look at a few of Israel's miraculous victories.

Crossing the Red Sea (Exodus 14). Israel's escape from Egypt is a good place to start. Through a series of miracles, God had just convinced a reluctant Pharaoh to release the Israelites from centuries of slavery. As Israel was marching towards the Red Sea, Pharaoh changed his mind and led his army in pursuit. Suddenly, the Israelites found themselves trapped between the sea and the approaching Egyptian army. Terror overtook them and they cried out to Moses (God's right-hand man at the time), protesting that it would have been far better to have remained slaves in Egypt than to escape just to die in the desert. Moses answered, "Do not be afraid. Stand firm and you will see the deliverance the Lord will bring you today. The Egyptians you see today you will never see again. The Lord will fight for you; you need only to be still." Then God miraculously divided the water "and the Israelites went through the sea on dry ground, with a wall of water on their right and on their left." As soon as they reached the other side, God made the sea come crashing down on "the chariots and horsemen—the entire army of Pharaoh that had followed the Israelites into the sea. Not one of them survived." Here's how the incident ended: "And when the Israelites saw the mighty hand of the Lord displayed against the Egyptians, the people feared the Lord and *put their trust in him* and in Moses his servant."

The moral of the story is clearly about trust, not violence. God didn't call the Israelites to fight for him. He called them to trust him by walking through the parted sea. Their victory depended on their willingness to trust God, not on their ability to use violence or be self-sufficient. In fact, this incident largely set the standard for God's involvement in Israel's warfare throughout the rest of the OT. Going forward, God would refer to it whenever he needed to remind the Israelites to trust him, doing so over eighty-five times throughout Scripture.

The Battle of Jericho (Joshua 6). In the first battle of Israel's conquest of the Promised Land, God miraculously caused the heavily fortified city of Jericho's walls to collapse. All Israel had to do was parade its army around the outside of the city while its priests blew trumpets. Then it charged in to easily overtake it. Butler puts the incident in perspective:

> Can you imagine the Allied Forces of World War II storming the beaches of Normandy with—not guns—but musical instruments? Or the Mongols marching up to the Great Wall of China and making—not war—but music? Or Canadians and Mexicans taking guitars and drums and marching along the US border as an act of war?
>
> This is not a battle strategy; it's a recipe for disaster.
>
> Unless God is the one leading the charge.[40]

Gideon defeats the Midianites (Judges 6 and 7). In response to Israel's request for deliverance from Midianite oppression, God commanded Gideon to "go in the strength you have and save Israel." But Gideon hesitated, saying "how can I save Israel? My clan is the weakest in Manasseh, and I am the least in my family." God responded with a promise: "I will be with you, and you will strike down all the Midianites, leaving none alive." So Gideon marched his men to a camp south of Midian. When he arrived, God made things even more difficult for him. He said to Gideon, "You have too many men. I cannot deliver Midian into their hands, or Israel would boast against me, 'My own strength has saved me.'" He had Gideon reduce his army from thirty-thousand men to ten-thousand by sending home every soldier who was afraid. But that was still too many, so he instructed Gideon to take his men to the water for a drink and send home all those who knelt down to drink instead of lapping the water from cupped hands. After that, only *three hundred* men remained. Nonetheless, God reiterated his promise to deliver the Midianites, who were "thick as locusts" and whose "camels could no more be counted than the sand on the seashore," into their hands. The next day that's exactly what he did. "Armed" only with trumpets and torches, Gideon's "army" marched to the edge of the Midianite camp and blew their trumpets. At once, "the Lord caused the men throughout the camp to turn on each other with their swords," and those who fled were killed or captured. God essentially did everything. Israel only had to trust. Thus, the moral of this story is the supremacy, dependability, and trustworthiness of God, not the ethics of violence.

Hezekiah breaks the Assyrian siege (2 Chronicles 32). When the mighty Assyrians invaded Judah, Judah's King Hezekiah told his people, "Be strong and courageous. Do not be afraid or discouraged because of the king of Assyria and the vast army with him, for there is a greater power with us than with him. With him is only the arm of flesh, but with us is the Lord our God to help us and to fight our battles." Then the king of Assyria laid siege to one of Judah's cities and sent intimidating messages to its inhabitants, warning them that their god would not save them any more effectively than the gods of all the other cities they had recently conquered. But King Hezekiah held strong and put his trust in God. Therefore, "the Lord sent an angel, who annihilated all the fighting men and the commanders and the officers in the camp of the Assyrian king. So he withdrew to his own land in disgrace."

Again, the takeaway here has nothing to do with the ethics of violence or any type of bloodlust on God's part. Here's what the passage itself says is the point: "So *the Lord saved* Hezekiah and the people of Jerusalem from the hand of Sennacherib king of Assyria and from the hand of all others. *He took care of them* on every side." As Yoder observed, "The battle call is not 'to the barricades!' but 'stand still and see the salvation of YHWH!'"[41]

Even when God doesn't do everything himself and instead has Israel do much of the fighting, the Bible always makes clear that God's involvement is decisive. The "one common denominator" that "runs through each successful battle" is that "victory is clearly the consequence of God's involvement in the battle," writes biblical studies professor Tremper Longman III.[42] "Human participation matters but is never determinative of the outcome."[43] Similarly, Chapman notes that "Israel's own military participation is viewed as either practically unnecessary or as merely providing support ... rather than ensuring victory in and of itself. The biblical pattern of discourse consistently attributes decisive military activity to Yahweh alone...."[44] God, not humanity, takes center stage. Let's look at three such examples.

Moses' staff overcomes the Amalekites (Exodus 17). When the Amalekites advanced on the Israelites at Rephidim, Moses instructed Joshua to gather some of his men and fight them. While they fought, Moses ascended a hill and raised his staff in the air. "As long as Moses held up his hands, the Israelites were winning, but whenever he lowered his hands, the Amalekites were winning." Eventually, "Joshua overcame the Amalekite army with the sword," but only because Moses' "hands remained steady" until then. Although the Israelite's did all the actual fighting, their victory was dependent not upon their own military prowess but upon Moses' symbolic act of trust.

God's hailstorm (Joshua 10). When the "five kings of the Amorites" joined forces to attack the city of Gibeon, God told Joshua, "Do not be afraid of them; I have given them into your hand. Not one of them will be able to withstand you." After marching all night, "Joshua took them by surprise" and God "threw them into confusion before Israel" so that Joshua's forces triumphed. But God wasn't done. As the enemy fled, "the Lord hurled large hailstones down on them, and more of them died from the hail than were killed by the swords of the Israelites." On that day, the biblical writer concluded, "*the Lord gave* the Amorites over to Israel."

David and Goliath (1 Samuel 17). Most of us know this story. God used an ordinary shepherd boy with a measly slingshot to defeat a heavily armored and well-equipped legendary warrior who stood almost ten feet tall, thereby scattering the mighty army who stood behind him. But what you may not have previously noticed is how David himself places the focus of the encounter on God's power and provision:

But David said to the Philistine, "You come to me with sword and spear and javelin; but I come to you in the name of the Lord of hosts, the God of the armies of Israel, whom you have defied. This very day the Lord will deliver you into my hand, and I will strike you down and cut off your head; and I will give the dead bodies of the Philistine army this very day to the birds of the air and to the wild animals of the earth, so that all the earth may know that there is a God in Israel, and that all this assembly may know that the Lord does not save by sword and spear; for the battle is the Lord's and he will give you into our hand." (1 Sam. 17:45-47 NRSV)

The OT is full of additional examples in which Israel's victories are directly attributed to God.[45] Over and over again, Israel's leaders told them it was God who fought for them, delivered the enemy into their hands, gave them the land, and drove its inhabitants out.[46] In fact, God himself frequently proclaimed those same things.[47]

Furthermore, after God delivered a victory, he would often instruct the Israelites to destroy the superior weaponry of their conquered foes, presumably so they wouldn't use it and begin trusting in it. For example, after God delivered the southern cities of Canaan into Joshua's hands, many of Israel's remaining enemies joined forces "with all their troops and a large number of horses and chariots—a huge army, as numerous as the sand on the seashore" to fight them (Josh. 11:4). But God said to Joshua, "Do not be afraid of them, because by this time tomorrow I will hand all of them, slain, over to Israel. You are to hamstring their horses and burn their chariots" (v. 6). So Joshua attacked and "the Lord gave them into the hand of Israel" (v. 8) Then, as God had commanded, Joshua "hamstrung their horses and burned their chariots" (v. 9) David did the same thing after he had defeated the king of Zobah and "captured a thousand of his chariots, seven thousand charioteers, and twenty thousand foot soldiers. He hamstrung all but a hundred of the chariot horses" (2 Sam. 8:3-4). It was like Israel had miraculously overcome its better-equipped enemies with a bunch of knives and then refused to take their guns.

Indeed, from day one, God apparently designed his entire military strategy around building trust. Let's review. First, he chose the nation of Israel not because it was big and strong but because it was small and weak. As Moses told the Israelites, "The Lord did not set his affection on you and choose you because you were more numerous than other peoples, for you were the fewest of all peoples" (Deut. 7:7). Second, he intentionally preserved Israel's weakness by prohibiting militarism and outlawing all fighting he didn't explicitly order. Third, he repeatedly commanded them not to be afraid of their more powerful enemies because *he* would take care of them.[48] Fourth, when God sent the Israelites into battle, he didn't equip them with the most or best weapons, soldiers, and strategies. Instead, he sent in the peasant militia and ensured they were vastly outnumbered and outgunned, even if that meant further reducing their already weak military strength or prohibiting them from adopting the superior weaponry of their vanquished foes. Occasionally he even told them to simply stand and watch while he did all the fighting. Fifth, despite all these handicaps, he always delivered a victory when he said he would. Every. Single. Time. If that's not a five-ingredient recipe designed specifically for baking trust, what is?

Throughout the OT, God also taught trust the old-fashioned way— with a carrot and a stick. Good things happened when the Israelites placed their trust in God and bad things happened when they didn't. In example after example, trusting in God led to victory, peace, blessings, and general wellbeing, while trusting in anything else (false gods, themselves, violence, foreign powers, etc.) led to defeat, destruction, pain, and suffering. For OT Israel, trust in God wasn't merely virtuous. It was pragmatic.

The prophets never let the Israelites forget it. They repeatedly sounded such warnings. "It is better to take refuge in the Lord than to trust in humans" (Ps. 118:8). "Fear of man will prove to be a snare, but whoever trusts in the Lord is kept safe" (Prov. 29:25). "Blessed is the one who trusts in the Lord" (Prov. 16:20). "Those who trust in the Lord are like Mount Zion, which cannot be shaken but endures forever" (Ps. 125:1). "Trust in the Lord with all your heart and lean not on your own understanding; in all your ways submit to him, and he will make your paths straight" (Prov. 3:5-6). "Do not put your trust in princes, in mortals, in whom there is no help. When their breath departs, they return to the earth; on that very day their plans perish. Happy are those whose help is the God of Jacob, whose hope is in the Lord their God" (Ps. 146:3-5 NRSV).[49]

The prophets' warnings often specifically mentioned militarism and violence. "Some trust in chariots and some in horses, but we trust in the name of the Lord our God. They are brought to their knees and fall, but we rise up and stand firm" (Ps. 20:7-8). "A king is not saved by his great army; a warrior is not delivered by his great strength. The war horse is a vain hope for victory, and by its great might it cannot save. Truly the eye of the Lord is on those who fear him, on those who hope in his steadfast love, to deliver their soul from death, and to keep them alive in famine" (Ps. 33:16-19 NRSV).[50]

Over and over again, the OT tells us Israel was victorious in battle *because it relied on God.*[51] Likewise, when Israel was defeated, it was *because it didn't trust God.*[52] "The nation's survival is not assured ... by horses and chariots," Yoder notes, "but by faith."[53]

In this sense, God's relationship with OT Israel was largely quid pro quo. His blessings were not unconditional. They were more contractual.[54] As theologian and professor Stephen G. Green puts it, "Yahweh's people thrive when they embody Torah but deteriorate when they turn away from the covenantal politics of Yahweh."[55] God offered them victory, peace, and prosperity, but they had to trust him to get it. When they misplaced their trust, the miraculous victories ceased, they lost God's protection, and the natural negative consequences of their violence kicked in. In a pattern reminiscent of Jesus' proclamation that "all who draw the sword will die by the sword" (Matt. 26:52), every time Israel trusted in militarism and violence they sowed the seeds of their own self-destruction, which usually came at the hands of their enemies. Or as God once explained to Joshua, "Israel has sinned; they have violated my covenant, which I commanded them to keep.... That is why the Israelites cannot stand against their enemies; they turn their backs and run because they have been made liable to destruction" (Josh. 7:11-12). "Obedience brings victory against the toughest opponents," observes Longman, "while disobedience means defeat even against the weakest."[56] Through such cause and effect, God methodically taught Israel to trust him.

This is illustrated perfectly by the story in which God sent an angelic warrior to slaughter 185,000 Assyrians while they slept. The mighty and brutal Assyrians were trying to conquer the entire Middle East and Israel was faced with determining how to defend itself. Should it simply give up and throw itself at Assyria's mercy? Should it build up its own military defenses? Should it enter into military alliances with its neighbors? Or should it turn to God? In other words, should it put its trust in Assyria, its own military might, the military strength of its neighbors, or God? According to the book of Isaiah, Israel tried each of the first three options and all of them ended disastrously. It wasn't until Israel took the prophet Isaiah's advice to place their trust in God instead of earthly things that they experienced victory and safety. When King Hezekiah finally prayed to God for his help, God sent an angel to kill the sleeping Assyrians.[57]

As it turns out, the OT views Hezekiah as one of the few "good" kings and does so *because he trusted God.* Here's how the prophet Jeremiah described his reign:

He trusted in the Lord the God of Israel; so that there was no one like him among all the kings of Judah after him, or among those who were before him. For he held fast to the Lord; he did not depart from following him but kept the commandments that the Lord commanded Moses. The Lord was with him; wherever he went, he prospered. (2 Kings 18:5-7 NRSV)

King Hezekiah pleased God not because he took matters into his own hands (i.e. not because he took responsibility for world events) but because he entrusted them to God. As the Psalmist wrote, "God's pleasure is not in the strength of the horse, nor his delight in the legs of the warrior; the Lord delights in those who fear him, who put their hope in his unfailing love" (Ps. 147:10-11).

This perspective also explains why God viewed Israel's request for a king in 1 Samuel 8 as a sign of distrust. Recall that the Israelites asked him for a king like the other nations had—a tangible, relatable, familiar, typical earthly king who they could see and touch and rely upon to militarily provide them with safety and security. To understand why God interpreted that request as a distrustful rejection of his own kingship, we need to look back to Deuteronomy 17. In it, God placed three restrictions on kings: (1) He "must not acquire great numbers of horses for himself or make the people return to Egypt to get more of them;" (2) "He must not take many wives;" and (3) "He must not accumulate large amounts of silver and gold" (Deut. 17:16-17). At first glance, these three criteria may seem a bit odd, but upon closer examination, they all revolve around the issue of trust. Theologian Charles E. Gutenson explains how:

First, the king that Israel would have was not to gather horses. Horses were the ancient Near Eastern equivalent of the B-1 bomber: fighting on horseback was the state of the art in contemporary weaponry. To be instructed not to hoard horses was to be instructed not to trust in one's own military might or cleverness.

Second, the king was instructed not to intermarry with those around him. At first, this seems likely to be about racial purity. However, the means of forming strategic alliances in the ancient Near East was through intermarrying. God is telling us that we are not to trust our own cleverness and strategies in protecting ourselves.

Finally, the king was not to spend time building a great economic empire. To do so would certainly mean falling prey to trusting in one's economic might as a means of exerting power over others. In short, each of these three points constitutes ways in which we trust in our own cleverness to protect ourselves against the threats that inhabit our world as humans. The biblical view of a king (only finally and fully to be realized in Jesus) is very different from our normal conceptions of kingship and of the power that national leaders wield.[58]

In other words, God prohibited a militaristic kingship because he wanted the Israelites to completely trust in him and when they requested a militaristic king he knew they had denied him that trust. The issue wasn't simply having a king. It was militarism—and therefore trust.

All of this leads to a crucial conclusion: The OT's holy wars were about trust, not violence or killing. God was teaching his followers to trust in him and him alone, not establishing the moral boundaries of acceptable violence or the criteria for fighting a just war. He was teaching them to trust him to take care of the things they thought they needed to take care of themselves. War was simply the classroom in which he taught. Because it was such an integral and commonly accepted part of ANE life, he used it to teach his foundational moral lessons, ones that laid the necessary groundwork for his future anti-violence, anti-killing, and anti-war lessons.

It's easy for us to get sidetracked today by our more advanced, post-Jesus moral perspective and consequently hung up on the violence that God committed and condoned. But as Yoder pointed out, "the ethics of bloodshed was not the issue. The issue was a new way of being created and preserved as a people: by God's intervention. God's people wait for God to intervene."[59] He elaborates:

> The phenomenon of holy war as a political and cultural experience in the early Hebrew period was, when properly understood, a new happening. It was not just war; it was something different. It had non-Hebrew analogues, but the creation of a people through God's act to save them in war was an event that has to be understood in terms that go beyond the simple moral question, is killing right or wrong? That was not the first question. The first question was, what does it mean to live by virtue of God's grace? The grace that we experience first in that story is God's grace in saving a people—by drowning the Egyptians—when the people could not save themselves. That was the first experience of divine salvation.[60]

> Therefore the violent story of the Old Testament is to be taken first as a case history of living as a people by grace. In that ancient culture, when they had not spent time refining ethical models, part of living by grace as a people was seeing God wipe out their enemies—and sometimes helping God do so.[61]

Or as Brueggemann puts it, Israel's "notion of God is one who will intervene and save, but who first must be addressed in trust."[62] Likewise, biblical scholar Ingrid E. Lilly writes, Israel's "engagement with the issues raised by human warfare" prompted it to see various "extremely important aspects of God's relationship with humanity," including his "capacity to defend and protect, to reverse oppression, to empower refugees, and to free humans from their bondage to the powers of the world."[63]

This is why the God-sanctioned wars in the OT were all about God's actions, not man's, and why, in this regard, they all shared three important attributes. First, Israel obtained God's permission and blessing before battle.[64] Over and over again before combat, God reassured them by saying things like "*I* will deliver the enemy into your hands," "*I* will give you the victory," and "When *I* destroy them" (Josh. 6-10). Second, Israel received divine help during battle, as we have repeatedly seen. Third, Israel praised God for giving it victory after battle.[65] In short, God was at center stage before, during, and after battle. These wars were all about demonstrating God's power, providence, dependability, and glory, not about the morality of human conduct in war or the human use of violence. Those lessons would come later.

In this sense, Israel's OT wars were much more of a religious ritual than an ethical lesson and killing in battle was much more of a religious sacrifice than a murder in the modern sense. Again, Yoder is instructive:

> Before being attacked, a Canaanite city would be "devoted to Yahweh," a ceremony which made of that entire city, including its living inhabitants, a sacrificial object. The bloodshed which followed the victory was not conceived as the taking of the individual lives of persons, each of whom could be thought of as a father or a mother or a child; it was rather a vast, bloody sacrifice to the God who had "given the enemy into our hands." The enemy has been put to death not because he has been conceived of personally as an object of hate but because in a much more ritual way he becomes a human sacrifice.[66]

Yoder goes on to describe Israel's warfare as "sacramental" and more of a "charismatic event" than "a result of strategic planning."[67]

When we step back and look at how Israel prepared for and fought its battles, it's hard to argue with him. Strict religious purity was enforced in the military camps.[68] The soldiers' bodies were kept holy through sexual abstinence.[69] Fighting was preceded by consecration, sacrifices, speeches given by priests, and assurances from God that he would give them the victory.[70] They carried the sacred Ark of the Covenant into battle in front of the army.[71] Prayers, religious songs, and celebrations occurred throughout the battle.[72] And then afterwards, the Israelites totally destroyed the enemy and its property as an offering to God, a religious practice known as "the ban" or *herem* in Hebrew.[73] As Green describes it, "The ban is a kind of sacrifice of dedication. It is the final act in the ritual conduct of a holy war, the handing over of the captives and the booty to Yahweh."[74]

Warfare was an act of corporate worship, not a lesson in the ethics of violence. It was a confessional endeavor, a demonstration of trust in God's sovereignty. "Thus," theologian Gerhard von Rad concludes, "we can indeed consider holy war as an eminently cultic undertaking—that is, prescribed and sanctioned by fixed, traditional, sacred rites and observances."[75]

Nonetheless, Israel's OT wars weren't *holy wars* as we understand the term today. They were Yahweh wars. There's a difference. A holy war is a war fought by humans to support a religious cause. A Yahweh war is a war fought primarily by God himself, and as Lilly points out, "The implication of the Yahweh war is that Yahweh's power is the only real human defense. Humans should therefore not seek out or even engage in military activity."[76] Or as Chapman notes, "the Old Testament tradition of 'Yahweh war' means exactly what it says: war belongs to God to prosecute, not humankind...."[77] In this regard, "ascription of warfare to God actually serves to limit rather than promote militarism on Israel's part."[78] Professor Willard M. Swartley concurs: "A first fundamental conviction is that God does not need us humans to fight against human enemies to win divine victory."[79] Because of the OT, "we know that we humans need not take God's battle into our own hands, that we need not control history's outcome, and that we need not take revenge on our enemies."[80] "It is mine to avenge; I will repay," says God (Deut. 32:35).

As hard as it is for us to understand today, even the practice of *herem* was anti-killing. It signaled God's sovereignty over life and stood as a reminder that humans should not kill without his permission. Nugent explains:

> Though it certainly offends modern sensibilities to speak about the death of humans as sacrifices, we must reckon with the fact that Scripture uses such language. Scripture does not do so to denigrate humans but to underscore that the Israelites were not participating in normal military bloodshed. God would not allow his people to wage war for material gain, imperial advancement, or ethnic cleansing. Rather, God emphasizes that only he has the right to take life and that the Canaanite battles, from the Israelite's perspective, were about obedience to God and thus worship.[81]

Plus, we must not lose sight of the fact that *herem* was one of God's cultural accommodations. According to Boyd, "there is, in reality, nothing particularly unique—let alone 'holy'—about the fact that ancient

Israelites believed that their deity wanted them to kill and, therefore, that they fought their battles under the banner of their God."[82] Similarly, according to Thompson, "we have clear archaeological evidence that this custom was commonplace among Israel's neighbors."[83] "I think we can safely conclude, therefore, that *herem* was not God's idea, but rather that it was a custom so deeply engrained that God not only had to tolerate it, but actively to retain it."[84] And don't forget, such religious rituals and sacrifices were among the OT practices Jesus explicitly abolished in the NT when he perfected the law.

Therefore, to the extent Israel's wars have something to say about the ethics of violence, killing, and war, they send a clear antiviolence message. Do not trust in violence. Do not rely on it for your safety or prosperity. Do not put your hope in it. It cannot save you. It only leads to pain, suffering, death, and destruction.

The irony is that people today cite the OT holy wars for the precise opposite purpose: to justify their use of and trust in violence, killing, and war, instead of God. Yoder lays it out:

> Negative legalism has said that since God commanded those wars back then, war must not be wrong in principle and our wars need not be wrong either. Yet the closer we look at the reports of wars that were commanded back then, the more we see that they are unique happenings, miracles, and sacrifices, in no way comparable to war as a regular instrument of national policy or to the use of an army as an institutional core of national polity. Only if wars today were commended by prophets and won by miracles would the wars of Yahweh be a pertinent example. As it is, taking them seriously would rather count on the other side. Israel was to trust Yahweh for national salvation, rather than using instruments like alliances with Egypt or the accumulation of horses. It is thus blatantly inappropriate to read those ancient stories as a document on whether war is sin, because that is not what they intended to document. What they intended to document is that Yahweh takes the side of his people: they can trust him for their continued existence. If that fundamental truth has any relevance for later times, and for the New Testament community, it would have to be precisely in the direction of trusting God for survival, rather than the lesser-evil arguments for war.[85]

At least this is how the Israelites themselves perceived the OT wars. The prophets didn't conclude, "God killed all the Canaanites so killing God's enemies is justified, maybe even preferable on occasion." Instead, they concluded, "God has always taken care of us, so we should trust in him *and not the sword.*" We should embrace the same anti-violence lesson.

Furthermore, not only is God's attempt to cultivate trust a central theme in the OT, but there's a sense in which it explains the entire OT narrative. It starts with humanity's first sin in the Garden of Eden. After creating the first humans, God commanded them to not eat from only one tree, the tree of the knowledge of good and evil, because it would cause them to die.[86] But then Satan claimed God had lied. If they ate of it, he told them, they would certainly not die but instead would become "like God, knowing good and evil" (Gen. 3:2-5 NRSV). So they ate. They disobeyed God because they believed him untrustworthy. Satan had convinced them God's rules were not for their good but only for God's good. According to Boyd, "This is the foundation of all sin: the lie that God is untrustworthy, the lie that God is not altogether loving and that he doesn't have our best interests in mind."[87] From that moment on, everything God did was aimed at proving himself trustworthy, even his use of violence.

That's why he formed his followers into the peculiar nation of Israel. His solution to the problem of distrust was to create a people who would trust in him for everything and thereby demonstrate to the rest of the world the unparalleled blessings of doing so. That is how Israel was to be a blessing to all other nations.[88] They were to be living proof that God is trustworthy, that he has our best interests in mind, and that obeying him is for our benefit, not just his.

Israel's formation began with God's call to Abraham to leave the relative security and comfort of his life in Babylon, which was the cultural center of the known world at the time, and trustingly follow him into the unknown. The primary purpose of such a call was to form Abraham's descendants into a nation that would trust in God instead of human power, particularly governmental power. "In calling Abraham out of Babylon," Nugent writes, "God was also calling him out of the apex of human power politics."[89] In other words, "The Israelites were called to be an exemplary culture over against the cultures of the earth, which were built upon the Babel model of humanly engineered unity, stability, and civilization."[90]

God knew "the greatest obstacle to becoming an exemplary nation that trusts [him] alone and orders its life according to his intentions is the self-preserving societal reflex of ordering life around hierarchical, sword-driven governmental structures....," writes Nugent.[91] That's why he formed his followers into a separate, vulnerable, largely defenseless nation. That's why he didn't give them a centralized government, a national defense strategy, a foreign policy program, a diplomatic network, or a means of amassing great wealth. That's why he "did not build his people into a nation that could aspire to the superpower status of neighboring empires" but at most "would be a relatively small and quirky nation that appears to the nations to have something of an unhealthy codependency upon their deity."[92] God wanted them to trust in him for everything, not in human power and not in government. Trust in him was supposed to be the core of Israel's identity.

No wonder Roth believes "the entire history of God's people in the Old Testament teeters on this question of trust."[93] It's hard to argue with him. The entire storyline seems specifically designed to showcase God's trustworthy attributes—his superior power, wisdom, control, intentions, and dependability.

Of course, this trust theme isn't limited to the OT. God's desire for trust and efforts to develop it spill over into and permeate the NT too. The relevant passages are too numerous to cite, so I will just quote Roth's synopsis:

> Over and over again, Jesus called on his disciples to put their security in God rather than in money or status or power. Paul repeatedly admonished the newly established churches to direct their loyalty to Christ alone. And the story of the early church is filled with stirring accounts of people whose resolute faith in Christ and trust in God was so deep that it led to their persecution and death.[94]

In other words, the same positive directive (trust in God alone) and all the same prohibitions (don't trust in yourself, don't trust in other men/kings/government, don't trust in military might, don't trust in violence, don't trust in riches, don't trust in false gods, etc.) found throughout the OT are also consistently reiterated throughout the NT.

But there is one key difference. God no longer asks his followers to trustingly employ violence. Instead, he now asks us to trustingly *not* employ violence. Whereas in the OT he asked his followers to trust him by waging war when they were vastly outnumbered and outgunned, he now asks us to trust him by *refusing* to wage war in all situations, even when others use violence against us. Whereas in the OT he asked his followers to trustingly fight with inferior weapons of violence, he now asks us to trustingly fight with wholly nonviolent weapons (i.e. love). Whereas in the OT God demanded that his followers entrust their lives to him by entering into battles greatly outmatched, he now demands that we entrust our lives to him by refusing to use violence for any reason, even to merely defend ourselves (e.g. do not resist an evil person and turn the other cheek). Whereas in the OT refusing to fight with violence was often a sign of distrust, it's now a sign of trust (and vice versa, fighting with violence has become a sign of distrust).

God still wants our complete trust. He just wants it in a different form. He still wants us to continue fighting his ongoing war against evil. He's just shifted what our fighting looks like. He still commands us to do radical things that require trust. He's just removed all violence from the equation. He still demands we trust him with our lives. He's just changed the manner in which we do so. He still uses underdogs in ways that highlight his sovereignty, providence, and trustworthiness. He's just using nonviolent ones now.

What the Israelites Saw

The Israelites would have viewed God's actions through rudimentary ethical glasses. They would have been focused on the introductory basics—who is this Yahweh character, what does he want, does he know what he is talking about, is he as powerful as he claims, will he take care of us as he has promised, can he be trusted, is obeying his weird rules really in our best interest, etc. They would have interpreted their ongoing history as the story of a unique God competing for their faith, trust, obedience, and worship, not as a post-Enlightenment-style course in human ethics. They would have been struck by how God intervenes in human history to save his people without their help, not by the fact that he utilized violence to do so.

They wouldn't have even thought of the moral questions we ask today. Such questions wouldn't have made sense to them. Our modern moral questions stand on the shoulders of other preceding questions and answers, the ones God was dealing with in the OT. At that time, ethics wasn't even a branch of knowledge yet. No one sat around studying the general moral principles that govern people's behavior. Humanity hadn't developed the concept of natural morality or drawn a distinction between universally right and universally wrong behavior. To paraphrase Yoder, ethics in the OT was subordinated to something else, something more than ethics.

For example, consider something as basic to us as the morality of killing. Asking questions like "Is killing wrong?" or "What does God's involvement in killing tell us about whether and how we can kill?" wouldn't have made any sense in the ANE. Killing in general wasn't a moral issue back then. It wasn't forbidden or even frowned upon yet. It was a regular, widespread, commonly accepted fact of life. It was taken for granted as a normal part of human existence, just like slavery and polygamy. Drawing a line between morally justified and morally unjustified killing wasn't on humanity's radar. When God intervened and began killing their enemies and commanding them to do the same, no one would have thought, "Hmmm. I guess this settles it. All killing isn't wrong. In fact, it looks like some killing isn't merely justified as a lesser evil but is actually a positive good. After all, God did it."

Of course, God gave the Ten Commandments to Israel relatively early in its national history and those commands included a command not to kill, but none of those commands were universally known general moral principles yet. They were merely part of God's special instructions to the uniquely theocratic nation of Israel. Thus, the command not to kill was just another Israel-specific civil law, like the commands to worship no other gods and to observe the Sabbath. No one had yet considered that such commands might apply to those outside of Israel. We know this because the OT itself never raises the issue. Not once during any of the subsequent holy wars in which God kills and orders killing does anyone question such killing or attempt to rectify it with the Sixth Commandment. No one would know to do so until after Jesus.

When we impose our modern, post-Jesus moral questions on OT events, we usually get into trouble. As we saw with Israel's wars above, we get derailed and end up missing the whole point. The story of God asking Abraham to sacrifice his son Isaac provides another example. Let's take a look.

God promised to make Abraham "into a great nation" and his offspring as numerous as the dust of the earth and the stars of the sky (Gen. 12:2).[95] Years later, when Abraham was ninety-nine years old, his wife Sarah was ninety, and they both were understandably questioning God's plans, God informed them they would soon give birth to a boy through whom God would fulfill his covenant.[96] Sure enough, within a year, Sarah miraculously bore him Isaac.[97] But then God did something seemingly counterproductive. When Isaac became a young boy, God said to Abraham, "Take your son, your only son Isaac, whom you love, and go to the land of Moriah, and offer him there as a burnt offering on one of the mountains that I shall show you" (Gen. 22:1-2 NRSV). Abraham faithfully complied, no questions asked. He went to the mountain, built an altar, placed Isaac on top of it, and then "reached out his hand and took the knife to kill his son" (Gen. 22:3-10 NRSV). But at that moment, God called out from heaven and commanded him not to lay a hand on the boy because he had sufficiently proven his willingness to obediently sacrifice his own son, his *only* son.[98]

What is going on here? We all know that to kill a child is the epitome of morally abhorrent, particularly when it's your own child and you are sacrificing him as part of some cultish ritual. And because we know that, we are inclined to interpret the story as God proving his unquestionable sovereignty by demanding obedience even when we find it personally painful and morally repulsive.

But that wouldn't have been Abraham's perspective. In his day, sacrificing your firstborn was standard operating procedure. Everyone did it. As Yoder explains, "It was as natural to sacrifice one's firstborn son, because of the prior claim of God on the fertility of one's wife and as a way of assuring her future fertility, as it was to sacrifice the firstfruits of the field and the flock for the same reason."[99] That's likely why Abraham didn't plead with God for Isaac's life, like he later plead for the lives of those living in Sodom and Gomorrah. Therefore, Yoder continues, we "misunderstand the Abraham story completely if we try to see in it the paradoxical command of a God telling a man to do something awful."[100] Likewise, we also misunderstand it if we get distracted by the sentimental connection between a father and a son, which is a much more modern phenomenon.

God was not testing Abraham's ethics or the strength of his emotional attachment to his son. In Yoder's words, the story is not about "whether killing is right or wrong" or "proof that that God is sovereignly unaccountable, or irrationally self-contradictory, or that His power is most clearly seen where our good sense and our sensitivity are summoned to bow blindly before Him."[101]

What lesson was God teaching? In a word, trust. The broader context and how the author of Hebrews interpreted it makes this clear.[102] For Abraham, the issue was whether he could trust God to fulfill his promise to make his descendants into a populous nation if his only son died after he and his wife were well past the age of child bearing. He was wondering if God could be trusted to uphold his end of the bargain, not how a good God could command him to kill an innocent child, particularly his own.

Therefore, analyzed in its proper context, the story is not about the morality of child sacrifice or killing in general. It's about trust. Here's Yoder again:

> The question "Is killing wrong?" is not the right question to ask about sacrificing Isaac. Killing was not wrong in the cultures of the Ancient Near East. Instead, the story invites us to ask who God is and what it means to listen to God. The wrongness of killing will come in due time, as the meaning of trusting God evolves.[103]

We must analyze God's OT actions and commands from the perspective of the ancient Israelites, not from our modern, post-Jesus perspective. We must interpret them the same way his intended recipients interpreted them. We must strive to learn the same lessons they learned. We must apply God's OT answers to the questions they were designed to address, instead of trying to force them into our modern moral framework. Instead of pulling God's OT actions out of context, generalizing them, and then directly applying them to our modern ethical issues, we must analyze them within their unique historical and cultural circumstances. That's how to properly determine what ethical lessons they have to teach us today.

Furthermore, we must view the biblical narrative in its proper chronological order. The moral conundrums of the OT only arise when we get the order wrong. As Yoder points out, most of the problematic approaches "begin to state the problem by looking *back* upon the Old Testament from the New.... But the story did not move that way.... It was rather a purposeful movement in the other direction."[104] He explains:

> If we look at the Old Testament from the perspective of the New we are struck by the difference, and the difference seems to lie at the point of whether killing is forbidden or not. But if we were instead to look at the events of the old story as they happened, moving toward the new, we should have been struck by quite another kind of consideration. It is therefore more proper, in reading the Old Testament story, to ask not how it is different from what came later, but rather how it differs from what went *before* or what prevailed at the time, and how it moves toward what was to come later. If we put the question in this way, we then find that the diversity of imperatives regarding killing is not the basic issue. What is most fundamentally at stake is rather an understanding of the covenant community and its relationship to God who has called it and promised it His care.[105]

To state it another way, the human story doesn't unfold in the sequential order most people have in mind when analyzing God's OT actions. God didn't (1) create humans, (2) declare killing and violence to be immoral, (3) participate in and command killing and violence, and then (4) reiterate that killing and violence are immoral. Such a sequence would create some major problems. But those problems never arise when we place the human story back into its actual order. God (1) created humans, (2) humans began using violence and killing, (3) God intervened to get them back on the right track, sometimes using violence to do so, and then (4) God sent Jesus to officially declare all killing and violence immoral.

God's actions in the OT only create ethical contradictions and conflicts when we view them through the lens of what hadn't happened yet, particularly the love, mercy, grace, and nonviolence of Jesus. Before him, most of the moral issues that draw our attention today simply weren't issues yet. It would take his life and teachings to make them so.

Summarizing the Pedagogical Role of the OT

Because of human nature, God had to take a pedagogical approach to teaching ethics. He had to work within the confines of human development. He had to start with the basics, structure his lessons to fit the relative ignorance of his beginner students, and then bring them along gradually. He had to teach humans how to grow up to be disciplined, responsible, successful, healthy adults, just like we must do with our children.

That's why God improved Israel's ethics but didn't immediately perfect them. That's why he temporarily accommodated some unethical cultural practices. That's why he forbid some behaviors in the OT that he now permits (like eating pork) and permitted some behaviors in the OT that he now forbids (like divorce and violence). And that's why he sent Jesus to finalize his ethical revelation. "Just as a mother gives milk and not 'strong meat' to her baby," Cavanaugh writes, "so God has nourished us through our infancy until we were ready to receive the full revelation of God in Christ."[106] Thompson elaborates:

> As circumstances change, as people grow or degenerate, God molds his message to the needs of the hour. For a people long enslaved in a pagan culture, the Sinai revelation was just what was needed—a little thunder and smoke to catch their attention. But as time went on, a fresh revelation became necessary to correct certain misconceptions about God and to shed fresh light on the path of his people.[107]

Therefore, God's OT actions played an indispensable role in the ethical education of the human race, but it was a temporary role. They laid the necessary groundwork for the future revelation of his universally and eternally applicable ethical rules in the life and teachings of Jesus, but they did not attempt or intend to teach such rules. They merely set the stage for them.

This is a crucial distinction. In the OT, God was teaching humanity to believe in him, to trust him, and to obey him, but he wasn't teaching precisely what to obey. That's what he sent Jesus to do. To oversimplify a bit, the OT teaches us that God desires complete obedience and is worthy of such obedience while the NT teaches us exactly what he wants us to obey. Consequently, looking to the OT for detailed instructions on how God wants us to behave is a misuse of the OT, one that usually produces theological confusion and sinful behavior.

So yes, God used violence to lay such ethical groundwork, but his purpose in doing so was to create the conditions under which his nonviolence rules could be received and implemented. He was constructing the historical, religious, and cultural foundation upon which Jesus' antiviolence message could be believed. Plus, he used violence to move his followers in the right ethical direction—toward nonviolence. Thus, far from supporting violence, the OT paves the way for condemning it.

Two final pedagogical points before we move on. First, note that we have applied this pedagogical approach to only a few of God's OT actions. If we had the time, we could use it to explain many more, including the weird cleanliness laws and Israel's intense tribalism. McLaren explains:

> What if people who live in the second-grade world of polytheism need to learn about one God as superior to others before they can handle the idea of one God as uniquely real? What if, in order to properly understand God's concern for social justice, they must first have a concept of God being pleased or displeased, and that concept can only be developed through the visceral reflexes of cleanliness and revulsion, which are in turn reinforced through ceremonial rules and taboos? What if the best way to create global solidarity is by first creating tribal solidarity and then gradually teaching tribes to extend their tribal solidarity to "the other"? What if, then, God must first be seen as the God of our tribe and then only later as the God of all tribes? What if we need to learn to find God in the face of our brother before we can find God in the face of the other, the stranger, even the enemy? And what if, until we find God in both our brother and the other, we can't truly say that we know God maturely?[108]

Second, notice there is no incremental revelation of God's ethical ground rules. For example, God never compromised on the necessity of obedience and trust. From day one, complete obedience and trust have always been right and even the slightest amount of disobedience or distrust has always been wrong.

Monster or Teacher?

Viewing God's actions from a pedagogical perspective not only helps explain why he used incremental revelation but also helps demonstrate why he's not a moral monster.

To move humanity forward, God had to do what every effective teacher must: meet his students at their current level. As it turns out, that level was relatively barbaric. Remember, this was not only pre-Middle Ages, pre-Renaissance, pre-Enlightenment, and pre-human rights but also pre-Jesus and pre-NT. There was no standard of comparison yet (i.e. Jesus) by which to universally denounce evils such as violence, killing, slavery, and war, let alone the more refined ethical issues we deal with today like intolerance, racism, and misogyny. The OT Israelites lived in a world in which sacrificing your firstborn child to the gods was a common practice, not the world we inhabit today in which merely spanking a child is taboo. By today's standards, humans were crude, uncultured, and morally immature. As Copan points out, "life in the Ancient Near East was much like the 'state of nature' described by philosopher Thomas Hobbes ... in his *Leviathan*: 'nasty, brutish, and short.'"[109]

To effectively communicate to humans in such a primitive moral state, God had to begin by speaking their language—the language of violence. Before it was a moral issue, violence was the universal human language. It was a way of life. Everyone spoke it and understood it. Consequently, before God could teach humanity a new language, he had to first speak to it in the language it understood. He had to speak to humans in violence before he could teach them to speak nonviolence. Again, God wasn't working with 4.0 honor students who had already taken the foreign language classes of Nonviolence 101, 201, and 301. He was working with brand new beginners who only spoke one primitive language—violence.

By using violence, God was employing the tactics of a good teacher. He was meeting humans where they were, establishing common ground with them, and communicating to them in a language they understood.

This is why God demonstrated his superiority by demonstrating his superior ability to wield violence, why he proved his trustworthiness by sending his followers into violent battles greatly outmatched and then single-handedly delivered the victory, why he revealed his desire for obedience by violently punishing disobedience, and why he even used violence to communicate his deep concern for justice, as McLaren explains:

> And what if, in order to understand the character of God that lies behind, beneath, above, and within the agency of God, we must similarly pass through some stages in which our understanding is imbalanced and incomplete? What if, for example, to view God as passionately committed to justice and goodness, we must first pass through a stage

in which we see God's passion for justice being expressed in the violent defeat of injustice? Or to say the same thing slightly differently: What if the only way to get to a mature view of God as nonviolently yet passionately committed to justice is to pass through an immature stage in which God appears to be both passionately and violently committed to justice? Don't we, as children, go through similar stages in coming to understand our parents?[110]

Note that meeting humanity where it was and communicating to it in ways it understood necessitated God getting his hands a little dirty. To help us out of the mud pit, he had to get a little muddy. He didn't create, celebrate, or even condone the pit or its mud, but he did reach down into it to pull us out. He sacrificed some of his purity to save us. He's not a moral monster for doing such a thing. He's a merciful Savior. He graciously and self-sacrificially dirtied himself by descending into the muck and mire to save us from an eternity of wallowing in our own ethical filth. He got involved in humanity's violence not because he likes violence but because he doesn't, because he knows it is antihuman and lovingly wanted to rescue us from it. That's the divine beauty in the midst of the OT's ugliness.

To explain it another way, given the pervasiveness of violence in the ANE and the fact that God was dealing with rational beings who possess free will, which he needed to respect, it was impossible for God to completely avoid becoming involved in violence. Just like none of us can truly free ourselves from being implicated in the violence our nation uses today if we want to remain citizens (after all, we vote for the politicians who wage it and pay the taxes that fund it), so too God could not truly free himself from being implicated in humanity's violence if he wanted to intervene into human history. And because he would be implicated in it in one way or another, he did the most antiviolence thing possible: he limited violence as much as possible and used it to lay the groundwork for his plan to abolition it.

As Boyd points out, "We may think of God as something like a heavenly missionary to our fallen world."[111] He elaborates:

> I have been acquainted with several people who have worked as missionaries to tribes in Third World countries that had not yet heard the gospel. I am told that serving in these contexts often requires a great deal of patience and flexibility. One sometimes encounters centuries-old customs such as "female circumcision" that are, by western Christian standards, utterly inhumane. The missionary cannot simply point out the inhumanity of these ancient customs and expect the tribe to abandon them. If the missionary ever hopes to have the tribe

eventually embrace the gospel and abandon their inhumane customs, they must rather initially accept the culture of the tribe as it is and gradually earn the right to be heard by patiently demonstrating God's love as they sow seeds of the gospel that they hope will bear fruit in the years to come. We might say that the missionary must, for a while, bear the sin of the tribe and take on the appearance of condoning a sinful custom if they ever hope to free the tribe from their bondage to their inhumane tradition.[112]

This is "why we find in Scripture the heavenly missionary accommodating false beliefs and inhumane practices that we now know he actually deplores."[113] He must temporarily do so "if he intends to gradually influence his people away from these practices and beliefs."[114]

The story of the OT is not the story of a wrathful, bloodthirsty, genocidal God entertaining himself by arbitrarily inflicting pain and suffering on innocent woman and children, as many biblically and historically ignorant critics contend. Rather, it's the story of a loving God descending to meet humans where they were (in a violent mud pit of their own making) so he could gradually and patiently help them move beyond their ethical adolescence into a better place, a place of loving, nonviolent Christ-like community. God's OT actions do reveal something about his character, but it's not a bloodlust or an inherent propensity for violence. Its traits like patience, trustworthiness, and sovereignty.

Likewise, the ethical concessions and imperfections in the OT were due to humanity's immaturity, not God's character. They were no more God's fault than the existence of evil is God's fault. Just like he chose to create free will and then deal with humanity's misuse of it, he chose to create humans who learn, grow, and mature and then deal with humanity's necessarily incremental progress. In the words of Pope Benedict XVI,

> ... biblical revelation is deeply rooted in history. God's plan is manifested progressively and it is accomplished slowly, in successive stages and despite human resistance. God chose a people and patiently worked to guide and educate them. Revelation is suited to the cultural and moral level of distant times and thus describes facts and customs, such as cheating and trickery, and acts of violence and massacre, without explicitly denouncing the immorality of such things. This can be explained by the historical context, yet it can cause the modern reader to be taken aback....[115]

Or as minister and professor James Orr explains, God's "revelation has to take man as it finds him, with his crude conceptions, his childlike modes of thought and expression, his defective moral ideas and social institutions, and has to make the best of him it can."[116] Therefore,

Thompson concludes, the OT God "was rough only insofar as he was dealing with rough people. But because the people were so very rough, God's actions have sometimes been misunderstood...."[117]

To put it another way, God's use of incremental ethical revelation tells us as much (or more) about humans as it does about God. Here's Thompson again:

> And when this rough lot of exslaves finally arrived at Sinai, the laws which God gave through Moses provide clear evidence that these people, cowering in mixed fear and awe about the mountain, were so deeply involved with cruel customs that instant abolition of such customs was out of the question. The best that could be done in some instances was a slight "humanizing" of some of the more barbaric aspects. And I use the term "humanizing" intentionally, for I think the laws of the Pentateuch must be seen, in the first instance, as revealing the kind of people God was dealing with, and then only in the second instance, as revealing the character of the God who had chosen these people.[118]

---

[1] Yoder, *The Original Revolution*, 1206.

[2] Sprinkle, *Fight*, 473.

[3] Thompson, *Who's Afraid of the Old Testament God?*, 431.

[4] Copan, *Is God a Moral Monster?*, 1034.

[5] Ibid., 1038.

[6] See also Matt. 13:10-11.

[7] Col. 1:25-26; Eph. 1:8-10; 3:8-11; Rom. 5:6.

[8] William T. Cavanaugh, *Constantine Revisited: Leithart, Yoder, and the Constantinian Debate*, ed. John D. Roth (Pickwick Publications, 2013), 2467, Kindle.

[9] Yoder, *The Original Revolution*, 1203.

[10] Boyd, *The Crucifixion of the Warrior God*, 399.

[11] Ibid.

[12] Nugent, *Endangered Gospel*, 1341.

[13] Timothy G. Gombis, *Holy War in the Bible*, ed. Heath A. Thomas, Jeremy Evans, and Paul Copan (InterVarsity Press, 2014), 1452, Kindle.

[14] Exod. 6:6-7; 7:5, 17; 14:4, 17-18; 16:11-12; Josh. 4:20-24.

[15] Deut. 4:2; 6:1-3, 17; 7:11; 8:1, 6, 11; 11:1; 12:32; 26:17; 27:10; Josh. 22:5; 1 Kings 8:61; 2 Kings 17:13; Lev. 20:8; 22:31; Prov. 7:1-2; Eccles. 12:13.

[16] Ezek. 12:25; Ps. 9:10; 22:4-5; 33:4; 57:10; 62:8; 86:15; 89:34; 100:5; 111:7-8; Prov. 3:5-6; Num. 23:19; Josh. 1:9; 21:45; 23:14; 1 Kings 8:20; 8:56; Deut. 7:8-9; 31:6; 32:4; Lam. 3:23; Gen. 21:1-2; Dan. 6:23.

[17] Exod. 16:1-36; Num. 11:1-9; Neh. 9:15, 20.

[18] Exod. 17:1-7; Num. 20:1-13; Ps. 78:15-20; Isa. 48:21; Ps. 105:41.

[19] Ps. 52:5-7; 62:10; Prov. 11:28; 23:4-5; Eccles. 5:10; Jer. 48:7; 49:4-5; Job 31:24-28.

20 Gen. 6-9, 17, 21; Exod. 3.

21 Judg. 15:15; Dan. 3, 6.

22 Joshua Ryan Butler, *The Skeletons in God's Closet: The Mercy of Hell, the Surprise of Judgment, the Hope of Holy War* (Thomas Nelson, 2014), 3766, Kindle.

23 Ibid., 2741.

24 2 Kings 17:32-39; Exod. 23:13; Lev. 26:1; Jer. 10:1-5; Deut. 4:22-24.

25 Exod. 20:4-5.

26 Ps. 40:4; Exod. 23:24-26; Deut. 8:19-20; Jer. 13:24-25; Ps. 97:7; Ezek. 23:49; Josh. 23:16, Josh. 24:19; 2 Kings 17:7-39; Judg. 2:11-15, 10:6-8; Num. 25:1-3.

27 Exod. 23:23-24; Deut. 12:29-30; 18:9-11.

28 Exod. 34:12-17.

29 Deut. 7:1-6, 16, 25-26; 20:16-18; Exod. 23:32-33.

30 Deut. 13:6-11.

31 If you have ever wondered why God described himself as a "jealous" God, this is why. He detests idolatry. See Exod. 20:5; 34:14; Deut. 4:23-24; 5:9; 6:14-15; 32:21, 26; Josh. 24:19; Ps. 78:58. Even the NT associates God's jealousy with the worship of false gods. For example, after warning the Corinthians about idolatry in their church, Paul asked them, "Are we trying to arouse the Lord's jealousy?" (1 Cor. 10:22). Of course, God's jealousy is not a covetousness for something that isn't rightly his but a holy desire for what rightfully belongs to him and him alone—trust, worship, obedience, and glory.

32 Deut. 32:15-18.

33 Yoder, *The War of the Lamb*, 1364.

34 Yoder, *Christian Attitudes to War, Peace, and Revolution*, 6058.

35 Yoder, *Revolutionary Christian Citizenship*, 69.

36 Sprinkle, *Fight*, 1320.

37 Ibid., 667.

38 Butler, *The Skeletons in God's Closet*, 3778.

39 Ibid., 3805.

40 Ibid., 3756.

41 John Howard Yoder, *For the Nations: Essays Evangelical and Public* (Eugene, OR: Wipf and Stock Publishers, 2002), 86.

42 Tremper Longman III, *Show Them No Mercy: 4 Views on God and Canaanite Genocide* (Counterpoints: Bible and Theology) (Zondervan, 2010), 2725, Kindle.

43 Ibid.

44 Chapman, *Holy War in the Bible*, 774.

45 For another example, see Barak's rout of the Canaanites in Judges 4 and 5.

46 Josh. 2:24; 3:10; 6:2, 16; 8:1, 18; 10:8-11, 14, 42, 19; 14:12; 23:5, 9-10; 24:7; Deut. 1:30; 4:37-38; 7:1; 9:1; 11:22-23; 19:1-2; 20:4; 31:3; Judg. 3:28; 4:7, 14-15; 7:9, 22; 18:10; 20:28, 35; 1 Sam. 5:11; 7:10; 14:12, 23; 17:46; 23:4; 24:4; 26:8; Exod. 14:14; 1 Kings 20:28; Num. 32:20-21.

47 Josh.; 11:6; 13:1-7; 24:11-13; Exod. 14:4, 18; 23:27-30; 34:11, 24; Lev. 18:24; 20:23; Deut. 7:23.

48 Deut. 7:17-24; 20:1-4; 2 Chron. 32:7-8.

49 See also Prov. 16:3; 28:26; Ps. 21:7; 37:5-6; 84:12; 112:6-8; Isa. 26:3; Jer. 17:5-8.

50 See also Isaiah 30:1-3, 31:1-3, and Hosea 12:1, which were quoted in the previous chapter.

[51] 1 Chron. 5:20; 2 Chron. 13:18; 16:8; Exod. 23:22.

[52] Hos. 8:14; 10:13-14; Amos 2:13-16; 3:11; 6:13-14; Jer. 5:17; 13:25; 2 Chron. 16:7.

[53] Yoder, *For the Nations*, 86.

[54] Deut. 7:12-15.

[55] Stephen G. Green, *Deuteronomy: A Commentary in the Wesleyan Tradition* (New Beacon Bible Commentary) (Kansas City, MO: Beacon Hill Press of Kansas City, 2016), 28.

[56] Longman, *Show Them No Mercy*, 2811.

[57] Isa. 37:16-20, 36-37.

[58] Charles Gutenson, *Christians and the Common Good: How Faith Intersects with Public Life* (Brazos Press, 2011), 1365, Kindle.

[59] Yoder, *Christian Attitudes to War, Peace, and Revolution*, 6063.

[60] Ibid., 6052.

[61] Ibid., 6068.

[62] Walter Brueggemann, *Peace* (Understanding Biblical Themes Series) (Atlanta, GA: Chalice Press, 2001), 28.

[63] Ingrid E. Lilly, *A Faith Not Worth Fighting For: Addressing Commonly Asked Questions about Christian Nonviolence* (The Peaceable Kingdom Series), ed. Tripp York and Justin Bronson Barringer (Cascade Books, 2012), 2717, Kindle.

[64] Judg. 20:18-28; 1 Sam. 14:36-37; 23:1-4, 9-12; 28:5-6; 30:7-8; 2 Sam. 17-24; 1 Kings 22:5.

[65] Josh. 10:42.

[66] Yoder, *The Original Revolution*, 1298.

[67] Ibid., 1305, 1306, and 1310.

[68] Deut. 23:9-14.

[69] 1 Sam. 21:5.

[70] Josh. 3:5; 1 Sam. 7:7-9; 13:7-12; Deut. 20:1-2, 13; Josh. 8:1, 18.

[71] Josh. 6.

[72] Longman, *Show Them No Mercy*, 2722 and 2750.

[73] Deut. 7:2; Josh. 6:17-19.

[74] Green, *Deuteronomy*, 106.

[75] von Rad, *Holy War in Ancient Israel*, 51.

[76] Lilly, *A Faith Not Worth Fighting For*, 2685.

[77] Chapman, *Holy War in the Bible*, 990.

[78] Ibid., 836.

[79] Willard M. Swartley, *Covenant of Peace: The Missing Peace in New Testament Theology and Ethics* (Grand Rapids, MI: Wm. B. Eerdmans Publishing Co., 2006), 377.

[80] Ibid., 378.

[81] Nugent, *The Politics of Yahweh*, 2539.

[82] Boyd, *The Crucifixion of the Warrior God*, 7175.

[83] Thompson, *Who's Afraid of the Old Testament God?*, 1790.

[84] Ibid., 1795.

[85] Yoder, *The War of the Lamb*, 1385.

[86] Gen. 2:16.

[87] Gregory A. Boyd, *Is God to Blame?: Beyond Pat Answers to the Problem of Suffering* (IVP Books, 2009), 174, Kindle.

[88] Gen. 18:18-19; 22:18; 26:4-5; 28:14; Gal. 3:8-9.

[89] Nugent, *The Politics of Yahweh*, 1031.

[90] Ibid., 1185.

[91] Ibid., 1187.

[92] Nugent, *Endangered Gospel*, 1000.

[93] Roth, *Choosing Against War*, 129.

[94] Ibid.

[95] Gen. 13:16; 15:5.

[96] Gen. 17:1-6, 17-22.

[97] Gen. 21:1-3; Heb. 11:11-12.

[98] Gen. 22:11-12.

[99] Yoder, *The Original Revolution*, 1258.

[100] Ibid., 1261.

[101] Ibid., 1269 and 1288.

[102] Heb. 11:17-19.

[103] Yoder, *Christian Attitudes to War, Peace, and Revolution*, 6083.

[104] Yoder, *The Original Revolution*, 1241.

[105] Ibid., 1245.

[106] Cavanaugh, *Constantine Revisited*, 2326.

[107] Thompson, *Who's Afraid of the Old Testament God?*, 304.

[108] McLaren, *A New Kind of Christianity*, 1807.

[109] Copan, *Is God a Moral Monster?*, 1642.

[110] McLaren, *A New Kind of Christianity*, 1818.

[111] Boyd, *The Crucifixion of the Warrior God*, 15743.

[112] Ibid., 15735.

[113] Ibid., 15747.

[114] Ibid., 26901.

[115] Post-Synodal Apostolic Exhortation *Verbum Domini* http://w2.vatican.va/content/benedict-xvi/en/apost_exhortations/documents/hf_ben-xvi_exh_20100930_verbum-domini.html.

[116] James Orr, *Revelation and Inspiration* (New York: Charles Scribner's Sons, 1910), 103.

[117] Thompson, *Who's Afraid of the Old Testament God?*, 1804.

[118] Ibid., 420.

6

A SET-APART PEOPLE

In addition to God's need to use incremental ethical revelation, his need for a distinct, set-apart people is another key to understanding his OT actions. Over and over again throughout the OT, he declared he had deliberately set Israel apart from all other peoples and nations.[1] Repeatedly, he referred to them as his "treasured possession," "my people," and a "holy nation."[2] And as Yoder notes, the word *holy* here "does not primarily mean morally pure; it means separated, set aside, consecrated."[3]

To set Israel apart, God instructed them to do almost everything differently. He gave them a unique diet (e.g. no eating of "unclean" animals, strict food prep guidelines), a unique religion (monotheism), unique religious rituals and ceremonies (e.g. specific festivals, the Sabbath, the Ark of the Covenant), unique civil laws (e.g. progressive protections for the vulnerable, limits on retaliation), a unique economic system (e.g. jubilee, limits on slavery, property rights for common citizens), a unique social structure (e.g. no earthly king, non-hierarchical), a unique foreign policy (e.g. no treaties, alliances, or intermarrying), and a unique military strategy (e.g. no standing army, no stockpiling of weapons). Alone, each of these characteristics would have made Israel noticeably different. Combined, they made it completely and radically set-apart.

Thus, the Torah was not simply a list of rules. It was a way of life. As Copan explains, "So what the Israelites did in their everyday lives— even down to their eating habits—was to signal that they were God's chosen people who were to live lives distinct from the surrounding nations."[4] Or as Green notes, "Another way of expressing what this collection of policies and practices are attempting to accomplish is that they are endeavoring to shape the identity of the people."[5] Yoder went even farther, calling God's "creation of a distinct community with its own deviant set of values and its coherent way of incarnating them" the "original revolution."[6]

So why did God set Israel apart? He did it to showcase himself to the world. "You are my servant, Israel, in whom I will display my splendor"

(Isa. 49:3). "But I have raised you up for this very purpose, that I might show you my power and that my name might be proclaimed in all the earth" (Exod. 9:16). "For as a belt is bound around the waist, so I bound all the people of Israel and all the people of Judah to me, declares the Lord, 'to be my people for my renown and praise and honor'" (Jer. 13:11). "I will be proved holy through them in the sight of many nations" (Ezek. 39:27). "Yet he saved them for his name's sake, to make his mighty power known" (Ps. 106:8). "It is not for your sake, people of Israel, that I am going to do these things, but for the sake of my holy name.... Then the nations will know that I am the Lord, declares the Sovereign Lord, when I am proved holy through you before their eyes" (Ezek. 36:22-23). "He did this so that all the peoples of the earth might know that the hand of the Lord is powerful and so that you might always fear the Lord your God" (Josh. 4:24).[7]

God needed a separate and distinct nation to bear witness to his existence, supremacy, power, and goodness. His revelation, his ability to teach the world about himself and his will, depended on it. Without a set-apart people, humanity would not have been able to distinguish God's actions from all the other spiritual and non-spiritual forces humans believed were operating in the world at that time. It would have erroneously attributed most of them to some other cause or combination of causes, and consequently, God's message would have gotten lost in the relative chaos of ANE life. Therefore, God needed to communicate through a set-apart people to prevent his message from being contaminated and corrupted by outside, pagan influences.

This is also why Israel's unique identity was based entirely on its special relationship with God. It was defined by God's will while every other nation was defined by the whims of its human king. It trusted in God and God alone while every other nation trusted in itself and its cornucopia of false gods. It wielded God's power while every other nation wielded mere human power. Its story was about God's gracious saving actions while every other nation's story was about self-glorifying human actions.

Furthermore, God didn't set Israel apart simply to show off. He did it to bless all peoples and nations.[8] He did it to introduce his redemption plan and prepare the way for Jesus. He did it so that all creation would eventually come to know and serve him.[9] He did it so that all humans could find salvation in him, the only place where it can be found.[10] He did it to rescue us from enslavement to Satan. In short, he did it to save the world.

That's why God was so strict about Israel's set-apartness. The fate of the entire world depended on it. That's why he inflexibly demanded their complete obedience to all of his instructions.[11] That's why he repeatedly commanded them not to follow the customs of the surrounding nations.[12] That's why he was so concerned with them separating the clean from the unclean in every area of life.[13] That's why he got so upset whenever they acted like everyone else (e.g. requesting a king like they had, adopting their military strategies, copying their religious practices, etc.). That's why he gave them their own territory (the Promised Land) and ordered them to purge it of all outside influences.[14] That's why he got angry when they didn't completely do so. That's why he punished them so severely when they violated his set-apart instructions, even kicking them out of the Promised Land, disbanding their nation, and sending them into political exile when necessary.[15]

That's also why God was so zealous about prohibiting interaction with false gods. Remember, God instructed Israel to destroy the idols of their conquered enemies *so they wouldn't be ensnared by them,* forbade Israel from making treaties with foreign nations *so they wouldn't be tempted to worship their idols*, prohibited Israel from intermarrying with foreigners *so they wouldn't be misled into serving false gods*, and even commanded the Israelites to kill any member of their own family who enticed them to follow other gods.[16] Christian apologist Greg Koukl explains:

> God's rescue plan to save mankind depended on the theological purity of Abraham's seed, Israel. The cancer of idolatry needed to be cut out for the patient—God's plan of redemption—to survive. Syncretism with pagan religions would have corrupted Israel's theological core. By purging the land of this evil, God ensured that redemption—forgiveness for the evils of any nation—would be available in the future for people of every nation.[17]

In fact, almost all the genocidal purging God ordered was specifically designed to protect Israel from distinctiveness-killing contamination by foreign idols.[18] For example, consider Moses' anger when he learned that his officers had allowed the Midianite women and children to live after burning down their towns and killing all the men. He said, "Now kill all the boys. And kill every woman who has slept with a man, but save for yourselves every girl who has never slept with a man" (Num. 31:14, 17-18). When we ignore the context and judge Moses' actions by today's moral standards, he looks like a monster. But notice the reason Moses himself gave for ordering the women killed: "They were the ones who followed Balaam's advice and enticed the Israelites to be unfaithful to the Lord in the Peor incident, so that a plague struck the Lord's people" (v. 16).[19] Obviously, Moses was reasonably concerned about idol contamination derailing God's entire world-saving plan. That's why he ordered his officers to take the necessary precautions to prevent the Israelites from engaging in such idolatry *again*.

Protection against idolatry also helps explain some of God's seemingly arbitrary laws. For example, God prohibited eunuchs from taking part in Israel's communal life.[20] Why? According to Thompson, "we now know from sources outside the Bible that Canaanite religion was violent and depraved" and that one of its customs "was the practice of male castration ... in connection with the 'official' worship practices!"[21] And because "there was real danger that Israel would attempt to imitate Canaanite practice," there was a "need for strong prohibitions, including categorical statements about male castration."[22] Similarly, "fairly recent discoveries have suggested that" the "prohibition against boiling a baby goat in his mother's milk (Ex. 34:26)" was "directed against Canaanite fertility practices," which were tied to the worship of their gods.[23]

God did what he had to do to keep his name holy, his message clear, and his world-saving plan moving forward. He told the prophet Ezekiel, "But for the sake of my name I did what would keep it from being profaned in the eyes of the nations in whose sight I had brought [the people of Israel] out" (Ezek. 20:14).

Of course, God also had additional reasons for doing most of what was just described. He wasn't only creating a set-apart people. As previously discussed, he was also doing things like establishing his superiority, teaching the basics of obedience, and developing trust. But producing set-apartness was a primary concern.

In fact, it's no exaggeration to say that set-apartness was the key to the whole endeavor. Without it, Israel was just another dime-a-dozen pagan nation. Without it, the path to Jesus would not have gotten paved, the other nations would not have eventually been drawn to God's love, and the whole point of God's intervention into human history would have been negated. Without it, nothing else God did mattered. Hence the drastic measures he undertook to ensure it. Green elaborates:

> Can God's people embody their special calling and identity if they are assimilated into the host culture in a syncretistic manner? Israel's unique purpose and calling would come under threat. The people would fail not only to be blessed but also to be a blessing to the rest of creation. The unmistakable difference between the holy people of Yahweh and the surrounding people groups would not be known. There would be no

comprehension of Yahweh and his purpose for the world; therefore, it was understood as essential for Israel to maintain a clear and unadulterated identity as God's holy and chosen people. This included eliminating all fallacious and misleading ideologies, values, and practices of counterfeit gods.[24]

Or as OT professor Eugene H. Merrill put it, Israel's "success depends on their obedience to the covenant (Deut. 7:12), especially the exclusive worship of their God (7:16) and the destruction of the nations intent on leading them astray (7:24–25)."[25] After all, the wisdom and beauty of God's plan can only be displayed to the world if his followers actually embody it.

Set-apartness is still the key today. Remember, Jesus reconfigured the identity of God's followers by denationalizing them and creating the church. But by doing so, he didn't repeal their set-apartness. He perfected it. The church is to be just as set-apart as the nation of Israel was and for many of the same reasons. Like Israel, we are "a chosen people, a royal priesthood, a holy nation, God's special possession" (1 Pet. 2:9). Like Israel, we have been commanded to "not conform to the pattern of this world" (Rom. 12:2).[26] Like Israel, we live lives of obedience as a means of glorifying God.[27] Like Israel, we have been set apart to bless all nations and we exist to bear witness to God so that all peoples may find salvation in him.[28] Like Israel, we exist not for ourselves but for others. And like Israel, we can only accomplish our mission by maintaining our set-apartness, by being *in* the world but not *of* it.

But unlike Israel, we are to embody God's fully revealed kingdom and perfect ethical ideal, which means we are to be set apart in different ways. Instead of being a uniquely theocratic, demilitarized, morally advanced nation that sometimes uses violence for specific and limited purposes, we are to be a transnational, interethnic, nongovernmental, geographically dispersed people that refuses to use violence for any purpose. Instead of being identifiable by our unique nationalistic characteristics, we are to be identifiable by our uniquely anti-nationalistic characteristics. Instead of being recognizable by *how* we employ violence, we are to be recognizable by our *refusal* to employ it. Instead of being distinct in our ability to control history, we are to be distinct in our trust of God's ability to control it. Instead of being distinguishable by our superior ability to dominate our enemies, we are to be distinguishable by our self-sacrificial love for them. Instead of being set apart by our racial, ethnic, and cultural differences, we are to be set apart by our racial, ethnic, and cultural inclusivity. Instead of protecting ourselves against contamination by unbelievers, we are to go out into the world and engage them in hopes of contaminating them with the love of Jesus. This is how God's followers participate in his ongoing, world-saving plan today.

As Yoder put it, Jesus did not "bring a vision of a new society that could be imposed from the top down. He did not bring a new constitution, a new set of laws, or new way to regulate global economic and social structures. What Jesus brought was a new way of being a distinctive and set-apart people."[29]

So yes, God used violence to ensure Israel's set-apartness. But he did it to move his followers to a place where they could be set apart by their nonviolence and thereby help him save the world from violence. God's ultimate goal has always been to save people, not to destroy them. The limited, temporary destruction of a few rebellious people was the means to that loving end. "Apparently," Chapman notes, "God was not able, given the violence of the world, to preserve Israel purely nonviolently although, even so, Israel's history witnesses to and moves toward nonviolence as it moves toward Christ."[30] Nugent elaborates:

> ... God carves out a people for himself—a people who will become his instruments of worldwide peace. During the early phases of this people's formation, a certain degree of violence will be required, albeit on a smaller scale, to preserve them, create space for them, and protect them against internal and external threats. God must creatively solve the problem of forging a people of peace in a world of war. The Yahweh wars are part of his solution. God delivers and sustains the Israelites with his own sword so they will not grow too accustomed to swords of their own. Such protection will only be required for a time. God will eventually scatter his people throughout the world so they can take his peace to the nations.[31]

Again, God didn't employ violence because he is wrathful, legalistic, and bloodthirsty. He did it because otherwise Israel's set-apartness, and by extension his entire loving plan, would have been compromised. Copan summarizes:

> If the Israelites hadn't done serious damage to the Canaanite religious infrastructure, the result would have been incalculable damage to Israel's integrity and thus to God's entire plan to redeem humanity. Much was at stake in creating the necessary context—including a set-apart people in a set-apart land—in order to bring about redemption and an eventually restored creation. Just as Frodo's success was precarious from start to finish, so was the journey from God's promise to Abram (Gen. 12) to the coming of the Messiah. God's plan involved a certain mysterious messiness, but this shouldn't deter us from seeing God's ultimate purposes at work.[32]

As always, we must not get sidetracked by our modern moral sensibilities and concerns. God did not intend the actions he took to set Israel apart to be a lesson on the ethics of violence any more than he intended them to be a lesson on the merits of political freedom of religion. For the same reasons we must not interpret God's fierce anti-idolatry in the OT as a condemnation of freedom of religion, we must also not interpret it as an endorsement of violence. Or as Green puts it, "The question that the text poses for Christians is not so much how or if when to use violence, but how to maintain an alien status to the host cultures that the church finds itself within."[33]

---

[1] Deut. 7:6; Lev. 20:24, 26; Ps. 4:3; 2 Sam. 7:23.

[2] Deut. 14:2; 26:19; 28:9; Lev. 26:12; 1 Kings 6:13; 8:53; 2 Kings 20:5; 1 Chron. 11:2; 17:21-22; Jer. 2:11; 31:1; Exod. 3:7; 10:6-7; 19:5-6; 22:31; Isa. 1:3; 62:12; 1 Sam. 2:29; Ps. 50:7; 135:4; Hos. 4:6; Joel 3:2; Amos 7:15; Mic. 6:3; Zeph. 2:8; Gen. 18:18-19.

[3] John Howard Yoder, *Radical Christian Discipleship* (Yoder for Everyone), ed. John C. Nugent, Andy Alexis-Baker, and Branson Parler (Herald Press, 2012), 1220, Kindle.

[4] Copan, *Is God a Moral Monster?*, 1504.

[5] Green, *Deuteronomy*, 34.

[6] Yoder, *The Original Revolution*, 356.

[7] See also Jer. 33:9; 2 Sam. 7:23.

[8] Gen. 12:3; 18:18; 22:18; 26:4; 28:14; Acts 3:25; Gal. 3:8.

[9] Ps. 22:27; 33:8; 48:10; 64:9; 67:7; 72:11; 86:9; 97:6; Isa. 45:22; 66:18, 23; Dan. 7:14; Zeph. 2:11; Hag. 2:7; Mal. 3:12; Rom. 14:11; 16:26; Phil. 2:10, 11; Rev. 15:4.

[10] Isa. 49:6.

[11] Deut. 4:5-8; 28:1-14; Lev. 20:22.

[12] Lev. 18:1-5, 29-30; 20:23; Jer. 10:1-2.

[13] Lev. 15:31; 20:24-26; Exod. 22:31.

[14] Deut. 20:16-17.

[15] Ezek. 36:16-32; 2 Kings 17:7-39; Judg. 2:11-15; 10:6-8; Num. 25:1-3.

[16] Deut. 7:1-6; 12:29-31; 13:6-11; 18:9-12; 20:18; Exod. 23:23-24, 32-33; 34:12-17; Ezra 9:1-4; Neh. 13:23-30.

[17] Greg Koukl, "The Canaanites: Genocide or Judgment?" posted January 1, 2013 at https://www.str.org/publications/the-canaanites-genocide-or-judgment#.WRB0z9LyuUk.

[18] Deut. 7:1-6, 15-16, 22-26; 20:16-18.

[19] Numbers 25:1-9 records the previous incident Moses was referring to.

[20] Deut. 23:1.

[21] Thompson, *Who's Afraid of the Old Testament God?*, 1108.

[22] Ibid.

[23] Ibid., 1160.

[24] Green, *Deuteronomy*, 31.

[25] Eugene H. Merrill, *Show Them No Mercy: 4 Views on God and Canaanite Genocide* (Counterpoints: Bible and Theology) (Zondervan, 2010), 1242, Kindle.

[26] See also 2 Cor. 6:14-18.

[27] Matt. 5:14-16; Eph. 1:3-6, 11-14; 1 Pet. 2:9, 12.

[28] Acts 3:25; 13:47; Gal. 3:8; Eph. 1:7-10; Matt. 24:14; 28:19; Isa. 49:6; Rom. 16:26; Rev. 15:4.

[29] Yoder, *Revolutionary Christian Citizenship*, 69.

[30] Chapman, *Holy War in the Bible*, 999.

[31] Nugent, *The Politics of Yahweh*, 2209.

[32] Copan, *Is God a Moral Monster?*, 4119.

[33] Green, *Deuteronomy*, 31.

7

THE CONQUEST OF CANAAN:
A JUST WAR

Although a cursory, surface-level reading of the Israelite's conquest of Canaan can make it appear morally indefensible, a more careful, contextual reading reveals an entirely just war.

The Legal Origins of the Conquest

To begin with, God owns all land, always has and always will. He created it and has declared himself sovereign over it. Just as we humans own whatever we create with our own labor and resources, so does God. Therefore, as Green notes, "He gives the land to whomever he chooses, because it is his to do with as he wills."[1]

Early in the biblical narrative, God did exactly that. He entered into a covenant with Abraham to make him and his descendants into a great nation and to give them the land of Canaan, i.e. the Promised Land.[2] On many occasions thereafter, he reaffirmed that promise to Israel's forefathers.[3]

God's promise to *give* the land to Israel may be more accurately described as a promise to *return* the land to Israel. In various places, the book of Genesis indicates Israel's ancestors (Abraham, Isaac, and Jacob) had occupied it first, even noting they had acquired title to some tracts by purchasing them from the prior owners.[4] At one point, God even told Abraham that his "descendants will come *back here*" (Gen. 15:16).

From the Israelites' perspective, the Canaanites[5] were the original trespassers and, at the time of the conquest, nothing more than squatters. They were occupying land to which the Israelites had not only a divine right (via their covenant with the land's true owner, God) but also, at least arguably, a legal right (via their prior possession).

God didn't promise the Israelites just any land. Nor did he let them attack or occupy whatever territory they wanted.[6] He restricted their conquest to lands they had a superior right to possess.

God's Patience with Canaanite Wickedness

Although Israel had a superior right to the Promised Land, God didn't immediately return it to them. He waited until the Canaanites became so wicked they lost any claim they might have had.[7] He waited until they had so abused the land, its inhabitants, and themselves that they deserved beyond all doubt to be kicked out. He waited until their injustice became so great that justice ardently demanded their eviction. And he didn't wait just a little while. He waited four hundred years![8]

In the meantime, God's own people paid the price for his patience. They spent those four centuries being oppressed and exploited in Egypt.[9] So the question is less "How could God be so cruel to the Canaanites?" and more "How could God be so merciful to them for so long and at the expense of his own people?" It is less "How could a good God order the conquest of Canaan?" and more "How could a good God wait so long to order it?" The answer, I believe, lies in God's loving, self-sacrificial nature, a nature he calls his followers to embody for the benefit of the world.

The OT repeatedly tells us how wicked the Canaanites had become by the time God evicted them. They were engaging in adultery, idolatry, sorcery, witchcraft, ritual prostitution, incest of all types, bestiality, and child sacrifice.[10] You read that right. They were not only having sex with their own mothers, fathers, sisters, brothers, sons, daughters, aunts, and uncles, they were having sex with animals. And to top it off, they were sacrificing their own children to false gods. Plus, they were a violent, aggressive, oppressive people, frequently attacking and exploiting the innocent and defenseless. And it wasn't just a few people involved in these practices. It was everyone. Nor were such practices sporadic. They were routine. No wonder God concluded they had so "defiled" the land it "vomited" them out (Lev. 18:25 NRSV).

When Israel infiltrated Canaan, it was not an idyllic paradise inhabited by peaceful, innocent, neighborly, indigenous people who mostly kept to themselves and who had acquired the land legally and were using it responsibly. Rather, it was inhabited by thoroughly wicked and profoundly corrupt tenants who were there illegally and who broke almost every rule in the book. Consequently, Israel's conquest of Canaan was not an impulsive overreaction from a raging, bloodthirsty, genocidal tyrant. It was the product of a mercifully patient but ultimately just landlord.

Not only did God use the conquest to return land to Israel, he also used it to punish the Canaanites for their wickedness.[11] As Seibert points out, "These texts draw a clear connection between Canaanite wickedness and their removal from the land."[12] Or as leading NT scholar N. T. Wright puts it, when the Canaanites were "ripe for judgment," God used "his people and their entry to the land as the means of that judgment."[13] Just as God had used the flood during the time of Noah and the plagues during the exodus from Egypt as instruments of punishment, now God was using Israel.[14] Of course, God also made it clear to the Israelites that he wasn't using them to punish the Canaanites because they were so righteous but rather because the Canaanites were so wicked.[15]

In that regard, God conditioned Israel's occupation of the land on its capacity to behave better than the Canaanites. Over and over again, he instructed them not to copy their sinful lifestyles,[16] told them their success in the Promised Land depended on their obedience,[17] and warned he would punish them if they adopted the Canaanites' wicked ways.[18] As Green concludes, "The claim of Deuteronomy is that the welfare of the people is dependent upon faithfulness to the political policies and practices of Yahweh...."[19]

Unfortunately, Israel eventually started behaving like the Canaanites and God punished them accordingly, just as he had warned.[20] He even used pagan nations to do so, just as he had previously used Israel against them.[21] In fact, he used much of the same harsh language against Israel— destroy, drive out, etc.[22] Ultimately, things got so bad God even evicted Israel from the land, just like he had the Canaanites.[23] Thus, not only was Israel held to the same standard as the Canaanites, it was arguably held to an even higher standard because God had chosen them to be a unique example of holiness.

God's Offer of Mercy to the Canaanites

On top of being bewilderingly patient with the Canaanites, God gave them multiple opportunities to flee or repent before punishing them. After all, he wouldn't have patiently held off on punishing them for four hundred years unless fleeing or repenting was a real possibility. First, he sent an angel and hornets to drive the Canaanites out ahead of Israel.[24]

Second, given Israel's ragtag, slow-moving, chariotless military, the Canaanites would have seen Israel coming from miles away, giving them plenty of time to head to the hills. Sometimes God even commanded Israel to use stalling tactics that provided additional time, as in the Battle of Jericho where he commanded it to march around the city each day for six days before finally attacking on the seventh.

Third, there's evidence Israel's reputation preceded it. For example, prior to the conquest, Moses told God that the Canaanites had already heard he was with them, a claim Rahab (the Canaanite prostitute who lived in Jericho and helped Israel conquer it) later substantiated.[25] Likewise, the Gibeonites apparently made a treaty with Joshua "because of the fame of the Lord your God," because they had "heard reports of him: all that he did in Egypt, and all that he did to the two kings of the Amorites east of the Jordan" (Josh. 9:9-11).

This makes sense. News of God's power would have spread like wildfire across the ANE after he miraculously liberated Israel from slavery in Egypt, not to mention his earlier displays of power during things like the destruction of Sodom and Gomorrah. After all, that was largely the point of many of the miracles he performed: to use Israel to make a name for himself across the known world. Here's Joshua's explanation for why God parted the Jordan River for the Israelites during the conquest of Canaan, just as he had previously parted the Red Sea for them during their exodus from Egypt: "He did this so that all the peoples of the earth might know that the hand of the Lord is powerful and so that you might always fear the Lord your God" (Josh. 4:24).[26]

Fourth, God spared those nations and tribes who repented.[27] The same was true for individuals, as Rahab exemplified. Sometimes the Israelites even went out of their way to spare the non-repentant but less-wicked inhabitants.[28]

Israel's conquest of Canaan was not a surprise attack. Only those who stubbornly ignored all the warning signs and refused to believe or flee were subjected to forceful eviction and, if they still refused, sometimes death. As Sprinkle puts it, "God's main concern was that there be no Canaanites living in His residence (unless they turn to Him, like Rahab). Any killing would be a result of their resistance, not Yahweh's insatiable thirst for blood."[29]

If death seems a bit harsh, remember that God had limited punishment options. As a homeless tribe of nomads, Israel didn't have any prisons in which to house the Canaanites or the infrastructure necessary to enslave them. Thus, God only had two options: chase them away or kill them. He repeatedly tried the former, but some refused to leave and chose death instead.

God's Restrictive Marching Orders

When the time was finally right, God sent Israel in to occupy the land, but not without important restrictions. First, he limited who they could fight by instructing them to not attack nations outside of the Promised Land.[30] Then he curbed how they were to fight by issuing a set of restrictive marching orders:

- Do not stockpile weapons, develop foreign alliances, accumulate a war chest, or maintain a standing army.

- If anyone is afraid or has recently built a new house, planted a vineyard, or gotten engaged, excuse them from fighting.

- Although you will be outmatched, do not be afraid because I will give you the victory.

- When you approach a city, give it an opportunity to peacefully surrender. If it does, you must not kill them but can turn them into forced labor. If it does not surrender, then attack it and kill all the men but spare the women, children, and livestock.[31]

Lastly, he issued one exception to those general rules: In the land you will make your home, kill everything that breathes.[32] "Otherwise," he warned, "they will teach you to follow all the detestable things they do in worshiping their gods, and you will sin against the Lord your God" (Deut. 20:18).

Although some of these orders offend our modern moral sensibilities, we must not forget that these instructions were radically progressive in their day, even revolutionary.

When reading these orders, we also need to bear in mind exactly who Israel was and exactly who it was attacking. The Israelites were not a numerous, well-supplied, well-trained, well-organized, well-established nation of Navy Seal-like warriors, and the Canaanites were not a small, defenseless, ill-supplied, untrained, unorganized, nomadic group of unsophisticated peasants, as many of the popular caricatures imply. Precisely the opposite.

Israel was a humble, ragtag collection of ex-slaves who had wandered the wilderness for the last forty years eating strange food, wearing strange clothes, and living a strange lifestyle. They were largely helpless, so much so they needed divine help daily just to feed themselves. Plus, they didn't have a standing army, let alone a well-trained one equipped with the latest military technology and staffed with experienced officers versed in contemporary military strategies. Nor were they numerous. In fact, God chose them to be his people precisely because they were "the fewest of all peoples" (Deut. 7:7-8 NRSV). The OT writers liked to point out how outnumbered Israel was, often declaring their opponents to be "as numerous as the sand on the seashore" (Josh. 11:4).[33]

The Canaanites, in comparison, were a well-equipped, highly trained, militarily advanced, aggressive, mighty, populous, and established collection of big, well-fed people who had been dominating the region for centuries. The Israelite spies who first scouted Canaan reported seeing strong, powerful people of great size living in large, fortified cities situated in a land flowing with milk and honey and stocked with abnormally large fruit.[34] In fact, they initially were so intimidated by them they longed to be slaves in Egypt again and refused God's command to invade, which they viewed as a suicide mission.[35]

When God ordered the Israelite conquest of Canaan, he wasn't ordering the school bully to pick on the class runt. Nor was he ordering a fair fight between two relatively equal opponents. He wasn't even ordering an underdog team like the Minnesota Twins to take on a powerhouse like the New York Yankees. Instead, he was ordering a mediocre high school team to take on the NBA champs. He was ordering a short, puny, shepherd boy with a sling shot and a few pebbles to take on a giant, muscle-bound, legendary warrior outfitted with the best armor and weaponry money could buy.

Israel didn't have a chance. It was spears versus machine guns, chariots versus F16s, rowboats versus destroyers. The contrast between the two nations couldn't have been more exaggerated. The Canaanites were in a different league. And that's exactly how God wanted it. He wanted the Israelites to rely on him for victory so the world would know *he* was in control.

A Non-Aggressive Conquest

We also need to keep Israel's objective in mind. It was not engaging in imperialism, colonialism, or empire building. It was not selfishly trying to expand its own borders or increase its own national coffers at the expense of other, weaker peoples. Instead, it was reclaiming its home. It was a group of refugees, an exploited and oppressed tribe of political exiles, trying to reestablish residence in the land of their ancestors.

Furthermore, Israel's battles were almost always defensive. Even if you view its physical entry into the land as aggressive (which requires ignoring its superior right to the land), Israel rarely attacked first. Many passages point out that Israel was being attacked, not attacking.[36] Other times the reactive nature of Israel's actions is deducible from previous passages. For example, remember when God sent an angle to kill 185,000 Assyrians while they slept? Well, it can be read as a response to Assyria's aggression. A couple of decades before, Assyria had attacked and captured the cities of Judah.[37]

Some of the Canaanite tribes even initiated contact by "attacking defenseless Israel as they were fleeing a situation in which they had been oppressively enslaved for hundreds of years," as Lamb describes it.[38] When Israel was "weary and worn out" from fleeing the Egyptians, the Amalekites dishonorably "attacked all who were lagging behind" (Deut. 25:17-18). Years later, God would remark, "I will punish the Amalekites for what they did to Israel when they waylaid them as they came up from Egypt" (1 Sam. 15:1-2). Lamb concludes, "The Israelites initiated none of these initial engagements because they were a wandering band of unarmed political refugees. The nations that attacked them were taking advantage of Israel's weak situation."[39]

Many other passages tell us the Canaanite tribes often joined forces to attack Israel.[40] In one example, they banded together to attack Israel's ally Gibeon, prompting Israel to come to its defense.[41]

In fact, when we take the entire context and history into consideration, it's reasonable to view Israel's "conquest" as a gradual, mostly peaceful, civilian-driven reestablishment of residency followed by aggressive Canaanite attempts at re-expulsion. Some passages even provide clear support for such a perspective: "Whenever the Israelites planted their crops, the Midianites, Amalekites and other eastern peoples invaded the country" and ruined "the crops all the way to Gaza and did not spare a living thing for Israel.... They invaded the land to ravage it. Midian so impoverished the Israelites that they cried out to the Lord for help" (Judg. 6:3-6).

Yes, as part of the re-occupation of their homeland, the Israelites started a few battles against a few enemy forts, but overall their re-entry into Canaan was much more of a gradual, civilian assimilation than a focused, military blitzkrieg. After all, the whole process took about a generation. Plus, the political structure of Canaan didn't lend itself to a quick, strategic, offensive campaign. Canaan wasn't a homogenous nation with a well-defined and universally agreed-upon geographic boundary. It wasn't like invading a foreign nation today. Israel wasn't crossing a clearly marked political border into a country wholly controlled by a single, unified group of people. Instead, the area was populated by many diverse tribes and clans, many of whom held competing claims to certain tracts and some of whom were largely nomadic. In this sense, the conquest was more akin to a Native American tribe repossessing its land after having been conquered by another tribe than it was like the European settlers' colonization of the Americas, let alone like the United States deciding to annex part of modern day Canada.

Israel's conquest of Canaan was much less aggressive than it might first appear to a new reader. As Chapman concludes, the "divinely authorized" wars were "primarily but not exclusively defensive actions."[42] Or as Yoder puts it, "although the infiltration of the Israelites into Palestine had about it a certain aggressive character, the actual holy war military operations tended to be defensive."[43]

Given who Israel was, who it was up against, what it was trying to achieve, what its marching orders were, and how most of the battles arose, Israel's conquest of Canaan wasn't much of a "conquest," despite what a surface-level reading of a few OT books might otherwise suggest.

A Limited Military Campaign

Similarly, to the extent we can call the conquest a military campaign, it was a severely limited one. It was limited in time. It only applied to a relatively short period in Israel's history. It was limited in location. It only applied to the land of Canaan. It was limited in scope. It only condoned the expulsion of the people from the land of Canaan so the Israelites could reestablish a home there as a set-apart people. And, it was limited in force. It was waged according to unusually restrictive rules of engagement from within a radically anti-militaristic society.

After Israel established residence in Canaan, its offensive maneuvers ceased, at least the God-sanctioned ones, and God never again commanded such a campaign. He never commanded Israel to take up residence elsewhere, destroy other peoples, or hunt down those he had supposedly ordered exterminated. He never even commanded it to expand its borders. It was one and done. God did, however, allow Israel to continue defending its home, but only for a little while.

Notice God never sanctioned national violence in general. He never told Israel he would support their selfish, nationalistic agenda. He gave them his agenda, supported them when they fulfilled it, and withdrew his support when they didn't. He only sanctioned their use of violence against *his* enemies and within the context of *his* world-saving plan. He used Israel for his divine purposes, not vice versa.

Israel's conquest of Canaan is the only time God ever sanctioned *human* warfare. He only ever sanctioned it for the Israelites and only for them to occupy and then defend the Promised Land. To state it more generally, he only sanctioned warfare for a few generations of people from one nation at one time in history in one geographic location for one divine purpose. Of course, God himself sporadically employed warfare-like violence outside of those parameters (e.g. the flood, killing the Egyptian firstborn, and destroying Sodom and Gomorrah), but he never sanctioned humans doing so. Any such human violence was either denounced by God or merely reported as occurring without any indication of his approval.

At the end of the day, Israel's conquest of Canaan was not only a speck on the timeline of human history but also only a small part of the OT story. As Wright reminds us, "we must understand the conquest ... within the limited span of history that it actually occupies (and not magnify it into the story of the whole Old Testament)."[44] It was "a unique and limited historical event...."[45] He elaborates:

> It is a caricature of the Old Testament to portray God as constantly on the warpath or to portray the conquest as simply "typical" of the rest of the story. It is not. The book of Joshua describes one key historical event, but it was finished. It should not be stretched out as if it were the background theme music for the rest of the Old Testament.[46]

Copan makes the same point: "As we've mentioned, this Yahweh warfare wasn't the standard for the other stages in Israel's history. It wasn't intended as a permanent fixture in Israel's story."[47] Seibert concurs: "Some people, especially those who are generally unfamiliar with the Old Testament, might conclude that virtually every Old Testament passage is terribly violent and ethically unacceptable. That would hardly be accurate."[48] In short, the conquest was a significant event in Israel's national story but it wasn't an all-encompassing one.

Now let's take a closer look at what God was trying to accomplish through the conquest.

A Just God

God is just. That is to say, he is fair and impartial and does what is right and good. "For the Lord is a God of justice" (Isa. 30:18 NRSV). "He loves righteousness and justice" (Ps. 33:5 NRSV). "He is the Rock, his works are perfect, and all his ways are just. A faithful God who does no wrong, upright and just is he" (Deut. 32:4). With him "there is no perversion of justice ... or partiality, or taking of bribes" (2 Chron. 19:7 NRSV). In fact, God is so just, and so perfectly just, that eventually all nations will come to him to settle their disputes—once and for all.[49]

Because God is just, he hates injustice. That is to say, he hates evil, violence, bloodshed, oppression, exploitation, falsehood, deceit, envy, greed, idolatry, and death.[50] Injustice makes him angry. It awakens his wrath.[51] In fact, love for justice and hatred of injustice are two sides of the same coin. To love one is to hate the other.

Because God hates injustice, he fights it. He judges it, punishes it, and sets it right. That's what it means to enforce justice. It means to declare something to be wrong (via judgment) and then make it right again (via punishment and restitution).

To put it another way, God is loving. That is to say, he desires the flourishing of his entire creation. Because he is loving, he hates unloving behavior, which thwarts flourishing. And because he hates unloving behavior, he combats it. He judges it, punishes it, and sets it right.

In fact, God's justice arises out of love. Love comes first. It precedes and produces justice. God lovingly wants everyone to be treated right. He wants everyone to have life and have it abundantly, to experience existence as he originally designed it, before Satan corrupted it. Consequently, he detests and combats all anti-flourishing behavior (i.e. all evil, sinful, disobedient, wicked, unloving, unjust behavior).

If God didn't love the world, he wouldn't get angry at injustice. If he didn't desire its flourishing, he wouldn't care about unjust, unloving, anti-flourishing behaviors like violence, exploitation, oppression, murder, rape, kidnapping, etc. Wright explains it well:

> Only one thing in the universe arouses God's anger, and that is – evil. Why? Because the very essence of evil is to resist, reject, and refuse the love of God. Evil is in essence rebellion against God's love. Evil seeks to frustrate all the good purposes that God's love seeks to achieve for his creation, and that makes God angry.[52]

To quote Boyd, "The fury of God's 'wrath' against sin, injustice, violence and everything else that destroys people is nothing other than the fury of his love for people."[53] Or as German theologian and professor Jurgen Moltmann puts it, "Love is the source and the basis of the possibility of the wrath of God. The opposite of love is not wrath, but indifference."[54]

Of course, there's always a temptation to define God's love in a way that excludes justice (or vice versa), but they belong together. Properly understood, they don't conflict. When God introduced himself to Moses, he described himself as "the compassionate and gracious God, slow to anger, abounding in love and faithfulness, maintaining love to thousands, and forgiving wickedness, rebellion and sin. *Yet he does not leave the guilty unpunished*" (Exod. 34:6-7).[55] Yes, God is loving and merciful, but he is also just. Yes, God is patient, but his justice doesn't wait forever.

God's righteous anger, judgment, and punishment are all good things. They aren't merely justified. They are morally praiseworthy. They don't contradict God's goodness. They are part of his goodness. It is good for him to get angry at the exploitation of widows, the oppression of foreigners, and the mistreatment of orphans. It is good for him to judge harmful, destructive, violent, unloving, anti-flourishing behavior to be wrong. It is good for him to punish and correct theft, slavery, murder, rape, and child sacrifice. He experiences such anger, conducts such judgment, and enforces such punishment because he is a good and loving God, not because he is a selfish, bloodthirsty, vengeful tyrant. He does such things because he cares about his creation, because he wants to heal it and restore its original harmony.

What would we think of God if he didn't have such a reaction to injustice? What would we think of him if he didn't get angry at such behavior, didn't judge it to be wrong, didn't punish it, and didn't eventually set it right? Wouldn't we accuse him of not caring, of being cold-hearted, of being unjust? Theologian Walter C. Kaiser, Jr. summarizes the issue:

> God's anger and wrath are his legitimate expressions of his abhorrence of all that is sinful, wrong, unjust, and against his very nature and being. God did not flare up with impetuosity against the Canaanites, but gave them centuries and millennia to get the point and right the wrong. In the end, he had to act or he would not be holy, just, righteous, and fair.[56]

As usual, Boyd is also on point: "There is no denying that the violence ascribed to God in the OT is deeply associated with the punishment of sinners. And there is no denying that God would be unjust, and the world would remain unjust, if God did not punish those who commit injustices against others."[57]

God's justice is an integral part of the central storyline of the entire biblical narrative.[58] God identifies injustice as an unwanted disease that has infected his good creation, promises he will eradicate it, and calls us to help him do so. As Wright observes, "The whole Bible, indeed, can be read as the epic account of God's plan and purpose to defeat evil and rid his whole creation of it forever. That, it can be argued, describes everything between Genesis 3 and Revelation 22."[59] Or as Swartley puts it, "The over-arching emphasis of Scripture presents God as Peacemaker who is also the Divine Warrior fighting against evil to establish and maintain peace and justice."[60]

God's Justice in the Conquest

Let's inspect how God's justice was at work in the conquest.

The story begins in Egypt, where the Israelites had been enslaved for four hundred years. With every passing day, they grew more tired of their oppression and increasingly cried out to God for help. God heard their pleas and had compassion.[61] He promoted Moses for the specific purpose of delivering them from bondage. Here's what he told Moses:

> The Lord said, "I have indeed seen the misery of my people in Egypt. I have heard them crying out because of their slave drivers, and I am concerned about their suffering. So I have come down to rescue them from the hand of the Egyptians and to bring them up out of that land into a good and spacious land, a land flowing with milk and honey— the home of the Canaanites, Hittites, Amorites, Perizzites, Hivites and Jebusites. And now the cry of the Israelites has reached me, and I have seen the way the Egyptians are oppressing them. So now, go. I am sending you to Pharaoh to bring my people the Israelites out of Egypt." (Exod. 3:7-10)

A few chapters later, God said to the Israelites,

> I am the Lord, and I will free you from the burdens of the Egyptians and deliver you from slavery to them. I will redeem you with an outstretched arm and with mighty acts of judgment. I will take you as my people, and I will be your God. You shall know that I am the Lord your God, who has freed you from the burdens of the Egyptians. I will bring you into the land that I swore to give to Abraham, Isaac, and Jacob; I will give it to you for a possession. I am the Lord. (Exod. 6:6-8 NRSV)

And that's exactly what God did. After liberating Israel from slavery, he sent them to reoccupy the land of their ancestors—Canaan. In doing so, he was kicking the Canaanites out, but he wasn't victimizing them. They weren't innocent bystanders or merely collateral damage. Remember, not only were they unjustly occupying Israel's homeland, they were ruling it with an oppressive iron fist while indulging in a lifestyle of unspeakable wickedness. And before ordering reoccupation, God patiently waited for Canaanite wickedness to reach the point of no return and mercifully gave them every opportunity to peacefully make room for a small, poor, weak, vulnerable tribe of recently liberated slaves who desperately needed a home. By ordering the conquest, God was not disrupting a tranquil, democratic, dignity-respecting, justice-enforcing, egalitarian community. He was expelling an exploitative, human-rights-violating, war-crimes-committing, evil nation.

Pause for a moment and note the justness of God's intervention in this series of events. Motivated by compassion for the victims of injustice (Israel), he liberated them from slavery (in Egypt) and returned them to their rightful home (in Canaan). In both the exodus and the conquest, God was simultaneously giving justice to the oppressed and punishing the oppressors. This two-pronged process of justice for Israel—liberation from slavery and then resettlement of their homeland—provides the framework for the majority of the OT narrative. And no matter what perspective we take, we see a God who enforces justice. Liberation from slavery was justice for the Israelites and punishment for the Egyptians. Likewise, resettlement of the Promised Land was justice for the Israelites and punishment for the Canaanites.

Don't overlook the role of compassion in this story, or its connection to punishment. God's compassion started the whole thing. It is what moved him to liberate the Israelites from slavery in Egypt in the first place.[62] And it is one reason God gave them a home in Canaan, a home where they could recover from four hundred years of oppression and be protected from additional persecution. As such, compassion was at the heart of why God punished the Egyptians and Canaanites. In an unjust world, compassion for one party often leads to punishment for another. They are two sides of the same coin.

Also notice God's actions were reactive. He didn't introduce violence into the story. Humans did. As little children who have been caught fighting like to say, "They started it." As Butler puts it, God's actions were simply "a holy, loving response to sin's vicious assault."[63] From this perspective, the entire conquest was reactive. Again, the conquest wasn't much of a conquest.

From a broad perspective, this pattern of humans causing great injustice and God compassionately intervening to enforce justice permeates the OT. The Israelites (or occasionally other people) sin by rebelling against God, their sin (which usually involves extensive violence) produces injustice (which is the natural consequence of sin), the victims of that injustice cry out for God's help, God hears those cries and compassionately delivers them (usually via violent means that also operate as punishment for the perpetrators of the injustice), and then the cycle begins anew. This happens over and over again throughout the OT—human sin produces injustice, injustice gives rise to cries for help, cries for help lead to divine compassion and deliverance, and then the pattern repeats. In fact, this is essentially the entire storyline of the book of Judges, particularly the first sixteen chapters.[64] Psalm 106 also provides a poetic overview of the cycle. It begins by acknowledging God's love, goes on to describe the cycle, and concludes by noting that God repeatedly delivers humans from injustice because he is so loving.

This same pattern of justice applies to all of God's seemingly indefensible acts of violence in the OT. To see how, we simply need to analyze them in context. For example, consider God's total destruction of the cities of Sodom and Gomorrah.[65] At the time, both cities were engaged in great injustices, including widespread mistreatment of the vulnerable.[66] After hearing the "great" cries of their victims, God sent two angels to check things out for himself. He didn't want to rush to judgment. Before doing so, however, Abraham asked God to spare the city if he could find merely ten righteous people in it, and God mercifully agreed. But the city was so wicked and violent not even ten could be found. In fact, when the two angels arrived in town, all the men of Sodom, the young and the old, tried to gang rape them. So God punished the city for its abhorrent injustices, but only after saving the one righteous family he found—Lot's family.[67] In short, God heard the cries of the victims of great injustice, had compassion on them, ensured the perpetrators of that injustice were beyond repair, mercifully relocated the only righteous people he could find, and then punitively destroyed the perpetrators, ending their egregious injustices.

The same is true for the flood and the killing of the Egyptian firstborn. When God destroyed the entire earth with a flood, he did so in response to widespread human injustice, particularly violence, and only after giving humanity plenty of time to repent, while also sparing the only righteous people he could find (Noah and his family).[68] When God killed all the Egyptian firstborn, he did so in response to their long-standing injustices (they had enslaved Israel for four centuries) and only after giving them plenty of opportunities to voluntarily change their ways (he had already performed nine separate miracles in an attempt to convince them to peacefully free Israel).[69]

God's Universal Justice

Throughout the conquest (and the entire OT), God wasn't concerned about justice only for his followers. He was concerned about justice for everyone. He persistently made it known that he didn't want Israel perpetrating injustice itself, particularly against the most vulnerable—widows, orphans, and foreigners. He repeatedly commanded Israel to not mistreat, take advantage of, or otherwise oppress such individuals.[70] Otherwise, he warned, you will be punished, sometimes even with death.[71] The reverse was true as well. If you want to prosper, he explained, you must act justly.[72] In fact, he went a step farther and commanded Israel to proactively do good to the poor and vulnerable—to treat them equally, give them justice, defend their cause, and serve them with loving acts of kindness.[73] Do these things for the weak and defenseless, God urged, because that is what I do, what I will do, and what I have done.[74] (By the way, he never said anything similar about violence.) And remember, at the time, these were revolutionary legal protections for the weak, defenseless, and poor. In many places today, over three thousand years later, they still are.

Furthermore, as we saw earlier, when Israel failed to do justice, God punished it just like he had punished Canaanite injustice.[75] In fact, the OT says much more about God's punishment of Israel than his punishment of Canaan. As Wright observes, "over the whole history of Old Testament Israel, far more generations of *Israelites* felt the judgment of God at the hands of their enemies than the single generation of *Canaanites* experienced the judgment of God at the hands of the Israelites."[76] Theology professor Branson Parler elaborates:

> In terms of sheer volume, the Bible talks far more about God's judgment on disobedient Israel through Assyria and Babylon than it does about God's judgment on the Canaanites. In terms of judgment and terror, the narrative in Joshua is quite tame in comparison to the covenant curses of Deuteronomy 28, which promise Israel that the destruction of one's family, land, and property will drive people mad, that the horror experienced by Israel will become a "byword among the nations," and that parents will cannibalize their own children. As Jeremiah laments, "With their own hands, compassionate women have cooked their own children, who became their food when my people were destroyed" (Lam. 4:10).[77]

When it came to enforcing justice, the God of the OT was not playing favorites. He was not concerned about justice for Israel alone. He was concerned about universal justice. He didn't merely despise the oppression of *his* people. He despised the oppression of *all* people. He didn't take Israel's side no matter what. He enforced justice no matter what. He didn't merely fight for Israel. He fought for justice. The battle was not between God's people and everyone else. It was between justice and injustice. Thus, as Creach puts it, "It would not seem an exaggeration to say that the Old Testament rests on a general assumption that God is intimately involved in warfare as a judge between the parties who have conflict."[78]

To state it another way, God's justice transcends nationalism. That's why when Joshua asked the commander of God's army whether he was for Israel or its enemies, he responded, "Neither" (Josh. 5:13-14). That's why God instructed the Israelites not to attack the lands outside of

Canaan, the lands they didn't have a moral right to possess.[79] That's why he didn't let the Israelites think they were superior to their enemies and why he didn't let them dehumanize the Canaanites.[80] That's why he held his chosen people to the same (or higher) standard and punished them with the same (or greater) intensity.

God hates injustice wherever it is found. He punishes the unjust whoever they are. As the NT writers would later observe, "God does not show favoritism" (Rom. 2:11; Acts 10:34), but instead he "judges each person's work impartially" (1 Pet. 1:17). God is so just he doesn't even favor the poor: "Do not pervert justice; do not show partiality to the poor or favoritism to the great, but judge your neighbor fairly" (Lev. 19:15). With God, "there is no injustice or partiality or bribery" (2 Chron. 19:7).

God's justice also transcends race. Contrary to the claims of some critics, the God of the OT was not a racist. He created all races in his own image, not just Israel.[81] He chose Israel as a means of blessing all races, not just Israel.[82] He instructed Israel not to oppress foreigners (i.e. people of different races and ethnicities), held it to the same moral standards as he held foreigners, and punished it as harshly as he punished foreigners. He showed mercy to anyone who repented, not just Israelites.[83] The NT even includes a Canaanite prostitute, Rahab, in Jesus' genealogy and holds her up as a model of faith and righteousness.[84] Remember, one of the many ways in which Jesus fulfilled the law was by offering membership in God's family to everyone, regardless of race, ethnicity, or nationality. As Paul would later famously write, "There is neither Jew nor Gentile, neither slave nor free, nor is there male and female, for you are all one in Christ Jesus" (Gal. 3:28).

God is not in favor of certain races or ethnic groups and against others. He is for good and against evil. He doesn't care about race. He cares about righteousness. He doesn't judge and punish race. He judges and punishes wickedness. The conquest was not racially or ethnically motivated. It was not an ethnic cleansing. It was justice—impartial, unbiased, unprejudiced, universal justice.

God's Plan for Worldwide Justice

Not only was the conquest an act of justice in itself, it was also part of God's bigger master plan for worldwide justice. It was part of his grand strategy to save the entire world from the injustice of sin itself.

In giving Israel a homeland, he gave it a place where it could exist as a set-apart people, where it could be free from idolatrous, message-diluting influences, where it could bear clear witness to God's existence, supremacy, power, goodness, and will, where it could plainly point others to God's love, where it could clearly communicate and introduce God's plan to redeem the world, where it could prepare the way for the world's Savior (Jesus), where it could pave a path by which all creation could come to know him, where it could reveal God's alternative kingdom and the blessings of life under his reign, where it could distinctly model true human community and show the world what God intended it to be, where it could unambiguously highlight the difference between the violence, oppression, falsehood, deceit, pain, envy, suffering, darkness, temptation, division, and death of the fallen kingdoms of the world and the peace, truth, light, joy, harmony, unity, freedom, solidarity, and servanthood of God's kingdom. Or as Jesus would later describe it, he was providing Israel a place where it could become a shining city on a hill, "the salt of the earth," and "the light of the world" (Matt. 5:13-16 NRSV).

By ordering Israel to occupy Canaan, God wasn't trying to force others to become his followers. He wasn't trying to eradicate his enemies. He wasn't trying to establish a base from which Israel could conquer and subjugate all other peoples. He wasn't trying to satisfy a lust for death and destruction. He was trying to save the world from death and destruction. He was trying to set Israel apart so it could be used to bless all peoples. As Wright observes, "The overall thrust of the Old Testament is not Israel *against* the nations, but Israel *for the sake of* the nations."[85]

One day all nations will come to recognize this. God's sovereign justice is so great and so universal that eventually all nations, even those like Canaan, will praise him for what he achieved in the OT, including what he accomplished through the conquest.[86] In Wright's words, "even the historical defeat of the Canaanites by Israel will ultimately be seen to be *part of an overall history of salvation* for which the nations themselves will praise God."[87]

This world-saving plan is the wider context within which we must view the conquest (and everything else in the OT). We must place it not only in the broader context of the entire OT but also in the broader context of the entire biblical narrative. We must not lose sight of the bigger picture of God's universal sovereign justice. We must not forget the whole reason for his intervention into human history, the whole reason why he formed Israel into a nation in the first place. Wright elaborates:

> This is the way in which God in his sovereignty chose to work within human history to accomplish his saving purpose for humanity and for creation, including me. I may not understand why it had to be this way. I certainly do not like it. I may deplore the violence and suffering

involved, even when I accept the Bible's verdict that it was an act of warranted judgment. I may wish there had been some other way.

But at some point I have to stand back from my questions, criticism, or complaint and receive the Bible's own word on the matter. What the Bible unequivocally tells me is that this was an act of God that took place within an overarching narrative through which the only hope for the world's salvation was constituted.[88]

The Goal of God's Violence

All of this reveals a lot about God's use of violence. Because violence is a specific type of injustice, God's attitude towards it is the same as his attitude towards injustice in general. He hates it. It makes him angry. Its destructive nature thwarts the flourishing he lovingly desires for his creation. So he combats it.

God's condemnations of injustice in the OT often specifically criticized violence. He said he detests the shedding of innocent blood, hates those who love violence or are bloodthirsty, gets angry at the widespread use of violence, and is saddened when violence fills the earth.[89] He wouldn't even let David, who he fondly called a man after his own heart, build the temple because he was a warrior and had shed blood.[90] He commanded Israel to "do no wrong or violence," to "not shed innocent blood," and to give up their "violence and oppression and do what is just and right" (Jer. 22:3; Ezek. 45:9). He declared those who use violence against the poor and righteous to be wicked.[91] He frequently punished people for using violence, often by giving them over to other people's violence.[92] And, as we saw earlier, he also often rescued the innocent from violence.[93] The God of the OT viewed violence as the fruit of wickedness and condemned both specific acts of violence and violence in general.

Solomon, who the Bible refers to as one of the wisest men to ever live, also repeatedly condemned violence.[94] "Do not envy the violent or choose any of their ways" (Prov. 3:31). Do not "walk in the way of evildoers" who "eat the bread of wickedness and drink the wine of violence" (Prov. 4:14, 17). "A violent person entices their neighbor and leads them down a path that is not good" (Prov. 16:29). "The unfaithful have an appetite for violence" (Prov. 13:2). "Blessings crown the head of the righteous, but violence overwhelms the mouth of the wicked" (Prov. 10:6). According to Solomon's vast wisdom, violence is foolish.

Such condemnations do not contradict what God was doing in the conquest, or anywhere else in the OT. Instead, they reinforce it. God was employing violence against violence. He was using violence to combat, suppress, and end violence. He was waging war on war. He did it not to dominate but to end domination, not to oppress but to eliminate oppression, not to exploit but to eradicate exploitation, not to violate human rights but to enforce human rights, not to take advantage of the weak but to protect them. He did it not out of bloodlust but out of a hatred for bloodshed.

So yes, God used and commanded the use of violence in the OT, but only in the service of justice, only to stop violence. His use of violence was always antiviolence. As Butler notes, "God exerts a *violence against violence*. God arises in holy love against sin's destructive power to contain it and to restrain its devouring impulse in order to protect the flourishing *shalom* of his world."[95] Swartley elaborates:

> To attribute violence to God is a misnomer, a misplaced indictment from Scripture's point of view. Rather, judgment is what characterizes the sovereign, holy God who punishes humans for sin and violence. God's redemptive acts stand in the service of bringing human violence to an end!... To attribute violence to God is to ... confuse human perversity with the divine prerogative to establish justice and shalom by punishing human violence. To put it bluntly, God's vengeance, however executed, stands against human violence.[96]

Also note God's use of violence was always reactive. It was always a response to human wickedness, which inevitably included some type of violence.[97] Remember, God created a nonviolent world, fallen humans introduced violence into it, God immediately condemned such violence, and then he set about combatting it. God isn't the author of violence. He is the author of nonviolence. He wasn't the first to use violence. He was the first to condemn it. He wasn't the first to kill. He was the first to outlaw killing. He doesn't inflict violence. He rescues people from it. He doesn't promote violence. He punishes it.

What if a Modern Ruler Did the Same?

How would we judge a human ruler who waged the same type of war today? What if the President of the United States freed a tribe of Africans from slavery in South Africa and returned them to the land of their ancestors by ordering its current inhabitants (who were themselves systematically committing all types of crimes against humanity and had been for centuries, like sacrificially burning children alive) to make room for the homeless ex-slaves or be evicted? What if when they refused, he empowered those ex-slaves to force the violent oppressors out via a restrained, narrowly tailored, temporary military campaign?

Not only would we not accuse such a president of being a jealous, unjust, vindictive, genocidal, bloodthirsty ethnic cleanser, to cite just a few of Richard Dawkins' descriptors, we would hail him as a hero. We would view such a war much like we view WWII today. We would call it "the good war." We would hold it up as an example of good triumphing over evil. We would refer to those who sacrificed for and participated in it as "the greatest generation." We would cite it as a demonstration of the proper use of violence. And the president who spearheaded it would become known as one of the greatest to ever live.

Yet many people today condemn God for doing essentially the same in the conquest. In doing so, they apply a double standard. Despite God's superior right to intervene in the misuse of his creation, his infinitely greater knowledge about the extent of injustice being perpetrated, his ability to more accurately judge the degree of violence necessary to combat such injustice, and his divine ability to do so impartially, they treat his just war decisions much less deferentially than they treat those of human rulers. Shouldn't our deference flow the other way? If anyone is in a position to accurately judge who has the right to go to war and what type of conduct within war is justified (the two sets of criteria within modern just war theory), wouldn't it be the all-knowing creator?

Likewise, many people today self-righteously condemn God for the violence he employed in the OT but fail to realize they employ or condone worse violence all the time, and often with much less justification. For example, Israel arguably never targeted civilian population centers (as we will explore in Chapter 11) or never did so except on a small scale during the conquest, but the United States has, even in its "good" wars. In 2001, U.S. foreign policy expert Walter Russell Mead estimated that (1) more German *civilians* were killed in the three-night bombing of Dresden than the number of American *soldiers* killed in all of WWI, (2) American bombs killed more than twice as many Japanese *civilians* in the last five months of WWII (*not including* those killed by the atomic bombs) than the number of American *soldiers* killed in all of its foreign wars combined, and (3) eight Vietnamese *civilians* died for everyone one American killed during the Vietnam War.[98] The Japanese and Vietnamese were surely guilty of much less injustice than the Canaanites, yet the United States killed proportionately more of them, including civilians. Thus, even by today's more advanced just war moral criteria, the conquest was more of a just war than any war the United States has ever fought. And to top it off, those who judge God's OT actions as morally inexcusable by today's standards fail to realize that the morally advanced viewpoint from which such condemnations arise only exists because of the moral groundwork God laid through the very same OT actions they condemn.

God can't win. On one hand, people who get self-righteously angry at and demand justice for relatively minor injustices (like racial epithets) condemn him for not doing more to stop human injustice. In fact, they cite God's failure to more severely crack down on injustice as a primary reason for not believing in him. They can't rectify a supposedly loving, all-powerful God with the amount of injustice that exists in the world. But then when those same people read about God cracking down on much greater injustices in the OT (like slavery and child sacrifice), they call him nasty names. In other words, when God intervenes to stop injustice, they call him vindictive, bloodthirsty, and imperialistic, and when he fails to intervene, they call him weak, uncaring, and unbelievable. Either way, he is labeled a moral monster. He is damned if he does and damned if he doesn't.

Conclusion

That's the extent of Israel's conquest of Canaan, which is arguably the worst God-sanctioned violence in the OT. When viewed in context, it loses most of its sensationalism doesn't it? It's not quite the controversy many critics would like it to be. It's maybe even a bit anticlimactic.

The conquest was not an arbitrary, selfish, or bloodthirsty campaign. It served multiple good and just purposes. It was a compassionate, loving, just response to human wickedness and violence. It was done on behalf of a poor, weak, and vulnerable people. It was an act of justice in its specific historical context and an act of justice in its broader world-saving context. It liberated a group of slaves, returned them to their homeland, and punished their oppressors while simultaneously advancing God's plan to unite and bless all nations.

The conquest was also not a murderous, genocidal, indiscriminate slaughter. It was executed in a restrained and just manner. God mercifully gave the perpetrators of injustice plenty of time and opportunity to change their ways and avoid punishment. When they refused, he didn't unleash the full weight of his destructive power on them. Instead, he sent in a ragtag group of militarily ignorant nomads operating under severely restrictive marching orders to gradually and methodically evict them.

To put it in terms of our modern just war theory, the conquest was just in its cause (*jus ad bellum*) and just in its conduct (*jus in bello*). It was fought to stop great injustice, it was properly declared by a lawful authority (it doesn't get any more lawful than God), it was fought with good intentions, it was fought as a last resort, there was a reasonable chance of success (our omnipotent God was fighting it, after all), and the means used were in proportion to the ends pursued. The conquest satisfied each of the official just war criteria as much as any war in human history ever has.

In fact, because God directly managed the conquest, it was just in a way that no human-led war ever can be. God saw and knew things we can't. He saw every single action, thought, and intention of every single individual on both sides of the war. He completely understood each person's degree of guilt and innocence. He knew more about them and their histories than they knew about themselves. In his infinite wisdom, he also knew exactly what type of violence to use and precisely how much. Consequently, we cannot compare God's justice to human justice because it surpasses all human understanding.[99] As the omnipotent creator of the universe, he knows exactly why to judge, when to judge, what to judge, and how to judge. Plus, his intentions are objective, selfless, and pure in ways ours can't be. God is a perfectly righteous judge.[100] But us? Not so much.

To state it another way, God's war was holy in ways ours can't be. As Butler explains, "God being the primary warrior is precisely what makes it holy. It is not a *holy* war unless God himself picks the fight and does the heavy lifting."[101] "A war initiated by human hands is not holy, so we shouldn't presume to fight in the many unholy wars of our world."[102]

Of course, none of this makes the God of the OT less violent, but it does show the character of his violence. It reveals it as restorative instead of destructive—and that makes all the difference. It's the difference between correcting a wrong and committing one, between restitution and theft, between imprisonment and kidnapping, and between controlled, selfless, remedial violence and impulsive, selfish, injurious violence. It's the difference between justice and injustice.

Dawkins clearly erred when he claimed the conquest was "morally indistinguishable from Hitler's invasion of Poland, or Saddam Hussein's massacres of the Kurds and the Marsh Arabs."[103] The only way to hold such an opinion is to ignore the historical, cultural, and literary contexts surrounding the conquest.

Lastly, and maybe most importantly, the conquest was not intended to teach us the ethics of violence. It was not performed to give us an example of how we should employ violence on behalf of God's kingdom or how we should treat our contemporary enemies. God was in the midst of laying his broad ethical framework, not teaching a specific lesson on the proper use of violence. He was teaching more fundamental lessons. He was establishing his existence and sovereignty, teaching the basics of obedience, and developing trust. He was showing the world he is for justice, for everyone. He was showing it he hates injustice and is doing something about it. He was showing us he fights injustice, but he was not teaching us how we should fight it. That lesson would come later in the person of Jesus, who would teach us to fight it not with violence but with self-sacrificial love.

We must not lose sight of the broader ethical context. The conquest occurred in the midst of God's incremental ethical revelation, which was a process that involved many temporary moral concessions and which was ultimately completed in Jesus' nonviolent life and teachings, including his denationalization of God's followers and the accompanying removal of national violence from their repertoire. Israel's violent occupation of a homeland was not an end in itself. Like so many other things in the OT, it was just another transitory step along the path of ethical progress.

To state it more plainly, Israel's conquest of Canaan in the OT does not justify our use of violence or war today. "Precisely because Yahweh wars are both a truly unique phenomenon when analyzed on their own terms and an integral part of a narrative that unfolds in the direction of Christ," writes Nugent, "we can now confidently say that they may never be waged again."[104] Because it was "unique to its time, place, and circumstances," Merrill adds, it must "not to be carried over to the age of the church."[105]

Even if we insist on employing the conquest as a model for our own warfare today by ignoring that it was a specific set of commands given to a specific group of people under specific circumstances at a specific point in history for a specific and temporary purpose, it still doesn't justify the types of nationalistic wars we want it to. It would only justify a war fought by exploited, homeless civilians who are seeking to reoccupy their homeland from Nazi-like occupiers by engaging them in battles as overwhelming underdogs who have to rely solely on God's miraculous intervention for victory. As an example, it might justify something like a Native American tribe's reoccupation of its homeland on the plains of South Dakota per God's direct orders and via his miraculous intervention, but it wouldn't justify the United States' overthrow of undemocratic rulers in the Middle East via superior military might. After all, as Butler notes, "Israel [was] a nation of fearful, intimidated slaves facing off with the mightiest imperial powerhouses of the ancient world, the extreme antithesis of *who* fights mainstream holy wars."[106] Kraybill elaborates:

> Christians have evaded the message of the Prince of Peace through several detours. One tempting excuse arises from warfare in the Old Testament. Didn't God send Israel into battle? At first glance this looks like a license to fight. Modern warfare, however, doesn't follow Old Testament strategies. When Yahweh commanded Israel to engage in military action, it was clear that Yahweh was the head warrior who would triumph. Thus military force was deliberately scaled *down* so any victory would be a miraculous one that would applaud Yahweh's divine intervention. If we took the ancient biblical model of warfare seriously, our modern armies would dramatically *reduce* their size and firepower and rely on God's miraculous intervention for victory![107]

To state it another way, the conquest only justifies wars that are directly run by God. His personal involvement is key. Merrill explains:

> If anything is clear in the foregoing review of this phenomenon, it is that such war was conceived by God, commanded by him, executed by him, and brought by him alone to successful conclusion. Among the attributes associated with his participation in Yahweh war are God's omnipotence, his infinite wisdom, and, above all, his holiness.[108]

Here's how Copan puts it:

> Some TV stunt shows warn children, "Kids, don't try this at home!" Likewise, we could say about Israel's "holy war" situation: "Don't try this without special revelation!" These matters aren't up to humans to decide. Yahweh-initiated battles were never intended for non-prophet organizations![109]

After all, not even God's own chosen nation could effectively wage war without his direct participation. Its attempts to do so led only to disaster.

To view it from yet another angle, the conquest battles were much more about God fighting for Israel than Israel fighting for God. They were about Israel waiting for God to work on its behalf instead of taking matters into its own hands on God's behalf. Butler puts it this way: "Mainstream holy war's motto is 'We will fight for God!' But Israel turns this motto on its head, shouting instead, 'God will fight for us!'"[110] That alone should caution us against attempting to wage "just" wars on God's behalf today.

The real irony is not only that many American Christians cite OT Israel's *God-run* wars to support America's *non-God-run* wars but that we cite God's OT efforts to destroy militarism to advance our own militarism. We cite God's OT violence to justify what that violence was trying to combat. We cite Israel's actions against Canaan to justify acting like Canaan. That's ironic. And tragic.

Simply put, *nothing* about Israel's conquest of Canaan, not its means or its ends, justifies our use of militaristic violence against our national enemies today.

---

[1] Green, *Deuteronomy*, 31-32.

[2] Gen. 12:7; 15:18-21.

[3] Gen. 17:8; 26:3; 28:13; 46:3; Exod. 3:8; 13:5; 23:31; 34:11-16.

[4] Gen. 13:12; 16:3; 23:16-20; 25:10-11; 26:6; 33:18-19; 37:1; 50:13.

[5] The "Canaanites" were a collection of nations who lived throughout the regions of Canaan, including but not limited to the Hittites, Jebusites, Amorites, Canaanites, Girgashites, Hivites, and Perizzites. See Deuteronomy 7:1.

[6] Deut. 2:1-19; Num. 20:14-21.

[7] Gen. 15:16.

[8] Gen. 15:13.

[9] Gen. 15:13.

[10] Lev. 18; Deut. 12:31; 18:9-13; Exod. 34:15; 2 Kings 16:3; Jer. 7:31; 19:5; Ezek. 16:20-21; 20:31.

[11] Deut. 9:4-5; Lev. 18:24-25; 1 Sam. 15:1-3.

[12] Seibert, *The Violence of Scripture*, 2287.

[13] N.T. Wright, *Evil and the Justice of God* (IVP Books, 2011), 588, Kindle.

[14] Gen. 6; Exod. 7-14.

[15] Deut. 9:4-6.

[16] Lev. 18:3-4, 24, 30; Deut. 6:1-25; 7:1-6; 12:1; 18:9.

[17] Deut. 6:1-3, 18-19, 24; 7:12; 13:17-18; 29:9; Lev. 18:5; Josh. 1:7.

[18] Lev. 18:28-29; Deut. 7:4, 9-10; 29:19, 24-28; 2 Chron. 7:19-20.

[19] Green, *Deuteronomy*, 27.

[20] 1 Kings 14:24; 2 Kings 17:7-23; 21:10-11; Ps. 106:34-46; Ezek. 5:5-8; 23:36-39; Jer. 5:17; 7:30-32; 19:3-6; 32:30-35; Josh. 7:1; 2 Chron. 28:1-4; 33:1-6; Isa. 63:10.

[21] Judg. 2:14-15, 20-21; 3:12-14; 6:1; Isa. 5:25-30; 10:5-19; 45:1; 46:11; Josh. 7:10-12; Num. 14:41-45; Jer. 5:19; 15:14; 20:4-5; 21:7; 25:8-11; 27:4-7; 34:21; Ezek. 21.

[22] 2 Kings 19:11; 2 Chron. 20:23; Judg. 21:10-11; Jer. 6:8; 9:16; 25:9-11; Lam. 2:5.

[23] 2 Kings 17:22-23; 23:27; Ps. 106:41-42; 2 Chron. 36:15-20; Jer. 9:13-16; 10:18; 16:13; 22:26; 24:10.

[24] Exod. 23:23, 27-28; 33:2; Deut. 11:22-23; Josh. 3:10; 23:5.

[25] Num. 14:14; Josh. 2:8-11.

[26] See also Exod. 9:16 and 14:17-18.

[27] Jer. 18:7-8.

[28] 1 Sam. 15:5-6.

[29] Sprinkle, *Fight*, 1074.

[30] Deut. 2:1-19.

[31] Deut. 17:16-20; 20:1-15.

[32] Deut. 20:16-17.

33 See also Judg. 7:12; 1 Sam. 13:5.

34 Num. 13:27-33; see also Exod. 3:8.

35 Num. 14:1-35.

36 Exod. 17:8; Num. 21:1-3, 21–33; Deut. 2:26-3:1; 2 Kings 18:13.

37 2 Kings 18:13; 19:35.

38 Lamb, *God Behaving Badly*, 968.

39 Ibid., 759.

40 Judg. 3:12-14; 6:33; 7:12; 10:11-12; Josh. 10:1-11; 11:1-5. See generally Josh. 5-11.

41 Josh. 10:1-11.

42 Chapman, *Holy War in the Bible*, 749.

43 Yoder, *The Original Revolution*, 1328.

44 Wright, *The God I Don't Understand*, 1498.

45 Ibid., 1565.

46 Ibid., 1562.

47 Copan, *Is God a Moral Monster?*, 3605.

48 Seibert, *The Violence of Scripture*, 299.

49 Isa. 2:1-4.

50 Prov. 6:17-19; 8:13; 15:9; 29:27; Ps. 5:4-6; Isa. 61:8.

51 Exod. 22:22-24; Jer. 32:30; Deut. 9:7; 2 Kings 17:17; Ps. 106:37-40.

52 Wright, *The God I Don't Understand*, 2372.

53 Boyd, *The Crucifixion of the Warrior God*, 3817.

54 Jurgen Moltmann, *The Crucified God: The Cross of Christ as the Foundation and Criticism of Christian Theology*, translators R. A. Wilson and John Bowden (Minneapolis, MN: Fortress Press, 1993), 272.

55 See also Num. 14:18

56 Walter C. Kaiser, Jr., *The Promise-Plan of God: A Biblical Theology of the Old and New Testaments* (Grand Rapids, MI: Zondervan, 2008), 110.

57 Boyd, *The Crucifixion of the Warrior God*, 9275.

58 See generally N.T. Wright's *Evil and the Justice of God.*

59 Wright, *The God I Don't Understand*, 901.

60 Swartley, *Covenant of Peace*, 51.

61 Exod. 2:23, 25.

62 Exodus 2:25. Likewise, when Stephen summarized the OT narrative in Acts 7 of the NT, he also specifically cited compassion as the reason why God delivered Israel from slavery in Egypt. See verse 34.

63 Butler, *The Skeletons in God's Closet*, 4652.

64 See also Isa. 30:18; 54:7-10; 1 Sam. 12:10; 2 Kings 20:6.

65 Gen. 18:16-19:38.

66 Ezek. 16:49-50; Gen. 13:13; Isa. 3:9.

67 Interestingly, what happened next in Lot's family confirms how thoroughly corrupt the cities had become. Shortly after fleeing Sodom, two daughters—from the most righteous family that could be found—got their father drunk and had sex with him.

68 Gen. 6-7.

69 Exod. 7-12.

[70] Exod. 22:21-22; 23:9; Zech. 7:10; Jer. 22:3; Deut. 24:14-18; Prov. 29:7; Lev. 19:33-34; 24:22; Amos 2:7; 4:1; 5:15; 8:4.

[71] Deut. 27:19; Prov. 17:5; Jer. 2:19; 21:12; 22:13; Mal. 3:5; Isa. 10:1-2; Exod. 22:23-24.

[72] Ps. 106:3; Jer. 7:5-7; 22:15-16; Deut. 7:9; 16:20.

[73] Isa. 1:17; Jer. 22:3; Zech. 7:9; Deut. 10:18-19; 14:28-29; 24:19-21; 26:12-13; Lev. 19:34; 23:22; Exod. 22:25-27.

[74] Deut. 10:18; Hos. 14:3; Ps. 72:12-14; 140:12; 146:7-9; Mic. 6:8; Jer. 22:16.

[75] Jer. 5:28-29; 6:6-7.

[76] Wright, *The God I Don't Understand*, 1677.

[77] Branson Parler, "Conquest, Exile, & Cross: Replacing Projection With Reality" posted February 24, 2014 at http://www.missioalliance.org/conquest-exile-cross-replacing-projection-with-reality.

[78] Creach, *Violence in Scripture*, 1165.

[79] Deut. 2:1-19.

[80] Deut. 9:4-6.

[81] Gen. 1:27.

[82] Gen. 12:3.

[83] Josh. 2 and 9; 1 Kings 17; 2 Kings 5.

[84] Matt. 1:5; Heb. 11:31; Jas. 2:25.

[85] Wright, *The God I Don't Understand*, 1768.

[86] Ps. 22:27; 48:10; 64:9; 86:9; 97:6; Isa. 2:1-2; 66:18, 23; Dan. 7:14; Mal. 3:12.

[87] Wright, *The God I Don't Understand*, 1898.

[88] Ibid., 1912.

[89] Prov. 6:16-17; Ps. 5:6; 11:5; Ezek. 8:17; Gen. 6:1-11.

[90] 1 Chron. 28:3.

[91] Ps. 37:14.

[92] Jer. 6:6-8; 7:5-7; 19:3-6; 22:13-17; Hab. 2:8, 17; Gen. 49:5-7; Zeph. 1:9; Joel 3:19; Hos. 1:4; Judg. 9:22-24.

[93] Ps. 72:12-14.

[94] 1 Kings 4:29-31; 10:23.

[95] Butler, *The Skeletons in God's Closet*, 4650.

[96] Swartley, *Covenant of Peace*, 395.

[97] Even if we could isolate an instance or two where God violently punished some type of wholly nonviolent human wickedness, his punishment would still be reactive from a justice perspective. Just like all human violence violates some human's rights and is therefore worthy of forceful correction, all human sin, whether violent or not, violates God's rights and is worthy of forceful correction. Therefore, whenever God uses violence to stop or punish sin, he is always using reactive force.

[98] Walter Russell Mead, *Special Providence: American Foreign Policy and How It Changed the World* (New York: Routledge, 2002), 218-19.

[99] Phil. 4:7.

[100] Ps. 7:11; 2 Tim. 4:8; 2 Thess. 1:5; Rom. 2:2.

[101] Butler, *The Skeletons in God's Closet*, 4539.

[102] Ibid., 4541.

[103] Dawkins, *The God Delusion*, 3884.

[104] Nugent, *The Politics of Yahweh*, 2561.

[105] Merrill, *Show Them No Mercy*, 1511.

[106] Butler, *The Skeletons in God's Closet*, 3748.

[107] Kraybill, *The Upside-Down Kingdom*, 2957.

[108] Merrill, *Show Them No Mercy*, 1277.

[109] Copan, *Is God a Moral Monster?*, 3429.

[110] Butler, *The Skeletons in God's Closet*, 2797.

8

Characteristics of the Old Testament God

Now that we have covered the basics of what God was doing in the OT and why, let's take a look at what it tells us about his character. Is he really the loving, compassionate, faithful, patient, gracious, forgiving God he claimed to be when he introduced himself to Moses?

Loving

A big-picture review of the OT reveals a loving God. He created a good and beautiful world, one full of love, joy, peace, and prosperity, one meant to be enjoyed by all of his creatures. But then humans corrupted it with sin. At that point, he could have simply walked away and left us to our own self-destruction. But he didn't. He loved us too much to abandon us. So he intervened into human history to put us on a path back to Eden. That was the whole point of his interactions with Israel. He lovingly used it to bless all creation. Thus, his intervention into human history itself was fundamentally an act of love. In fact, the only reason the OT exists is because God chose to lovingly rescue humanity from its enslavement to sin. As the Israelites said over and over throughout the OT, "Give thanks to the Lord, for he is good. His love endures forever."[1]

Interestingly, the Bible never explains why God loves. It simply says he does. It simply says that is who he is. He is love.[2] And the source of love.[3] The Bible doesn't go any farther back than that. Love is its starting point. According to it, love is the foundation of everything God has ever done in and for the world.

Love is so central to Christianity the Bible explicitly says we can't know God unless we love, we can't live in God or have God live in us unless we love, without love we are nothing and have nothing, to inherit eternal life we must love, love binds all the virtues together in perfect unity, love is greater than faith and hope, love indicates faith is real, love conquers all, love is what identifies us as Christian, to love is our supreme and sole moral obligation, and love has *always* been the heart of Christian ethics.[4] In Christianity, love is everything.

Relational

God's love for humanity makes him a relational God. In fact, he created humans for relationship—with him, his creation, and each other. He speaks to humans, listens to them, converses with them, pleads with them, walks with them, suffers with them, and enters into covenant with them. That's why the Bible refers to him as a father, lover, and friend. He is a living, interactive, participatory God.

Of course, throughout history, God has related to humans in different ways (e.g. directly in the OT, through Jesus in the NT, through the Holy Spirit since then, etc.) and not always in ways his followers might prefer, but he always has *related* and always will. That's the point: God cares enough to relate. As the awestruck psalmist humbly observed, "When I look at your heavens, the work of your fingers, the moon and the stars that you have established; what are human beings that you are mindful of them, mortals that you care for them?" (Ps. 8:3-4 NRSV).

In addition, God's relationship with OT Israel was uniquely personal and historically unprecedented. As Berman notes, "The degree to which the Bible envisions an intimate relationship between the individual Israelite and the Almighty is distinct in the ancient Near East."[5] In contrast to the neighboring cultures wherein "honor is bestowed unilaterally by inferior to superior," "the biblical texts invoke a paradigm in which honor was a value reciprocally bestowed by each party."[6] In fact, the OT writers often compared God and Israel's relationship to a marriage:

> To be sure, in these cultures, the gods were routinely seen to have spouses or consorts. Yet these were universally divine spouses—goddesses—thus forming an analogy between the cosmic family and the ruling family of the king. For these cultures to conceive of the marriage between a god and a human, or group of humans, would have been as unthinkable as for us to imagine the marital union of a human and a cat. Yet we find the marriage metaphor invoked time and again in the prophecies of Hosea, Isaiah, Jeremiah, and Ezekiel.[7]

Referencing the work of Yochanan Muffs, Berman adds:

> In the neighboring cultures of the ancient Near East, man was merely a servant of kings. In the Bible, he is transformed into a servant king in relation to a beneficent sovereign, a wife in relation to her benefactor-husband. God seeks from Israel "love," in both the political sense of loyalty between parties to a treaty and in the sense of a faithful, intimate relationship between man and wife.[8]

Or as Boyd puts it, "the most distinctive, and arguably the most beautiful, aspect of Yahweh's covenant with Israel is that it is repeatedly characterized as a marriage covenant."[9] (No wonder God gets so angry at idolatry. It's akin to the intense anger we would feel if our spouse had an extramarital affair.)

Here's the most important point: God enters into relationship with humans out of love and grace, not out of a desire to control or dominate. Given his omnipotence, he exerts little control over our lives. He has the utmost respect for free will, which he created. He lets us make our own choices, and it's evident throughout the entire OT. For example, when Israel asked for a human king, God granted their request even though he viewed it as a rejection of his kingship and knew it would end in disaster.

God is so relational he even lets humans influence his actions. For example, when God set out to destroy Sodom as punishment for its irredeemable injustices and Abraham asked him to spare the entire city if he could find fifty righteous people in it, God graciously agreed.[10] Then Abraham kept negotiating with God until he reduced the number to forty-five, then forty, then thirty, then twenty, and finally ten.[11] In a similar exchange, Moses convinced God to forgo the punitive destruction of the Israelites after they had repaid God for liberating them from slavery and sustaining them in the wilderness by promptly engaging in idolatry.[12] Likewise, when the leaders of an Israelite religious assembly rebelled against God, Moses persuaded God to punish only the leaders and not the entire assembly.[13]

Amazingly, Abraham and Moses, arguably the two OT actors who knew God the best, felt comfortable enough with him to openly and directly challenge his plans. They wouldn't have done so had they viewed him as a domineering tyrant liable to strike them dead at any minute for any reason whatsoever, or no reason at all. They (and many other OT characters) also *wanted* to spend time with God and have a personal relationship with him, which wouldn't have occurred had he been a cross between Adolf Hitler and Darth Vader, as some critics insinuate.

Prayer provides additional proof of God's relationality. It only exists because he is relational. It is an inherently interactive and conversational endeavor. It allows him to speak to us and us to speak to him. And in the process, it allows us to influence his actions. The OT is full of examples of prayer doing precisely that.[14] After all, Boyd notes, "a relationship in which one party is powerless is not a genuinely interpersonal relationship."[15] Therefore, "Scripture teaches that God created a world in which he has significantly bound himself to the prayers of his people."[16] He elaborates:

John Wesley only slightly exaggerated the truth when he concluded that "God will do nothing but in answer to prayer." The biblical narrative is shaped by God's response to prayer. From Cain's plea for leniency (Gen 4:13-15) to the Israelites' cry for liberation (Ex 2:23-25; 3:7-10; Acts 7:34), from Moses' cry for help at the Red Sea and against the Amalekites (Ex 14:15-16; 17:8-14) to Hezekiah's prayer for an extension of life (2 Kings 20:1-7), and from Abraham's prayer for a son (Gen 15:2-6; 17:15-22; 21:1-3) to the lepers prayer for healing (Mt 8:2-3), the biblical narrative is woven together by examples of God moving in extraordinary ways in response to the prayers of his people.

James sums up the general teaching on prayer when he says that "the prayer of the righteous is powerful and effective" (Jas 5:16).[17]

Faithful

Unwavering faithfulness is another prominent characteristic of the God of the OT. Time after time, the Israelites rejected God's guidance. Time after time, they failed to fulfill their covenantal obligations. Time after time, they repaid his acts of kindness with disobedience. Time after time, they defiantly brought disaster upon themselves and those around them. But God never gave up on them. He never abandoned them. He kept giving them another chance, kept bailing them out. He continued to comfort them, protect them, fight for them, and bless them. For example, after God kicked Adam and Eve out of the Garden of Eden, he made clothes for them and helped Eve bear a child.[18] After Cain killed Abel, God protected him from those who wanted to inflict vengeance on him.[19] After the Israelites rejected God's kingship by requesting a typical earthly king, God not only granted their request but genuinely tried to help their kings succeed. God did these things out of compassion, not because the Israelites had kept their end of the bargain. They hadn't. They had so stubbornly persisted in their rebellion that Moses called them "a stiff-necked people" (Deut. 9:6).

Most importantly, God did not let Israel's (or anyone else's) rebellion thwart his plan for worldwide salvation. Over and over again, he graciously repurposed their destructive behavior for good. He patiently and persistently reworked it into his redemptive strategy.

God's unwavering faithfulness to humanity despite its continuous unfaithfulness to him is a core theme of the OT. Or as N. T. Wright explains it, "Central to the Old Testament picture of God's justice in an unjust world, then, is the picture of God's faithfulness to unfaithful Israel."[20] The Israelites themselves recognized it and repeatedly praised him for it.[21]

The bad news is the OT reveals our human inability to be faithful to God, but the good news is it also demonstrates he is faithful to us anyway. Despite our defiance, he keeps pursuing us, keeps wooing us back. Despite our propensity for self-destruction, he keeps working things out for our good, keeps leading us back to true life. He is faithful even when we are not. That's a beautiful thing.

Merciful

The God of the OT was also merciful. That is to say, he was compassionate, gracious, and forgiving. The OT writers repeatedly declared it.[22] In fact, one OT prophet, Habakkuk, blatantly accused him of being too lenient on the unjust.[23]

Despite the Israelites' persistent rebellion, God repeatedly showed them mercy.[24] His mercy often manifested itself in the lessening or complete withholding of deserved punishment, often only because humans asked him to.[25] On many occasions, he even explicitly declared his intention to have mercy on anyone who would simply repent.[26] In fact, Paul confirmed in the NT that God, in his mercy, largely let sin go unpunished in the OT.[27] He was as flexible with punishments as he was steadfast with blessings.

God also frequently had mercy on non-Israelites. When Rahab, a Jerichoan prostitute, helped hide the two Israelite spies from the king of Jericho, God spared her and her family from the destruction he brought upon the rest of the city.[28] After God miraculously delivered the Aramean army into Israel's hands, God's prophet instructed Israel's king to not only spare them but also to give them something to eat and drink and then send them home.[29] When Israel started feeling superior, the prophet Amos reminded them God had mercifully led the Philistines out of Caphtor and the Arameans out of Kir just has he had led Israel out of Egypt.[30] On one occasion, God used the compassion of an enslaved Israelite girl and the miracle-working hands of his prophet Elisha to mercifully cure the leprosy of an enemy commander named Naaman.[31] The Psalmist's proclamation rings true: "The Lord is good to all, and his compassion is over all that he has made" (Ps. 145:9 NRSV). And as you can see, Jesus' command to love our enemies, not just our neighbors, has its roots in the OT.[32]

Sometimes the God of the OT was so merciful towards his enemies it angered his followers. Consider the story of Jonah.[33] God commanded him to preach repentance to the despised Assyrian capital of Nineveh.

After initially refusing and trying to flee to Tarshish, Jonah complied. He proclaimed to the Ninevites, "Let everyone call urgently on God. Let them give up their evil ways and their violence. Who knows? God may yet relent and with compassion turn from his fierce anger so that we will not perish" (Jon. 3:8-9). Amazingly, they followed Jonah's advice and "turned from their evil ways," so God "relented and did not bring on them the destruction he had threatened" (v. 10). And that made Jonah angry. He viewed God's mercy as unjust. He said to God, "That is what I tried to forestall by fleeing to Tarshish. I knew that you are a gracious and compassionate God, slow to anger and abounding in love, a God who relents from sending calamity" (Jon. 4:2). In other words, Jonah became angry with God because he wanted to see his enemies receive the punishment they were justly due, but instead God had mercy on them.

Unlike Jonah, God doesn't want to see anyone punished. He takes no pleasure in it. "For he does not willingly bring affliction or grief to anyone" (Lam. 3:33). He wants everyone to repent and avoid punishment, particularly death.[34] "As surely as I live, declares the Sovereign Lord, I take no pleasure in the death of the wicked, but rather that they turn from their ways and live. Turn! Turn from your evil ways!" (Ezek. 33:11). That's why he pleads with us to repent. "Repent! Turn away from all your offenses; then sin will not be your downfall. Rid yourselves of all the offenses you have committed, and get a new heart and a new spirit. Why will you die, people of Israel? For I take no pleasure in the death of anyone, declares the Sovereign Lord. Repent and live!" (Ezek. 18:30-32). God "longs to be gracious" to us (Isa. 30:18). That's why he is so slow to anger and so patient with our disobedience. He doesn't want "anyone to perish, but everyone to come to repentance" (2 Pet. 3:9). "Like water spilled on the ground, which cannot be recovered, so we must die. But that is not what God desires; rather, he devises ways so that a banished person does not remain banished from him" (2 Sam. 14:14). "For God did not appoint us to suffer wrath but to receive salvation through our Lord Jesus Christ" (1 Thess. 5:9). And he desires such salvation for *everyone*. He "wants all people to be saved and to come to a knowledge of the truth" (1 Tim. 2:4). He wants us all to "have life, and have it to the full" (John 10:10). He sincerely wants each of us to choose what is truly in our best interest: him.

If God enjoyed punishing us, he could justly do so much more often and much more harshly. Every time we sinned, he could promptly and thoroughly punish us. In fact, if he so desired, he could be constantly punishing us. Justice would allow it. That he doesn't tells us a lot about how merciful he is.

God is so merciful we've come to take it for granted. We've gotten so used to him not punishing us for our sins we've come to feel entitled to it. He has so freely shown us mercy we now think he is violating our rights when he doesn't. Like a child whose parents almost never tell him no, we've been spoiled by God's ever-present, unending, boundless mercy.

We have forgotten "the wages of sin is death" (Rom. 6:23). We have forgotten "sin, when it is full-grown, gives birth to death" (Jas. 1:15). We have forgotten God warned Adam and Eve they would certainly die if they disobeyed him by eating the forbidden fruit.[35] We have forgotten we all have sinned and consequently all deserve death, to paraphrase Paul.[36] We have forgotten death is the just punishment for sin and salvation through Jesus is a *gift* from God.[37]

Or maybe it's just that we have been so corrupted by sin we can't see how egregiously wrong it is and therefore mistakenly judge God's punishments as too harsh. Maybe it's our standard of measurement that's off, not his. Maybe it's that our judgment of sin isn't severe enough, instead of his punishment being too severe. Maybe it's that we don't take sin seriously enough, instead of him taking it too seriously. Maybe our thinking that God's punishments are sometimes too harsh says more about us than it does about God.

We shouldn't be shocked God punishes some people. We should be shocked he lets anyone go unpunished. We should be shocked at how often he shows mercy and how rarely he punishes, not that he sometimes does punish. We should be surprised he doesn't dispense punishment and death more quickly and frequently, not that he allowed sin to produce instant death a few times, as with Uzzah in the OT (who unlawfully touched the Ark of the Covenant) and Ananias and Sapphira (who lied to God) in the NT.[38]

When we realize that all sin deserves death, even the Flood appears merciful.[39] When human wickedness passed the point of no return by locking itself into an irredeemable pattern of perpetual self-destruction, God didn't destroy the earth or annihilate the human race. Instead, he cleansed the world of everyone who was unwilling to help him restore justice and saved the only family who was—Noah's family. Then he promised to never enact such a widespread cleansing again and committed himself to more peaceful means of accomplishing his earthly purposes. To use Isaiah's words, he made a "covenant of peace" with humans (Isa. 54:9-10). Out of that covenant, he called Abraham to birth the nation of Israel for the benefit of all humankind. In this sense, the Flood was an act of mercy that produced a promise of even greater mercy.

Nugent compares God's decision to flood the earth to a doctor taking care of "a terminally ill pregnant woman whose body is rapidly deteriorating."

> The most loving thing for the doctor to do—and the very thing the mother would want—is to take the life of the dying mother so the child may live. In the same way, taking the life of all creatures that were wrapped up in destroying this world may have been the only way for God to allow all creatures to repopulate and refill the earth.[40]

In other words, the flood was designed to make the world a healthier place.

There's even a sense in which death can be an act of mercy. After all, isn't that how people who commit suicide view it? They are so miserable in this life they believe nonexistence or whatever the afterlife holds can't be any worse. As Nugent puts it, "To live forever in a state of sin is a dreadful form of torture (the movie *Groundhog Day* comes to mind). Eternal enmity with the animal kingdom, eternal scratching at hardened soil, eternal domination of the strong over the weak—none of this is what God had in mind for this world."[41]

Here's the most amazing part of God's mercy. Buckle up, this is earth-shaking. Ultimately, God is so merciful he offers to forgive all of our injustices *for free*. All we need to do is accept. All we need to do is sincerely acknowledge that we have wronged God and others, ask him to forgive us, and request his help in doing better. That's it. Mercy received. There's no need for repayment or purification through punishment. If we stand before the cosmic judge and admit our crimes, he will not impose a just sentence on us. Instead, he will set us free.

Note that God doesn't have to be merciful to be good. He would still be a good God if he simply enforced justice. But God is more than simply good and just. He is loving. And that's why he offers us what we don't deserve: the gift of grace.

We are sometimes tempted to view God as cruel only because we are asking the wrong questions. We are asking entitled, spoiled kid questions. We should be asking why a perfectly holy God is so often tolerant of unholiness, not why he sometimes isn't. We should be asking why God is so frequently merciful, not why he occasionally enforces justice. We should be asking why God is so often compassionate, gracious, and forgiving to those who spite him, not why he sometimes appears to be otherwise. We should be asking why an all-powerful God continues to offer mercy to those who continually reject him, not why he sometimes allows them to suffer the natural consequences of their own choices. We should be asking why God doesn't allow sin to instantly produce death more often, not why he infrequently does. We should be asking why God didn't immediately kill Adam and Eve when they sinned, not why he so cruelly kicked them out of Eden for it. We should be asking why God spared Cain's life after he murdered Able, not why he so cruelly condemned him to a life of restless wandering.[42] We should be asking why God allowed the thoroughly corrupt Canaanites to occupy the Promised Land for four hundred years while Israel was enslaved in Egypt, not why he eventually employed violence to kick them out.

We should be asking better questions.

Patient and Slow to Anger

In addition to being merciful, the God of the OT was also patient and slow to anger.[43] Let's look at a few examples.

Before cleansing the earth with a flood, God patiently waited until "the wickedness of the human race" became so great "that every inclination of the thoughts of the human heart was only evil all the time" and then had Noah preach repentance for an additional *century* while he built the ark (Gen. 6:5-7).[44] And even then, humanity's persistent rebellion made God more sad than angry.[45] Before kicking the Canaanites out of the Promised Land, God patiently waited four hundred years for their wickedness to reach a point of no return, and then he waited over five hundred years before doing the same to Israel.[46] Before destroying the city of Jericho, God made the Israelites march around it for six days to ensure its inhabitants had multiple opportunities to surrender. When God asked Moses to help him rescue the Israelites from slavery in Egypt and Moses responded with a flurry of distrustful questions, he graciously answered those questions and didn't get angry until Moses finally and rebelliously asked him to send someone else.[47] And even then, God didn't smite Moses in his anger but instead appeased him by sending his brother Aaron to help.

God's patience and slowness to anger in these instances is not atypical. It is representative of his behavior throughout the entire OT. He never reacted impulsively or fell victim to the heat of the moment. He always behaved like a coolheaded, dispassionate, objective judge who carefully reviewed all the evidence before passing judgment and imposing a sentence. His punishments were always preceded by plenty of warnings and ample opportunities to repent and receive mercy.

The OT is not the story of God constantly punishing humans, of him continually moving from one punitive outburst to another with little or no interaction in between. Nugent explains:

> God's pronouncement [of the curses] in Genesis 3 is not the beginning of a string of wrath-filled actions that an angry God unleashes upon his wayward creatures. It is not as if God first curses the original sinners, next floods the earth, then annihilates the Canaanites, and eventually anyone else who rubs him the wrong way. One doesn't have to be a Jew or a Christian to see that this sort of interpretation gets the story all wrong.[48]

In fact, after studying the OT in detail, I have come to share Thompson's perspective: "It now seems strange to me that the Old Testament God has the reputation of having a short fuse. A God of incredible patience is a much more accurate description."[49]

Notice the issue here isn't whether God ever got angry. Anger isn't bad per se. The issue is why he got angry and what he did with his anger. In the OT, he only got angry about injustice and always used that anger to compassionately enforce justice.

Again, God is a just God. Yes, he is also merciful, but he can't be merciful all the time. Yes, he is also patient, but he can't be patient forever. At some point, he has to combat injustice. At some point, he has to teach humanity about the consequences of sin. At some point, he has to take a stand against evil and proclaim, "Enough!" Otherwise, he's not just, and if he's not just, he's not loving because love is both just and merciful.

Not Legalistic

The God of the OT was not legalistic in any sense of the word. For starters, his laws were a gift to the recently liberated nation of Israel. After centuries of enslavement, the Israelites needed legal guidance. They had become dependent upon their oppressors and had forgotten how to self-govern. In that context, God's laws were indispensable. They provided order and stability to a brand-new nation. They were definitely not intended to oppress. God had just freed the Israelites from oppression.

Not only was the existence of God's legal system a blessing, so was its unique structure. The laws he issued were well-defined, knowable, and unchanging. Unlike the laws of all other ANE nations, they were not hitched to the whims of a selfish, earthly king. They came from the benevolent creator, not some fallen mortal. They were designed to protect people's dignity, not advance a king's personal interests. They also applied equally to all citizens and were radically egalitarian for their time. Thus, their very shape promoted Israel's well-being.

Furthermore, God didn't impose a great number of laws on the Israelites. In total, he issued approximately 613 commands. By contrast, the United States, also known as the "land of the free," has so many different types of laws (statutes, case laws, regulations, ordinances, etc.) on so many different levels (federal, state, county, city, etc.) governing so many different aspects of everyday life (everything from how much water your toilet can use when flushed to how large of a soda you can buy at your local convenience store) it's essentially impossible to count them all. Federal tax laws *alone* number over 70,000 pages and comprise over 10,000,000 words. That's about thirteen times the amount of words in the entire Bible. In contrast to the thousands of volumes our nation's laws fill, God's OT laws don't even fill one. In fact, our government adds many more laws *each year* than the Bible has in total.

Nor was God puritanical. He commanded a lot of pleasurable activities. The first thing he instructed humans to do in the Bible was to have lots of sex: "Be fruitful and multiply, and fill the earth and subdue it" (Gen. 1:28 NRSV). The second thing he told humans to do was to freely enjoy the fruit from all the trees in the Garden of Eden, except the one tree whose fruit was harmful.[50] Later, he ordered the Israelites to rest for an entire day every week, even making it one of the Ten Commandments.[51] He also commanded them to celebrate numerous festivals every year, some of which were a week long.[52] On one occasion, he told them to use their tithe to buy "cattle, sheep, wine or other fermented drink, or anything you wish" so they could eat and rejoice (Deut. 14:22-27). Within just the first two books of the Bible, God essentially told the human race to have lots of sex, enjoy lots of good food, get lots of rest, and throw lots of rad parties. That sounds like a generous God who wants his followers to enjoy the gifts of his creation, not a legalistic one who delights in subjugating them.

In fact, the OT explicitly tells us that God desires our flourishing, that he wants what is best for us and has a plan to achieve it. "'For I know the plans I have for you,' declares the Lord, 'plans to prosper you and not to harm you, plans to give you hope and a future'" (Jer. 29:11).

To use the Hebrew term, God desires *shalom* for us. According to Swartley, that word "occurs well over 200 times" in the OT and "has many dimensions of meaning: wholeness, completeness, well-being, peace, justice, salvation, and even prosperity."[53] Therefore, in desiring shalom for us, God desires our total flourishing—material, physical, psychological, and spiritual—on both a personal and social level.

God's desire to see us flourish is why he created the world in the first place. He wanted us to experience its beauty and majesty. He wanted to share his infinite love with us. That's also why when things went awry he intervened to restore the world to its original state of flourishing, first through OT Israel, then through Jesus in the NT, and now through the work of the Holy Spirit.

Everything God does, from his laws to his warfare activities, is designed to promote our flourishing. He enforces justice because it promotes flourishing and combats injustice because it inhibits it. He commands us to be kind, patient, generous, and forgiving to others because such things promote their flourishing and orders us to refrain from coveting, stealing, exploiting, and murdering because such things inhibit it. He even sent his son Jesus to earth so we "may have life, and have it to the full" (John 10:10). As German theologian and martyr Dietrich Bonhoeffer declared, "Jesus calls men, not to a new religion, but to life."[54] And not just temporal life, but eternal life.

God himself repeatedly explained that he issued his laws *for the purpose of promoting Israel's flourishing*. He declared, "I am the Lord your God, who teaches you what is best for you, who directs you in the way you should go" (Isa. 48:17). "Be careful to obey all the law my servant Moses gave you; do not turn from it to the right or to the left, that you may be successful wherever you go" (Josh. 1:7). In passage after passage, he told the Israelites that obeying his laws would bring many blessings, including peace, prosperity, safety, and longer lives.[55] As OT scholar Ronald Clements explains, the book of Deuteronomy "emphasizes that the purpose of the law was not to bind Israel to a set of arbitrary restrictions, but to guide it towards the fullest enjoyment of life."[56] Over and over again as God was promulgating his laws, he instructed the Israelites to obey them "so it may go well with you," "so that you may prosper in everything you do," "so that you may enjoy a long life," "so that you may live and prosper and prolong your days in the land," etc.[57]

The OT writers echoed the sentiment. They continually reminded the Israelites that God designed his laws for their prosperity.[58] Multiple OT writers compared those who follow God's laws to a thriving, well-nourished plant.[59] In the NT, Jesus made a similar comparison when he said the one who follows his instructions is "like a wise man who built his house on rock" and the one who doesn't is "like a foolish man who built his house on sand" (Matt. 7:24-27 NRSV). One house withstands the storms of life and the other doesn't.

One merely needs to read God's OT laws to see how they contributed to human flourishing. Pull up a list of them on the internet and look at the underlying values they promoted. They encouraged things like gratefulness, respect for property, obedience to parents, forgiveness, sexual purity, equal treatment before the law, and generosity towards the poor. They discouraged things like adultery, prostitution, incest, bestiality, rape, holding grudges, taking revenge, the exploitation of widows, militarism, and dishonesty. All such laws clearly promoted the common good in one way or another.

Just take a step back and look at what God did and didn't command. They were hardly the commands of a moral monster. As Nehemiah noted, God "gave them regulations and laws that are just and right, and decrees and commands that are good" (Neh. 9:13). It's hard to deny the goodness of laws that promote justice and combat injustice. Occasionally, you may not like to be restricted by such laws, but I bet you're always glad others are.

Over time, even many of God's seemingly arbitrary laws have been proven beneficial. For example, because of advances in science, we now know that God's strict cleanliness laws promoted health by preventing the spread of disease. We also now know that circumcision has many health benefits, like a decreased risk of urinary tract infection and penile cancer.

Of course, a few of God's OT laws still seem pretty random to us today, but given the cultural gap, the obvious goodness of all of his other laws, and the ongoing pattern of scientific vindication, it's reasonable to assume they served some type of beneficial purpose in their time. Lamb explains:

> Why does God care whether or not the Israelites wore clothes that blended wool and linen [Deut. 22:9-11]? Is Yahweh really so high control he wants to tell his people exactly what they can wear? (God should have given a command not to wear stripes with plaids. I would have benefited from that during my twenties.)
>
> While commands about clothing may seem bizarre and unnecessary, these types of laws are culturally specific, addressing particular problems from their context. Imagine how advice given in a 2010 sermon about lust would sound to a reader in the year 5010: "Don't buy

Sports Illustrated in early February, and avoid the red-light district."
Most males today understand that the *SI* swimsuit issue comes out right
after the Super Bowl and that in a certain section of town they can
expect to find prostitutes, but in three thousand years (roughly how
distant we are from these Old Testament laws) this sound advice for
avoiding sexual sin won't make sense. It would seem random, like a
command not to wear wool and linen.

Commentators suggest that the wool and linen command might be
connected to practices of magic, so an equivalent command might be,
"Don't play with a Ouija board," or it may have to do with prostitution,
comparable to "Avoid the red-light district." We really don't know what
is behind these laws, but since the vast majority of the Old Testament
laws make sense and are obviously good laws, it is reasonable to assume
that there is a particular societal problem that these types of laws are
addressing.[60]

But what about God's anti-idolatry laws? What about the laws that
required the Israelite's to worship him and him alone, the laws that
demanded their complete and sole allegiance, and the laws that imposed
the death penalty on those who adopted other religions? Surely those laws
didn't promote flourishing. Surely those laws reveal a narcissistic,
egotistical, self-obsessed, vainglorious, and ultimately insecure God.

I don't think so. If God alone knows and desires what is best for us,
it makes sense that he would steer us towards such knowledge (i.e.
towards him) and away from destructive falsehoods (i.e. away from false
gods) via things like anti-idolatry laws. It also makes sense that he would
glorify himself as a means of drawing us to him and consequently to what
is best for us. Without highlighting himself, how else would we find such
knowledge? And if he truly wants what is best for us, it makes sense he
would take drastic measures to guide us towards it via things like zero
tolerance policies and severe penalties for violations. In fact, wouldn't we
accuse God of being heartless if we knew he possessed such wisdom but
never attempted to pass it along? Wouldn't that be the selfish, egocentric
thing to do?

God issued his OT anti-idolatry laws because he knew all other gods
wouldn't and couldn't satisfy the Israelites. He issued them because he
knew that their true flourishing could be found only in relationship with
him. He issued them because he not only wanted Israel to experience such
a relationship but also because he also wanted it to demonstrate its beauty
to the rest of the world so it too might come to experience it. He issued
them for the benefit of all humanity, not for his own self-gratification.

In this sense, God was treating us like we treat our young children.
He insisted the Israelites believe in, trust in, and obey him above all others

for the same reasons we insist our children believe in, trust in, and obey us above all others. We demand their primary allegiance and complete submission because we know them better, love them more, and want what is best for them more than anyone else, not because we are egotistical. We do so because we truly and deeply want them to be as successful and happy as possible.

This parent-child analogy applies to more than just God's anti-idolatry laws. It applies to all of his laws. Generally, God gave the Israelites laws for the same reason we give our children rules. We lovingly want them to flourish and know we possess superior knowledge about how to do so. So we impose our wisdom on them in the form of rules until they gain the experience and maturity necessary to make their own choices. We know some behaviors are beneficial and others are destructive, so we instruct accordingly. And we do so out of love and for their good, not because we are spiteful or legalistic or enjoy seeing them suffer. Sometimes we so desperately want to see them flourish we practically beg them to heed our wisdom, just like God occasionally did with the Israelites.

Likewise, God disciplined the Israelites for the same reason we discipline our children. We want to see them mature into responsible, self-controlled, well-adjusted, healthy, highly-functioning, successful adults. As every parent knows, it's much harder to enforce rules that develop character than it is to let our children do whatever they want. Spoiling them is much easier than training them. But it's not good *for them*. So we exert the effort to discipline them. And we do so because we have their best interest in mind, not because we enjoy causing them pain.

A plethora of biblical passages, mostly from the OT, employ this parent-child analogy. Like a good father, they proclaim, God rebukes and disciplines those he loves.[61] He instructs us, teaches us, and counsels us with a "loving eye" (Ps. 32:8). In fact, to be disciplined by God is to be blessed.[62] Thus, the wise embrace God's discipline, but the foolish spurn it.[63] One lengthy NT passage is worth quoting in full:

> And you have forgotten the exhortation that addresses you as children—
>
> "My child, do not regard lightly the discipline of the Lord,
>   or lose heart when you are punished by him;
> for the Lord disciplines those whom he loves,
>   and chastises every child whom he accepts."
>
> Endure trials for the sake of discipline. God is treating you as children; for what child is there whom a parent does not discipline? If you do not have that discipline in which all children share, then you are illegitimate

and not his children. Moreover, we had human parents to discipline us, and we respected them. Should we not be even more willing to be subject to the Father of spirits and live? For they disciplined us for a short time as seemed best to them, but he disciplines us for our good, in order that we may share his holiness. Now, discipline always seems painful rather than pleasant at the time, but later it yields the peaceful fruit of righteousness to those who have been trained by it. (Heb. 12:5–11 NRSV)

Of course, just as our children sometimes don't understand some of our rules, we sometimes don't understand some of God's. But just as our children's understanding isn't required for them to flourish, ours isn't either. Only our obedience is. Plus, if we do our job well, someday our children will understand our rules, just as we all gradually come to better understand God's.

Another helpful analogy for understanding the beneficial nature of God's laws (particularly his universally applicable moral commands) is that of the operating manual. God is like the inventor of a complex, high-performance race car and his laws are its operating manual. He designed, engineered, and built the car, gave it to us as a gift, and then handed us instructions on how to properly operate it. Some of the instructions, the absolute basics, are interwoven into the vehicle itself. They are largely intuitive, and almost everybody understands them as soon as they enter the car. In life, we call such instructions the natural law. The more detailed instructions, however, the instructions about how to achieve optimal performance, are contained in the written manual found in the car's glove box. In life, we call such a manual the Bible.

Although God desperately wants us to use the car properly and thereby maximize our enjoyment of it, he doesn't control our use of it. He grants us a license to operate it however we want. He doesn't force us to drive correctly or even perform routine maintenance.

God does, however, allow us to suffer the natural consequences of disobeying his instructions. Sometimes the negative effects are immediate and drastic (e.g. if we drive too fast in the rain or on gravel, we crash) while other times they don't show up for years (e.g. if we fail to change the oil regularly, the engine gradually erodes). In the short term, violating some of God's instructions might even be kind of fun. It might seem harmless and provide some temporary pleasure. But if we do it too often or for too long, we eventually wreck the car or it breaks down. Ultimately, we violate the designer's instructions at our own risk.

On the other hand, perfect operation doesn't guarantee a flawless experience either. We live in an interconnected world and are surrounded by factors outside of our control. We aren't the only ones on the race track and we can't control the weather. Following God's instructions ensures our automotive experience will be as favorable as possible. And consequently, the more everybody follows God's instructions (including how to properly share the road with others, not just how to operate our own vehicle), the more everybody will have a positive experience. As Gutenson points out, "God's intentions always aim toward long-term flourishing for all humans. As our Creator, the way God intends us to structure our common lives will lead to the best environment for human flourishing for the most people."[64]

Notice one other thing here: God doesn't punish us. He doesn't crash the car or erode the engine. He doesn't do anything. He simply allows us to suffer the natural consequences of our destructive, self-sabotaging behavior. He passively allows our misuse of the car to run its natural course. When the Bible speaks of God's "wrath" and "punishment," that's what it means. It's not meant to be taken literally, as if God personally tortures us when we disobey his commands. He doesn't. He doesn't have to. Our violations of his ethical instructions (i.e. our sin, disobedience, evil, injustice, etc.) are self-punishing.

In other words, God doesn't say to us, "If you disobey me, I will destroy your car." Instead, he says, "If you disobey me, *you* will eventually destroy your car." There's a difference. An important one.

The Bible is full of verses that reflect this cause-and-effect relationship, this intrinsic and organic connection, between disobedience and self-destruction. "The wicked are brought down by their own wickedness" (Prov. 11:5). "The evil deeds of the wicked ensnare them; the cords of their sins hold them fast. For lack of discipline they will die, led astray by their own great folly" (Prov. 5:22-23). "But am I the one they are provoking? declares the Lord. Are they not rather harming themselves, to their own shame?" (Jer. 7:19). "Your own conduct and actions have brought this on you. This is your punishment" (Jer. 4:18). "Your wickedness will punish you; your backsliding will rebuke you" (Jer. 2:19). "But you have planted wickedness, you have reaped evil, you have eaten the fruit of deception" (Hos. 10:13). "Do not be deceived: God cannot be mocked. A man reaps what he sows" (Gal. 6:7). "Whoever sows injustice reaps calamity, and the rod they wield in fury will be broken" (Prov. 22:8). "Because you have plundered many nations, the peoples who are left will plunder you" (Hab. 2:8). "The violence of the wicked will drag them away, for they refuse to do what is right" (Prov. 21:7). "'Put your sword back in its place,' Jesus said to him, 'for all who draw the sword will die by the sword'" (Matt. 26:52). "But those who fail to find me harm themselves; all who hate me love death" (Prov. 8:36).[65]

This self-punishing aspect of sin also applies to hell. Hell is not a place God sends people. It is a place of self-exclusion. It is a place people *choose* to live instead of choosing to live under God's reign, where only love is allowed. If you choose to act unlovingly, he kicks you out of his kingdom (to protect others from your unloving behavior).

To use one more analogy, God's universally applicable ethical instructions operate just like the physical laws of nature, including those of physics, biology, and economics. When someone violates the law of gravity by jumping off a two-story building, his bones break. When someone violates the laws of biology by failing to eat enough good food or drink enough water, his body deteriorates. When someone violates the laws of economics by spending more than he earns, his financial health declines.

The same cause and effect exists in the moral universe. When we violate the laws of morality, destruction follows. When someone refuses to forgive, he experiences negative psychological effects. When someone lives by violence, he increases his risk of dying by violence. When someone becomes a drunk, he suffers hangovers, liver disease, lowered productivity, and often broken relationships. When someone is sexually promiscuous, he increases his risk of venereal diseases, broken relationships, retaliation from jealous spouses, and unwanted pregnancies—while also decreasing his ability to trust, remain faithful, and emotionally connect through sex. But when someone commits himself to a monogamous marital relationship, none of those consequences arise and everybody (he, his spouse, their children, their community, and society as a whole) is better off physically, emotionally, psychologically, and financially.

God has interwoven both physical and moral laws into the fabric of life, and the negative consequences of violating his moral laws are as real as the negative consequences of violating his physical ones, even if they usually aren't as obvious, immediate, or direct. "And as is true in all areas of life," writes Boyd, "when we live in contradiction to reality, we invariably end up bringing harm, and ultimately death, on ourselves."[66] Christian apologists Norman L. Geisler and Frank Turek explain it well:

> Like the physical universe, the moral universe is governed by unforgiving laws that we do not have the power to alter. No one would claim, for example, that a child could become physically and emotionally healthy by eating literally anything he wanted to eat including battery acid, arsenic, and lead paint chips. There are natural

physical limits on what one can and cannot eat. In the same way, there are natural *moral* limits to what one can and cannot do. Human beings have natural limits that, if ignored, lead to injury, disease, or death.... Indeed, the Moral Law recognizes nature's unforgiving moral limits and prevents us from destroying ourselves and others when we obey its precepts.[67]

If you still doubt the connection between obedience to God's ethical instructions and human flourishing, imagine a society in which nobody obeys his basic moral commands regarding theft, murder, adultery, and bearing false witness. Needless to say, it wouldn't be a happy place. On the other hand, as biblical scholar Dallas Willard points out, "even a fairly general practice of them [the Ten Commandments] would lead to a solution of almost every problem of meaning and order now facing Western societies."[68] He makes the same point about Jesus' teachings: "If we only put them into practice, along the lines previously discussed, most of the problems that trouble human life would be eliminated."[69] Secular philosophers, historians, and ethicists have long made the same point about virtue in general.

God's commands are life's operating manual. They are his provision for our orderly flourishing, both individually and collectively. They are, as Pastor Matt Chandler notes, "about lining people up with how he designed the universe to work."[70] Consequently, obeying them isn't only moral. It's also wise. More specifically, his commands to love and do justice aren't only right. They are also profitable. God should know. He created the game of life and its rules. When we violate those rules, things break down, harm ensues, and flourishing recedes. Theology professor Miroslav Volf summarizes:

> Christians have traditionally understood their faith not as a religious add-on to life but as itself constituting an integrated way of life. Correspondingly, Christian wisdom in one sense is that faith itself—an overarching interpretation of reality, a set of convictions, attitudes, and practices that direct people in living their lives well. Here "living well" means living as God created human beings to live, rather than living against the grain of their own true reality and the reality of the world. Wisdom in this sense is an integrated *way of life* that enables the flourishing of persons, communities, and all creation. Human beings are wise if they walk in that way.[71]

In fact, Volf adds, "A vision of human flourishing—and resources to realize it—is the most important contribution of the Christian faith to the common good."[72]

For all these reasons, the OT writers viewed God's law as a gift. Here are a few snippets from one psalmist: "The law from your mouth is more precious to me than thousands of pieces of silver and gold" (Ps. 119:72). "Your word is a lamp for my feet, a light on my path" (Ps. 119:105). "Your statutes are wonderful; therefore I obey them. The unfolding of your words gives light; it gives understanding to the simple. I open my mouth and pant, longing for your commands" (Ps. 119:129-131). "Great peace have those who love your law, and nothing can make them stumble. I wait for your salvation, Lord, and I follow your commands. I obey your statutes, for I love them greatly" (Ps. 119:165-167).

According to Willard, "The ancient writers knew well the desperate human problem of knowing how to live, and they recognized the law revealed by Jehovah, Israel's covenant-making God, to be the only real solution to this problem."[73] For example, upon receiving God's laws, Moses recognized their goodness almost immediately:

> You must observe them diligently, for this will show your wisdom and discernment to the peoples, who, when they hear all these statutes, will say, "Surely this great nation is a wise and discerning people!" For what other great nation has a god so near to it as the Lord our God is whenever we call to him? And what other great nation has statutes and ordinances as just as this entire law that I am setting before you today? (Deut. 4:6-8 NRSV)

Paul would later concur in the NT: "I agree that the law is good" (Rom. 7:16). "In my inner being I delight in God's law" (Rom. 7:22). As Yoder observed, Paul viewed the law as "a gracious arrangement made by God for the ordering of the life of his people while they were awaiting the arrival of the Messiah."[74] It's hard to argue with him. Other than the Savior himself, is there a gift greater than the wisdom of how to live life well?

Of course, since the beginning, Satan has tried to convince humans otherwise. When God told Adam and Eve they could freely enjoy the fruit from all the trees in the Garden of Eden except for just *one*, Satan tried to make God look bad by twisting his words. He asked Eve, "Did God really say, 'You must not eat from *any* tree in the garden'?" (Gen. 3:1). When Eve corrected him by explaining they were only restricted from eating the fruit from one tree because doing so would kill them, Satan responded with a lie: "'You will not certainly die,' the serpent said to the woman. 'For God knows that when you eat from it your eyes will be opened, and you will be like God, knowing good and evil'" (Gen. 3:4-5).

Notice Satan's modus operandi. God gave the first humans almost complete freedom. He told them to eat all the fruit they wanted from any tree in the forest except one and that was only because he knew its fruit would harm them. But Satan subtly reframed the situation in an attempt to label God legalistic and tyrannical. His statements implied God's instructions were (1) restrictive instead of nearly the exact opposite and (2) ill-intentioned instead of for their good. Unfortunately, the first humans fell for it—and many of us continue to do so.

This is life's great tug of war. God commands one thing while Satan tempts us to do the opposite. God instructs us to pursue righteousness (i.e. kindness, patience, forgiveness, generosity, humility, servanthood, etc.) while Satan urges us to pursue fame, fortune, and power. And both claim to have our best interests in mind. Ultimately, each of us must decide who we will believe and obey. As far as I can see, God's way leads to true, deep, and lasting satisfaction while Satan's path leads to fleeting moments of shallow pleasure. The evidence is all around us.

Simply put, God's OT laws were not legalistic, overbearing, controlling, vindictive, self-serving, or arbitrary. They were a blessing. They were not issued out of anger. They were given in love. They were not arbitrarily chosen. They were specifically designed to promote human flourishing. They were not meant to make humans sacrifice their own interests. They were intended to show them what was truly in their own interest. They were nothing less than the creator's instructions on how to live the longest, happiest, most peaceful, most prosperous, most fulfilling life possible. Far from being punitive, they were a gracious gift God entrusted to the Israelites for their own good. To condemn God for issuing such laws is pure foolishness.

Had the Israelites been able to consistently obey God's laws, they would have become the set-apart people he had intended and their unparalleled flourishing would have attracted other nations to him. To use Jeremiah's words, they would have brought God "renown, joy, praise and honor before all nations on earth," nations in such awe they would "tremble at the abundant prosperity and peace" God provides (Jer. 33:9).

And of course, all of this is just as true for Jesus' commands, maybe more so. They are a loving gift, not a burden. As Jesus explained, "Take my yoke upon you and learn from me, for I am gentle and humble in heart, and you will find rest for your souls. For my yoke is easy and my burden is light" (Matt. 11:29-30). Much lighter than the weight of sin.

Conclusion

When we view *all* of God's OT actions within their proper cultural, historical, and literary contexts, the God that emerges is not the detestable figure many critics claim, but a positively good and praiseworthy God. When we take a step back and look at how God responded to human wickedness *in total*, we see a wise, caring, and patient father, protector, and deliverer, not a cold-hearted, self-interested, vindictive dictator. When we look at the *entire* OT story instead of only its most violent incidents, we see a God who created a good world, gifted it to humans, and then lovingly went out of his way to put it back on the right track after humanity had violently derailed it. When we look at the *whole* picture, we see a God who remained faithfully committed to patiently, graciously, and lovingly working with and through humans to restore the world to its originally intended harmony. Even his decision to use incremental ethical revelation, as opposed to dropping off a list of relatively counterintuitive rules one day and immediately enforcing them with an iron fist, demonstrates such things.

We don't have to look to the NT to find a good, compassionate, faithful, patient, gracious, merciful, forgiving, just, loving God. We simply need to slow down long enough to carefully read the OT.

---

[1] Ps.136:1; see also Ps. 100:5; 106:1; 107:1; 118:1-4, 29; 1 Chron. 16:34; 2 Chron. 5:13; 7:3; 20:21; Ezra 3:11.

[2] 1 John 4:8.

[3] 1 John 4:7.

[4] 1 John 3:10, 11, 14; 4:7, 8, 12, 16; 1 Cor. 13:1-3, 8, 13; Luke 10:25-28; Jas. 2:5, 17; Col. 3:14; Gal. 5:6, 14; 1 Pet. 4:8; John 13:35; Matt. 22:36-40; Mark 12:28-34; Rom. 13:8-10; 2 John 1:5; Deut. 6:4-9; Lev. 19:18.

[5] Berman, *Created Equal*, 1012.

[6] Ibid., 966.

[7] Ibid., 972, citing Hos. 2:4-10; Isa. 1:21; 54:5-8; 57:3-10; 61:10-11; 62:4-5; Jer. 2:2, 20; 3:1-5; 3:6-25; 13:27; 23:10; Ezek. 16, 23.

[8] Ibid., 1009.

[9] Boyd, *The Crucifixion of the Warrior God*, 6930.

[10] Gen. 18:20-26.

[11] Gen. 18:27-33.

[12] Exod. 32:7-14; Num. 14:11-20; Deut. 9:11-25.

[13] Num. 16:20-35.

[14] Num. 11:1-2; 2 Sam. 24:25; 1 Kings 21:27-29; 2 Kings 20:1-7; 2 Chron. 7:14; 12:5-7; Ezek. 22:29-31; Jer. 26:19.

[15] Boyd, *Is God to Blame?*, 1391.

[16] Ibid., 1354.

[17] Ibid., 1377.

[18] Gen. 4:1.

[19] Gen. 4:15.

[20] Wright, *Evil and the Justice of God*, 683.

[21] Deut. 7:8-9; Ps. 89:1-2; 100:5 105:8; 106:43-46; 145:13, 17-18; Lam. 3:22-23; 1 Chron. 16:15.

[22] Deut. 4:31; Ps. 86:15; 103:10, 13; Lam. 3:22-23; Isa. 63:7.

[23] Hab. 1:3-4, 13.

[24] Neh. 9:27; Ps. 78:38; 106:43-46.

[25] Gen. 18:20-26; Exod. 32:7-14; Deut. 9:11-25; Num. 11:1-2; 14:11-20; 16:20-35; Isa. 38:1-6; 2 Sam. 24:16, 25; 1 Kings 21:27-29; 2 Kings 20:1-7; 1 Chron. 21:15; 2 Chron. 12:5-7; Amos 7:1-6; Jer. 26:19; 42:9-10; Joel 2:12-14.

[26] Jer. 18:7-8; 26:3, 13; 2 Chron. 7:14.

[27] Rom. 3:25-26.

[28] Josh. 2, 6.

[29] 2 Kings 6:8-23.

[30] Amos 9:7.

[31] 2 Kings 5:1-14.

[32] See also Prov. 25:21 and Jer. 29:7.

[33] Jon. 1-4

[34] Ezek. 18:23.

[35] Gen. 2:16-17.

[36] Rom. 3:23.

[37] Rom. 6:23.

[38] 2 Sam. 6:2-11; Acts 5:1-11.

[39] Gen. 6-8.

[40] Nugent, *Endangered Gospel*, 821.

[41] Ibid., 665.

[42] Gen. 4:1-12.

[43] Exod. 34:5-7; Isa. 65:2; Num. 14:18; Joel 2:13; Neh. 9:17; Nah. 1:3; Jon. 4:2; Ps. 86:15; 103:8; 145:8.

[44] See also 1 Pet. 3:19-20; 2 Pet. 2:5.

[45] Gen. 6:6.

[46] Gen. 15:13; 2 Kings 17:7-23; 25:1-30.

[47] Exod. 3:7-4:17.

[48] Nugent, *Endangered Gospel*, 615.

[49] Thompson, *Who's Afraid of the Old Testament God?*, 564.

[50] Gen. 2:16-17.

[51] Exod. 20:8-11; Deut. 5:12-15.

[52] Exod. 23:14-17; Deut. 16:1-17.

[53] Swartley, *Covenant of Peace*, 28.

[54] Dietrich Bonhoeffer, *Letters and Papers from Prison* (London: SCM Press, 1971), 362.

[55] Lev. 18:5; Josh. 1:8; Jer. 7:23-24; Prov. 1:33; 3:1-10; 10:27; 14:34; 16:20; 29:18; Ps. 34:8-14; 112:1-3; 128:1-2; Isa. 32:17-18.

[56] Ronald Clements, *God's Chosen People: A Theological Interpretation of the Book of Deuteronomy* (Valley Forge, PA: Judson Press, 1969), 58.

[57] Deut. 4:40; 5:29, 33; 6:1-3, 18-19; 7:12; 8:1, 11-14; 11:8-22; 13:17-18; 28:1-14; 29:9; 30:8-10.

[58] 1 Kings 2:3; Deut. 6:24; Deut. 10:12-13.

[59] Isa. 58:11; Ps. 1:1-4; Jer. 17:7-8.

[60] Lamb, *God Behaving Badly*, 1217.

[61] Deut. 8:5; Prov. 3:11-12; 13:24; Jer. 9:7; Rev. 3:19.

[62] Ps. 94:12; Job 5:17.

[63] Prov. 10:17; 12:1, 15; 13:1, 18; 15:32.

[64] Gutenson, *Christians and the Common Good*, 1089.

[65] See also Prov. 26:27; Hos. 8:7.

[66] Boyd, *The Crucifixion of the Warrior God*, 17357.

[67] Norman Geisler and Frank Turek, *Legislating Morality: Is It Wise? Is It Legal? Is It Possible?* Reprint Edition (Eugene, OR: Wipf and Stock Publishers, 2003), 114.

[68] Dallas Willard, *The Divine Conspiracy: Rediscovering Our Hidden Life in God* (HarperCollins, 2009), 1221, Kindle.

[69] Ibid., 5301.

[70] Matt Chandler, *The Scriptures Testify about Me: Jesus and the Gospel in the Old Testament*, ed. D. A. Carson (Crossway, 2013), 1613, Kindle.

[71] Miroslav Volf, *A Public Faith: How Followers of Christ Should Serve the Common Good* Reprint Edition (Brazos Press, 2011), 1672, Kindle.

[72] Ibid., 1111.

[73] Willard, *The Divine Conspiracy*, 2708.

[74] John Howard Yoder, *The Politics of Jesus* (Grand Rapids, MI: Wm. B. Eerdmans Publishing Co., 1994), 215.

9

OUR MORAL STANDARD

Regardless of what you think of the God of the OT, he does not call us to obey or imitate him. Instead, he calls us to obey and imitate Jesus. The Bible makes this clear on every level.

The Historical Context

Remember, the Bible is a narrative. In general, it's the story of the world. More specifically, it's the story of God creating and then intervening into human history. Ethically speaking, it's the story of God gradually and incrementally revealing his moral standards to humanity until he eventually completes them in the life and teachings of Jesus. As such, it demands to be read as a developing story, not as a bullet list of static commands, a fixed constitution of laws, or a comprehensive encyclopedia of do's and don'ts.

The OT plays an indispensable but *temporary* role in the biblical narrative. To oversimplify a bit, it gets the story moving and sets the stage for the NT. It tells the story of how God created the world, how Satan corrupted it, and how God used various individuals and the nation of Israel to begin restoring it. As part of that initial restorative process, God personally issued many direct commands to those parties. Such commands served various purposes and included everything from specific, onetime-only individual and national actions (like building an ark and attacking a particular foreign enemy) to a long list of detailed laws governing all aspects of daily life.

But God never intended for his OT commands to be universally or eternally applicable. The commands were not general pronouncements. They weren't directed at all humankind. They weren't even directed at future believers. Instead, each was narrowly aimed at a particular individual or at the theocratic nation of ancient Israel—a nation specifically chosen and directly ruled by God for a distinct purpose. As such, they don't apply to God's followers today.

We seem to understand this on an individual level but lose sight of it on a national level. For example, most of us realize that God's OT commands to individuals like Noah or Abraham don't apply to us today. Only the insane believe they should build an ark like God commanded Noah or sacrifice their son on an altar like God commanded Abraham. We intuitively understand that God gave those commands to specific people under specific circumstances at specific times for specific, temporary purposes. But for some reason, when it comes to the more general OT commands given to the larger nation of Israel, like using violence for nationalistic purposes, we ignore such context. Regardless, the same contextual analysis and conclusion applies. God's commands to the nation of Israel were given to a specific people under specific circumstances at a specific time for specific, temporary purposes. Therefore, for the same reason we need not build an ark or sacrifice our sons on an altar, we also need not enforce the death penalty or violently defeat our national enemies.

To put it another way, because you and I are not citizens of OT Israel, God's commands to OT Israel do not apply to us today. It's that simple. You and I are Christians, not OT Israelites. In fact, there was no such thing as a Christian in the OT. By definition, to be a *Christian* means to follow the ways of *Christ*, not those of OT Israel. That's why God's followers weren't called Christians until after Jesus' life, death, and resurrection.[1]

In short, the historical context surrounding all of God's OT commands, including everything from the civil laws to the warfare instructions, indicate they don't apply to us today.

The Theological Context

Examining the theological context surrounding God's OT commands yields the same conclusion. God issued commands to the OT Israelites as part of a covenant with them—and only them. He promised he would bless them, he would bless the world through them, they would be his "treasured possession" and a "holy nation," and they would occupy the Promised Land *if* they would faithfully obey his commands, which he subsequently revealed through Moses.[2] As such, God's commands and Israel's obedience to them were both elements of a particular, unique religious contract.

Furthermore, not only was the covenant within which God issued his OT commands not a universally binding covenant, it was also temporary.[3] It wasn't even eternally binding on the parties to it. It served a specific, short-term purpose, and God never intended it to do or be anything else. It was never his complete and ultimate plan for all of humanity. That's why the OT is littered with prophesies about our patient and faithful God making a new, and this time, everlasting covenant.[4]

Right on cue, Jesus came to earth to replace the old covenant with a new, superior, eternal one, one "established on better promises" (Heb. 8:6).[5] First, he transcended the old covenant by fulfilling it, not abolishing it.[6] In doing so, he "set aside" the old covenant and rendered it "obsolete" and "outdated" (Heb. 7:18; 8:13; Eph. 2:15). Note, however, he did so not because it was bad, but because it's good and necessary purpose had been fulfilled. It had run its intended course.

Second, Jesus became the means by which God established a new covenant. (Although we refer to the two sections of the Bible as the Old and New Testaments, we could just as accurately refer to them as the Old and New Covenants.) Through Jesus, whom the Bible calls the "mediator" of the new covenant,[7] God offered all individuals (not just Israelites) a new way to overcome sin and reenter right relationship with him. By his death on the cross, Jesus atoned for our sins and his blood became the blood of the new covenant.[8] To accept God's new covenant offer, all we need to do is believe. The perfect obedience required by the old covenant is no longer necessary. The new covenant is a relationship with God based on grace and faith instead of the works of the law. More succinctly, it's salvation by grace through faith in Jesus. "For the law was given through Moses; grace and truth came through Jesus Christ" (John 1:17). And, unlike the old covenant, the new covenant is eternal.[9]

When God established this new covenant, he also completed his ethical revelation. In Jesus, he finally and definitively revealed his perfect, eternal, and universally applicable moral code. In other words, as part of this new covenant, Jesus superseded Moses as the authoritative source of God's ethical instructions. The entire NT makes this clear. Everyone in it declared it.

Jesus declared it. When he taught people to obey, he pointed them to his own commands, not the OT's. In the Great Commission, he proclaimed that "all authority in heaven and on earth" had been given to him (not Moses) and then instructed his disciples to teach others to obey him (not Moses) (Matt. 28:18-20). He repeatedly stated that those who love him will obey his commands (not Moses').[10] He said everyone who hears his words (not Moses') and "puts them into practice is like a wise man who built his house on the rock" (Matt. 7:24).[11] He referred to John the Baptist as greater than anyone who had been born before him, which obviously included Moses, and then he claimed to be greater than even him.[12] Jesus even refused to obey many OT commands himself, like the one that required stoning adulterous women.[13]

God declared it. When Jesus, Moses, and Elijah were standing on the mountain together in front of the disciples, God commanded the disciples to listen to Jesus, not Moses or Elijah or even his own OT commands.[14]

The post-gospel writers declared it. The author of Hebrews proclaimed that Jesus is greater and more authoritative than Moses.[15] "But in fact," he also wrote, "the ministry Jesus has received is as superior to theirs as the covenant of which he is mediator is superior to the old one...." (Heb. 8:6). Paul insisted that he and all other Christians are no longer subject to the Mosaic Law but instead are now under Jesus' law.[16] He referred to the Mosaic Law as "transitory" and consequently much less glorious than Jesus' eternal law.[17] He warned the Thessalonians that God will punish those who "do not obey the gospel of our Lord Jesus," not the laws of Moses (2 Thess. 1:8). In fact, some Jews even tried to kill Paul because he taught that the OT commands no longer need to be obeyed.[18] Likewise, Peter proclaimed that the OT commands no longer apply because of Jesus.[19]

Even Moses declared it. Before Jesus had even been born, Moses said, "The Lord your God will raise up for you a prophet like me from among your own people; you must listen to everything he tells you" (Acts 3:22). That prophet was Jesus, the same Jesus who told the Jewish leaders, "If you believed Moses, you would believe me, for he wrote about me" (John 5:46).

The Law of Jesus replaced the Law of Moses. God calls us to be Jesus' disciples, not Moses' or Joshua's or David's. Ethically speaking, God gave Jesus (not Moses) the final word. The ethics of the Sermon on the Mount supersede the ethics of the OT, not vice versa. As Hays puts it, "If irreconcilable tensions exist between the moral vision of the New Testament and that of particular Old Testament texts, the New Testament vision trumps the Old Testament."[20] Again, it's not that the Law of Moses was bad, just that its good and necessary but also temporary purpose had been fulfilled.

Therefore, the theological context surrounding God's OT commands reveals that they don't apply to us today. God issued them as part of a temporary (and now expired), non-universally applicable covenant between himself and the Israelites, a covenant to which we were never parties. Even if we had been, Jesus changed the rules of the game by fulfilling, rendering obsolete, and replacing the old covenant and its commands with the new covenant and its commands. You and I are now under that new covenant (the covenant of Christ) and consequently its new laws (the laws of Christ).

To claim otherwise, to claim that something God commanded in the OT trumps what Jesus commanded in the NT, fails to acknowledge the significance and purpose of Jesus and reverses the clear direction of biblical progress. God's OT commands were never meant to provide humanity with a universally and eternally applicable code of conduct, but Jesus' were. The Law of Moses served an indispensable but temporary purpose: to point the way to Jesus. Or as Lasserre put it, the OT "speaks to us of Jesus Christ, not of morality."[21] The Law of Jesus, on the other hand, serves an eternal purpose: to teach us how to embody God's kingdom on earth.

Additional Explicit Instructions

If the historical and theological contexts aren't enough to convince you that Jesus is our moral standard, the Bible gets even more explicit. Not only does it clearly order us to *obey* Jesus' commands (not God's OT commands), it just as clearly orders us to *imitate* Jesus, not the God of the OT. Again, everyone in the NT declared it. Jesus commanded us to mimic him and him alone.[22] So did the apostles.[23] Similarly, the NT writers frequently referred to God's followers as "the body of Christ," not the body of the OT God.[24] And as Boyd points out, one thing that means is "that we are to do exactly what Jesus did."[25]

As Yoder astutely observed, "No theme is more widely present in the New Testament than that Jesus reveals what God wants of the believer."[26] "Jesus did in the world what we are supposed to be doing in the world."[27] Or as C. S. Lewis so plainly put it, "The whole purpose of becoming a Christian is simply ... to become a little Christ."[28] Again, that's one primary reason why God's followers are called *Christ*ians.

Here's another way to look at the issue. Because the Bible contains conflicting commands and includes conflicting behavioral examples, we have to come up with some way of choosing between them. And if we have to choose, why not let the Bible choose for us? Why not let it tell us which of its commands to obey and who in it to imitate? Is there a more reasonable approach? In fact, the only objective way of solving the problem is to do exactly that. Any other solution is us subjectively choosing based on our own personal preferences, which are usually more influenced by our fallen desire for safety, comfort, and control than a sincere intention to do God's will regardless of the cost.

Jesus is the Answer

Despite all the good, essential things the OT accomplishes, it does not provide us with a perfect moral standard. For that, God sent Jesus. He is our ethical ideal, our moral compass, our one and only code of conduct. He is the perfect example of how to do God's will, which is precisely what he came to earth to do.[29] We are to obey and imitate him, not Moses, not the OT Israelites, and not the God of the OT. We are to be his disciples and no one else's. Everything and everyone in the Bible declares it: the historical context, the theological context, Moses, the NT writers, Jesus, and even God himself. The Bible couldn't have made it any clearer. All we need to do is obey it.

To claim otherwise, to claim that we are to obey or imitate any of the OT characters, is to dishonor Jesus. After all, Jesus himself proclaimed that whoever believes in him and loves him will do what *he* said and did.[30]

Of course, there is one exception to the general rule that God's OT commands do not apply to us today. It's so obvious it's almost not worth mentioning, but to be thorough, here it is: We are subject to the OT commands that are also part of the new covenant.

Generally, two types of OT commands fit that criteria. First, for obvious reasons, we are subject to the OT commands Jesus ratified. For example, he affirmed most (if not all) of the Ten Commandments.[31] Second, we are subject to the OT commands that are part of the natural law (i.e. eternally valid and universally applicable moral precepts that all humans inherently know on some level) because they always have been and always will be binding. For example, we are subject to God's OT commands to not murder, steal, commit adultery, covet, and give false testimony because those behaviors were wrong before God gave Moses the Ten Commandments and they remain wrong despite the expiration of the old covenant. As you've likely just noticed, many of the OT commands that are part of the new covenant fit both criteria—Jesus endorsed them and they are part of the natural law. To clarify our general rule, God's OT commands do not apply to us today *unless* Jesus also commanded them or they are written on our hearts.

One last caveat: Concluding that the vast majority of God's OT commands do not apply to us today does not denigrate the OT or diminish its continued importance. You don't have to believe its commands still apply to believe it—all of it—is still "God-breathed and is useful for teaching, rebuking, correcting and training in righteousness," as Paul famously proclaimed all Scripture is (2 Tim. 3:16-17).

For example, the OT tells us a lot about God and his character: that he is the creator, the supreme and sole authority, the source of all morality, and the ruler of the entire universe. It shows us how he interacts with humans. It reveals our human purpose and what he wants most from us: obedient relationship. It exhibits the significance of being set apart from the world, being in it but not of it. It helps us identify sinful behavior.[32] It displays God's holiness and our sinfulness. It demonstrates our fallen condition and our inability to cure it without his help. In doing so, it points us to our need for Jesus and the beauty of his saving, sacrificial love. Likewise, it reveals how the new covenant is based on God's grace. It gives us hope.[33] It reveals what God generally thinks about specific issues like marriage and divorce. It informs our understanding of the NT and its commands. In short, the OT and its commands teach us many invaluable lessons about who God is, what he wants, what he is doing in the world, and how we fit into his plan.

The entire OT, including all of its commands, is still an essential, relevant, valuable, and useful component of Christianity and always will be. But for determining how God wants us to behave in a post-Jesus world, the NT is our guidebook. As the ethicists say, the OT commands are informative but the NT commands are normative. Recognizing and applying that fundamental biblical tenet is the key to clearing up much of the confusion surrounding what God wants from us, his present-day followers.

What This Means for Our Use of Violence

All of this is as true for the OT's violence as it is for everything else in the OT. It occurred within an evolving narrative. It was part of special religious contract between God and a specific group of people in a specific place at a specific point in history. It served a good and necessary purpose within that unique covenant, but it was never intended to teach or demonstrate universally or eternally applicable moral principles. It played an indispensable but *temporary* role, a role that is now obsolete. Yes, as Ecclesiastes 3:1-8 says, "There is a time for everything, and a season for every activity under the heavens," including "a time to kill" and "a time for war," but the time for such things has come and gone. Or to borrow an analogy from Paul, "When I was a child, I talked like a child, I thought like a child, I reasoned like a child. When I became a man, I put the ways of childhood behind me" (1 Cor. 13:11).

Even if the old covenant was still in effect today, it would not justify our use of violence because the United States is not the OT theocratic nation of Israel. Our nation, as amazing as it is, is not God's treasured possession. U.S. citizens are not God's chosen people. The U.S. military is not God's army. Our great country is not the Promised Land.[34] You cannot get from "the OT Israelites used violence for historically specific purposes under God's personal direction" to "Christians today can use U.S. military violence for wholly different purposes in the absence of God's personal direction" without committing an egregious act of contextual violence, murdering proper biblical interpretation, and nuking basic Christian theology.

Simply put, the OT provides *no* support for using violence today. God's commands to use violence in the OT do not justify our use of violence today any more than his command to Abraham to sacrifice his son as a burnt offering justifies our use of child sacrifice. Likewise, God's own use of violence in the OT does not justify our use of violence today any more than his causing parents to cannibalize their children justifies us forcing our enemies to cannibalize theirs. The OT provides no more support for waging war today than it does for imposing the death penalty on those who commit adultery, worship other gods, or work on the Sabbath. All justification for such violence must come from the life and teachings of Jesus, and any such justification must be sufficiently unambiguous to overcome the OT's overarching antiviolence posture, not to mention Jesus' similar posture.

One final point before we move on. The Bible contains evidence that Jesus might even expect us to perform greater feats of nonviolence than even he did. He told his disciples, "Very truly I tell you, whoever believes in me will do the works I have been doing, and they will do even greater things than these, because I am going to the Father" (John 14:12-14). Shortly thereafter, he added, "I have much more to say to you, more than you can now bear. But when he, the Spirit of truth, comes, he will guide you into all the truth" (John 16:12-13). So not only are we supposed to mimic Jesus' nonviolence, we might actually be expected to surpass it.

Such an expectation makes sense from a resource standpoint. Jesus was given the gargantuan task of radically altering humanity's ethical trajectory, but he wasn't given much time to do it. He only lived about thirty-three years and was engaged in public ministry for only the last three. He also wasn't given much, if any, help. Prior to his death and resurrection, his disciples were a much greater drain on his ministry than an aid to it. They were struggling to understand the ethical shift themselves, so helping Jesus propagate it was out of the question. Thus, there's a sense in which Jesus barely had enough time and resources to change our path, let alone make it very far down that path himself. We the church, on the other hand, have centuries to study, understand, test, and implement Jesus' teachings and much more help in doing so, in the form of both the Holy Spirit and multitudes of fellow Christians. From this perspective, we should accomplish more.

Slavery is a prime example. Jesus wasn't able to eradicate it in his short, revolutionary lifetime. But his followers eventually were after centuries of gradual moral progress in the direction Jesus had pointed them. Cavanaugh elaborates:

> Although the story comes to an unsurpassable climax in the events of Jesus' life, death, and resurrection, it might take a while for humanity to come to grips with those events.... Sometimes it takes a lot of maturity through hard experience for the church to get it right. Arriving at the doctrine of the Trinity took several centuries of argument. The ban on slavery and the embrace of religious liberty took far longer. The Christian critique of war that has gathered so much momentum and authority since the second half of the 20th century might not be—as some politically conservative commentators fear—the selling out of the church's "just war" tradition to a wooly liberalism but rather a new stage in the fruition of the Gospel. Whatever the case, the pedagogical model need not be strictly linear and progressive, as every parent and teacher knows. The Christian understanding is subject to reversals and detours, though in the long run it may be that something is learned in the process.[35]

Although God's ethical revelation is complete, our embodiment of it isn't. We are still growing and maturing, still learning how to faithfully put his ethical ideal into practice. In many respects, we've come a long way, but in others, there's still much work to do. Nonetheless, the history of slavery gives me great hope. It was once institutionalized and taken for granted but is now largely extinct. Its story makes me wonder what we take for granted today that will no longer exist in a few hundred years. Eating animals? Taxation? I don't know, but to borrow Martin Luther King, Jr.'s words, I believe "The arc of the moral universe ... bends toward justice." You and I live within that arc, and it's our job to continue bending it in the same direction Jesus did—towards greater and greater nonviolence.

---

[1] Acts 11:26.

[2] Exod. 19:3-6; 23:31; Deut. 4:40.

[3] Gal. 3:19, 24.

[4] Jer. 31:31-34; 32:38-40; Ezek. 16:60-62; 37:26; Isa. 55:3.

[5] See also Gal. 3:23-25; 4:21-31.

[6] Matt. 5:17.

[7] Heb. 9:15; 12:24.

[8] Matt. 26:28; Mark 14:24; Heb. 9:15, 10:29; Col. 2:14.

[9] Jer. 32:38-40; Ezek. 16:60-62; 37:26; Isa. 55:3. For more on the transition from the old covenant to the new, read the book of Hebrews, which discusses it at length.

[10] John 14:15, 21, 23; 15:14.

[11] See also Luke 6:46-48.

[12] Matt. 11:11; John 5:36.

[13] John 8:1-11.

[14] Matt. 17:1-5.

[15] Heb. 3:1-6.

[16] 1 Cor. 9:20-21; Gal. 2:15-16; 3:23-25.

[17] 2 Cor. 3:7-11.

[18] Acts 21:17-36.

[19] Acts 15:5-11.

[20] Hays, *The Moral Vision of the New Testament*, 9415.

[21] Lasserre, *War and the Gospel*, 24.

[22] John 13:15, 34; 14:12; 15:12.

[23] 1 Cor. 3:11; 11:1; 1 Pet. 2:21; Phil. 2:5; 1 John 2:6; 3:16; Col 2:6; 3:17; Eph. 5:1-2.

[24] Rom. 12:4-5; 1 Cor. 10:17; 12:12-27; Eph. 4:4; 5:30; Col. 1:18, 24; 2:19.

[25] Gregory A. Boyd, *The Myth of a Christian Nation: How the Quest for Political Power is Destroying the Church* (Zondervan, 2009), 382, Kindle.

[26] Yoder, *The War of the Lamb*, 1588.

[27] Yoder, *Christian Attitudes to War, Peace, and Revolution*, 3297.

[28] C. S. Lewis, *Mere Christianity* (New York: Harper Collins, 2001), 177.

[29] John 6:38.

[30] John 14:12, 15, 21, 23; 15:14.

[31] Matt. 4:10; 19:16-19; Mark 10:19; Luke 18:20; Eph. 6:2; Rom. 13:8-10.

[32] Rom. 7:7.

[33] Rom. 15:4.

[34] If these facts offend you, if they strike you as anti-patriotic, if you think they smell of a left-wing conspiracy, you've probably turned the United States into an idol.

[35] Cavanaugh, *Constantine Revisited*, 2357.

10

MAYBE GOD DIDN'T DO IT

Up to this point, we have assumed that God did what the OT says he did. We have assumed he performed, ordered, and sanctioned all the violence the OT attributes to him. And despite taking those descriptions at face value, we have discovered that the God described therein is still a good, loving, and just God, one who clearly hates violence but sometimes employs it in limited ways to further his antiviolence agenda.

In this chapter and the following, we will explore some of the historical, cultural, literary, and theological reasons for questioning whether God actually engaged in the violence the OT says he did. In other words, we will review evidence for concluding that God not only wants us to refrain from using violence but that he refrains from using it himself, despite what the OT says.

The underlying issue here is how to determine God's true character. We can't simply "look to the Bible" because it contains enough different portraits of him to allow us to concoct whatever type of God we want, as NT professor Bradley Jersak explains:

> Even if we restrict our inquiry into the nature of God to the Bible, we are likely to find just the kind of God that we want to find. If we want a God of peace, he's there. If we want a God of war, he's there. If we want a compassionate God, he's there. If we want a vindictive God, he's there. If we want an egalitarian God, he's there. If we want an ethnocentric God, he's there. If we want a God demanding blood sacrifice, he's there. If we want a God abolishing blood sacrifice, he's there.[1]

Given the conflicting portraits of God in the Bible, how do we know what he is really like? To what more specific criteria should we turn to discern his true nature? How do we decide whether the OT's depiction of him as a mighty warrior who violently slays his enemies or the NT's depiction of him (in Jesus) as a wholly nonviolent servant who willingly suffers violence and lays down his life for his enemies is a more accurate representation?

This is a crucial issue. How humans view God lies at the heart of the entire biblical narrative. Since the beginning, God and Satan have been locked in a tug of war over God's character, competing against each other to sell their conflicting viewpoints to humanity.[2] In the Garden of Eden, God commanded Adam and Eve to not eat the fruit of the tree of the knowledge of good and evil because, he claimed, it would cause them to die. But then Satan sold them a different story. He claimed God lied, that eating the fruit would not cause them to die but instead would cause them to become like God, knowing good and evil. And so the historic struggle began—God claiming his commands are in humanity's best interest and Satan claiming they aren't, God trying to convince humans he is trustworthy and Satan claiming he isn't, God claiming he is benevolent and Satan claiming he is selfish, etc. In other words, Satan's initial strategy to cause humans to sin was to alter their view of God. And he's been working at it ever since.

This is what Satan does. He distorts the truth. He attempts to lead "the whole world astray" (Rev. 12:9). He is "full of all kinds of deceit and trickery" (Acts 13:10). According to Jesus, "there is no truth in him. When he lies, he speaks his native language, for he is a liar and the father of lies" (John 8:44). Satan's power is the power of deception. Boyd explains:

> From this perspective, we could describe the entire biblical drama of God working to restore us to himself as a conflict between God's truth and Satan's deception. From start to finish, God is working to restore humanity into a right relationship with himself by delivering us from the false conception that "the ancient serpent," who is "the accuser" and "the deceiver of the nations," has used to enslave us since our fall in the garden (Rev 12:9, cf. 20:2-3, 7-8).[3]

To put it another way, a distorted view of God's character is the root of all sin. In Boyd's words, "our alienation from God and our bondage to Satan is most fundamentally anchored in the fact that we have been seduced, to one degree or another, into sharing Satan's jaded and untrustworthy view of God, as the story of Adam and Eve graphically illustrates."[4] Simply put, "the foundation of all that separates us from God is a false picture of God," which is why "everything hangs on the question, Where do we find the true picture of God?"[5] In this sense, our reconciliation with God (i.e. our salvation) largely depends on our obtaining an accurate conception of him.

Furthermore, our conception of God's character has an immense practical impact on how we live our lives. According to pastor and theologian A. W. Tozer, "what comes into our minds when we think about God is the most important thing about us" because "we tend by a secret law of the soul to move toward our mental image of God" and "no religion has ever been greater than its idea of God."[6] "For this reason," Tozer concludes, "the most portentous fact about any man is ... what he in his deep heart conceives God to be like."[7]

Inevitably, our lives reflect what we believe about God, and that's particularly true of violence. If we believe he uses violence against his enemies and to advance his agenda, we will be inclined to do the same. History testifies to it.

Unfortunately, this tendency exists despite God's clear commands to mimic Jesus and not his OT actions. We typically look to God's character instead of to his commands to determine whether, how, and why we should use violence. We are inclined to do as (we perceive) God does, not as he says.

So how do we solve this dilemma? How do we avoid being misled by Satan? How do we discern God's true character? Thankfully, the Bible gives us an unambiguous, definitive answer: Jesus.

God is Like Jesus

According to the Bible itself, God's character is most accurately revealed in the person of Jesus. He is the clearest picture we have of what God is really like. He is God's own self-revelation.

In fact, God isn't partially like Jesus. He isn't even mostly like Jesus. He is exactly like Jesus. The author of Hebrews described Jesus as "the radiance of God's glory and the *exact representation* of his being" (Heb. 1:3). Jesus himself said, "The one who looks at me is seeing the one who sent me" (John 12:45). Likewise, Paul called Jesus "the image of the invisible God" (Col. 1:15; 2 Cor. 4:4). Jesus is "the word of God in its fullness" (Col. 1:25). "For in Christ," he wrote, "all the fullness of the Deity lives in bodily form" (Col. 2:9).[8]

Jesus claimed he was sent by God to do and say exactly what God wanted. "I have come here from God. I have not come on my own; God sent me" (John 8:42).[9] "I do nothing on my own but speak just what the Father has taught me. The one who sent me is with me; he has not left me alone, for I always do what pleases him" (John 8:28-29). "Very truly I tell you, the Son can do nothing by himself; he can do only what he sees his Father doing, because whatever the Father does the Son also does" (John 5:19). "For I did not speak on my own, but the Father who sent me commanded me to say all that I have spoken.... So whatever I say is just what the Father has told me to say" (John 12:49-50).[10] These claims—to be directly sent by God, to act directly on God's behalf, to say only what

God wants said, and to do only what God wants done—are made by no other person in the Bible.

Jesus also claimed that to know him is to know God. To the Pharisees, he said, "If you knew me, you would know my Father also" (John 8:19). He told his disciples, "If you really know me, you will know my Father as well. From now on, you do know him and have seen him" (John 14:7). And then when one of his disciples who still didn't get it responded by saying, "Lord, show us the Father and that will be enough for us," Jesus attempted to remove all doubt. He answered:

> Have I been with you all this time, Philip, and you still do not know me? Whoever has seen me has seen the Father. How can you say, 'Show us the Father'? Do you not believe that I am in the Father and the Father is in me? The words that I say to you I do not speak on my own; but the Father who dwells in me does his works. Believe me that I am in the Father and the Father is in me; but if you do not, then believe me because of the works themselves. (John 14:9-11 NRSV)

Or as John the apostle put it, Jesus "has come and has given us understanding, so that we may know him who is true. And we are in him who is true by being in his Son Jesus Christ" (1 John 5:20). As Boyd deduces, "This means that in knowing Jesus, we are not knowing someone 'one step removed' from God. In knowing Jesus we are knowing God *himself*, God in his eternal essence. In seeing Jesus, we are seeing the very heart of God."[11]

In fact, Jesus claimed he was the *only* way to truly know God. He said, "All things have been committed to me by my Father. No one knows the Son except the Father, and no one knows the Father except the Son and those to whom the Son chooses to reveal him" (Matt. 11:27). Or as the author of 1 Timothy put it, "there is one God and one mediator between God and mankind, the man Christ Jesus" (2:5). We must also not forget one of Jesus' most famous proclamations: "I am the way and the truth and the life. No one comes to the Father except through me" (John 14:6).

In various ways, the NT claims that before Jesus no one truly knew God. John the apostle claimed no one had "ever seen God" until Jesus "made him known" (John 1:18).[12] Paul claimed God had kept his perfect wisdom and true character hidden until he revealed them in Jesus.[13] And Jesus himself told his disciples they were getting to see and hear things no one before them had: "For truly I tell you, many prophets and righteous people longed to see what you see but did not see it, and to hear what you hear but did not hear it" (Matt. 13:17).

Furthermore, Jesus wasn't merely a full and perfect *portrayal* of God. He *was* God. Or as Jersak articulates it, "Jesus is not just a filter through which God is seen—Jesus *is* that God."[14]

The NT writers often explicitly proclaimed it. The author of John's gospel proclaimed that Jesus "is himself God" (John 1:18). In his letter to Titus, Paul referred to Jesus as our "God and Savior," as did the author of 2 Peter (Titus 2:13; 2 Pet. 1:1). Other times, the NT writers bestowed labels on Jesus that implicitly made the same point. They often called Jesus the "Son of God," which was their way of highlighting his divinity (as opposed to his humanity, which they highlighted by calling him the "Son of Man"). According to Matthew's gospel, Jesus was to be called "Immanuel," which means "God with us" (Matt. 1:23). John's gospel put it this way: "In the beginning was the Word, and the Word was with God, and the Word was God" (John 1:1). And in Jesus, "The Word became flesh and made his dwelling among us" (John 1:14). This is what it means to refer to Jesus as the "incarnation" of God. It is to literally call him the enfleshment of God. In contrast to the spoken words, dreams, and miracles through which God revealed himself in the OT, through Jesus he revealed himself in human form. Jesus was God come to earth in person. There are many more examples we could explore, as Boyd explains:

> This same truth is reflected in the remarkable way NT authors ascribe titles and attributes to Jesus that were previously reserved for Yahweh. Among other things, Christ is portrayed as the Creator (John 1:2; Col 1:15–17, Heb 1:2–3; cf. Gen 1:1), the judge of the whole world (e.g., Matt 25:31–46; 2 Cor 5:10; cf. Gen 18:25; Joel 3:12), the heavenly "bridegroom" in search of his bride (Matt 9:15, 25:1; Mark 2:18–20; John 3:25–30; 2 Cor 11:2–3; Eph 5:22–25; Rev 19:7–9; cf. Isa 49:18, 54:1–8, 62:5; Jer 2:2; 3:1, 6–9, 14; 16:9; Ezekiel 16; Hos 2:16), the "alpha and omega, the beginning and the end" (Rev 1:8, 21:6, 22:13; cf. Isa 41:4, 44:6), and the one to whom "every knee will bow and every tongue confess is Lord" (Rom 14:11; Phil 2:10; cf. Isa 45:23).[15]

Even Jesus himself claimed to be God. "I and the Father are one," he declared (John 10:30). "Very truly I tell you," he announced, "before Abraham was born, I am!" (John 8:58). At least the Jewish leaders, high priests, and Pharisees thought Jesus claimed to be God. On many occasions, they tried to put him to death for such blasphemy.[16] Yet Jesus never refuted the charge, not even when faced with death. Similarly, when doubting Thomas finally acknowledged Jesus as "My Lord and my God," Jesus didn't rebuke or correct him. He didn't say, "Oh no, I'm only a prophet," or "Don't dishonor God like that. I'm just a teacher." Instead, he commended Thomas for his realization.[17] Thus, although Jesus never directly said, "I am God," everything he did indicated he believed he was God. Plus, had he not been so indirect with his claims of divinity, his already-cut-short public ministry would have likely been cut even shorter.

Jesus isn't merely one picture of God among many equally revealing pictures. He is *the* picture of God. He isn't merely the best picture the Bible gives us. He is the culmination of them, the one to which all others point, and the one that supersedes all others. He is not merely one of many equally authoritative "words" of God. He is *the* Word of God.[18]

Jesus is the means by which God won the battle with Satan over his own character. He is the means by which God decisively dispelled Satan's lies about him. Jesus removed the veil that Satan had hung between us and God. Hence, "Just as the lie about God is the foundation for all sin," writes Boyd, "so too the truth about God, revealed in Jesus Christ, is the foundation for all wholeness."[19] This is one way in which God used Jesus to defeat evil. He used him to defeat Satan's power of deception and expose him as the liar and deceiver, the untrustworthy one.

According to the Bible itself, God's character is fully and perfectly revealed by Jesus, not by the OT authors, not by Moses, not by the book of Revelation, not by the Pope, and not by philosophizing theologians. We are accustomed to saying that Jesus is like God, but it's more accurate to phrase it the other way around: God is like Jesus. God is Christlike. The Bible is very clear on this. Just as it unambiguously asserts we are to obey and mimic Jesus instead of the OT Israelites or the OT God, it unambiguously asserts that Jesus is the most accurate picture of God we have, not the OT. Therefore, if you want to know what God is really like, look at Jesus.

Jesus answers all our questions about God. What is God like? Jesus. How does God treat people? Jesus. How does God handle his enemies? Jesus. What does God think of violence? Jesus. How does God fight and conquer evil? Jesus. How does God want *us* to treat people, handle our enemies, use violence, and fight evil? Jesus. Everything we need to know about God is found in Jesus.

All Scripture is Ultimately About Jesus

The Bible also tells us that everything in Scripture ultimately testifies about and points to Jesus. To the Jewish leaders who were questioning his authority, Jesus said, "You study the Scriptures diligently because you think that in them you have eternal life. These are the very Scriptures that testify about me, yet you refuse to come to me to have life" (John 5:39-40). And then he added, "If you believed Moses, you would believe me, for he wrote about me" (John 5:46). As theologian and seminary president Albert Mohler points out, Jesus effectively said, "you cannot read those [OT] words without reading of me. You cannot read the Law without reading of me. You cannot read the History without reading of me. You cannot read the Psalms without reading of me. You cannot read the Prophets without reading of me."[20] And as theology professor C. S. Cowles notes, in making such a claim, Jesus "infuriated his Jewish opponents by declaring that the Scriptures existed primarily to bear witness to him."[21]

Similarly, to a couple of his followers who struggled to believe in him shortly after his death, Jesus appeared and said, "How foolish you are, and how slow to believe all that the prophets have spoken! Did not the Messiah have to suffer these things and then enter his glory?" (Luke 24:25-26). And then "beginning with Moses and all the Prophets, he explained to them what was said in all the Scriptures concerning himself" (Luke 24:27). Soon thereafter, Jesus told his disciples, "Everything must be fulfilled that is written about me in the Law of Moses, the Prophets and the Psalms," and then "opened their minds so they could understand the Scriptures" (Luke 24:44-45). Remember, Jesus also proclaimed, "Do not think that I have come to abolish the Law or the Prophets; I have not come to abolish them but to fulfill them" (Matt. 5:17). Thus, according to Jesus, Philip was correct when he told Nathanael, "We have found the one Moses wrote about in the Law, and about whom the prophets also wrote—Jesus of Nazareth, the son of Joseph" (John 1:44-45).

Paul concurred. According to him, Jesus is the fulfilment of God's plan to save the world, which is "to reconcile to himself all things" (Col. 1:20) and "bring unity to all things in heaven and on earth under Christ" (Eph. 1:10). "All things have been created through him and for him. He is before all things, and in him all things hold together" (Col. 1:16-17). "For no matter how many promises God has made, they are 'Yes' in Christ" (2 Cor. 1:20). Indeed, many NT passages reveal that Jesus fulfilled the OT's prophecies about God's promised Messiah.[22]

And it's not only the Scriptures that exist to bear witness to Jesus. We, the church, do too.[23] So does the Holy Spirit, which the Bible sometimes even calls the Spirit of Jesus.[24] According to the author of 1 John, "This is how you can recognize the Spirit of God: Every spirit that acknowledges that Jesus Christ has come in the flesh is from God, but every spirit that does not acknowledge Jesus is not from God," but instead "is the spirit of the antichrist" (4:2-3).

Furthermore, it's not only the Bible that says this about Jesus. According to Boyd, "all early Christian thinkers ... believed that since everything in Scripture was spoken by 'the Spirit of Christ,' the one message that unites Scripture and that is uniformly communicated through its diversity is nothing other than Jesus Christ."[25] The same is true for the church's greatest theologians – Augustine, Luther, Calvin, Barth, etc. They all believed that all of Scripture ultimately exists to bear witness to Jesus and that all of it was fulfilled in him.

While the Bible was written by many authors across many generations, it all points in a one direction: to Jesus. Pastor Bill Johnson summarizes:

> The entire Old Testament points to Jesus. He is the central figure of ALL Scripture. Both the Law and the Prophets declared His role as Messiah, showing how Jesus would fulfill God's redemptive plan. The stories, prophecies, and laws all pointed to Him at various levels in the same way that a highway sign points to an upcoming city from varying distances. The sign is real and significant, but in itself it is not the reality we are looking for. It points to something greater than itself. In this case we must not worship the sign of the Old Testament. Neither can we afford to be distracted by it, as though in some way it contained a greater reality than the message of the Messiah Himself. These signs serve their purpose by taking us to Jesus. A freeway sign never defines the city, and neither should the Old Testament be made to redefine who Jesus is. He is the fulfillment of both the Law and the Prophets. The nature of His life and purpose is clear and must not be diluted or dismantled by unresolved questions from the Old Covenant.[26]

For as Pastor Brian Zahnd points out, "Jesus is what the Law and Prophets were always trying to say but could never fully articulate."[27]

This Jesus guy is pretty important. The Bible says none of these things about anyone else. In fact, to believe these things about Jesus is what it means to be Christian. It is why we worship Jesus, not the Bible. It is why we are Christians, not Biblicists. As Jersak concludes, "The Scriptures ultimately bear witness to Christ, and Christ perfectly bears witness to God. While we are searching the Bible to find out what God is like, the Bible is all the while resolutely pointing us to Jesus."[28] Or as Pastor Conrad Mbewe succinctly puts it, "The whole Bible—from Genesis to Revelation—is about [Jesus]."[29]

At the end of the day, because Jesus claimed to fulfill all Scripture and to perfectly represent God, we have a choice to make. Either (1) we believe Jesus and therefore believe that God is like Jesus, even when the OT contradicts him, or (2) we don't believe Jesus and therefore must conclude he was delusional. To state it more bluntly, either we believe

God is like Jesus or we believe Christianity is largely a farce. The Bible doesn't leave us with any other option. On its own terms, it doesn't allow us to conclude that God is partially like and partially unlike Jesus. We don't get to pick and choose what God is like. Jesus chose for us. Either Jesus was who he claimed to be or he was tragically wrong, and all of basic Christian theology is too. As self-professed believers in Jesus, shouldn't we take his word for it? For that matter, as self-professed believers in the divine inspiration of Scripture, shouldn't we take Scripture's word for it? After all, only Jesus claimed to fully and perfectly reveal God. The OT never made such a claim.

All Scripture Must Be Interpreted Through Jesus

Because of all this—because Jesus is the perfect picture of God and the fulfillment of all Scripture—we must interpret the entire Bible through him. We must read all of it, especially the OT, through the lens of Jesus, not vice versa. As we study it, we must fix our eyes, thoughts, and hearts on Jesus, not on Moses, OT Israel, or even the OT God.[30] In Boyd's words, "we must never think of the revelation of God in Christ as merely *part* of God's total revelation. Rather, everything before Christ must be read in the light of Christ."[31] We must give Jesus' revelation "interpretive priority over all preceding revelations."[32] "The WHOLE of the Hebrew scriptures," asserts N. T. Wright, "have to be read through the lens of the messianic and God-unveiling events concerning Jesus."[33]

To state it another way, Jesus is the key to proper biblical interpretation. He is the password by which we gain access to a correct understanding of everything written in Scripture. He is the ticket that gets us admitted into the concert of biblical truth. Or as Paul put it, Jesus is the solution to knowing "the mystery of God" and unlocking "all the treasures of wisdom and knowledge" (Col. 2:2-3; Eph. 1:8-10; 3:8-11). He is "wisdom from God" and "the wisdom of God" (1 Cor. 1:22-24, 30; 2 Cor. 4:6; Eph. 3:10). In fact, Paul went so far as to claim we are reading Scripture with a veil over our eyes and hearts unless we are reading it through the lens of Jesus.[34] In other words, Paul believed Scripture could *only* be correctly understood through Jesus.

Paul wasn't alone. According to Boyd, all the NT writers believed Jesus' revelation trumped all else, including the OT writer's originally intended meanings.[35] They "placed the OT under the revelation of God in Christ and read it in the light of this revelation and as a witness to this revelation."[36]

Not surprisingly, the post-biblical early church adopted the same approach. "While early Christian thinkers did not generally consider the original meaning of passages in the OT to be irrelevant," Boyd notes, "they nevertheless considered it to be merely 'preparatory' for the fuller meaning that was unlocked when these passages were interpreted in the light of Christ."[37] The same is generally true for the church throughout its history.

This makes sense. If all Scripture points to Jesus and Jesus fulfills all of it, then he must be the key to properly understanding it all.

Here's another way to look at it. Without granting Jesus deference, without acknowledging that God's revelation in him is more authoritative than his revelation in the rest of Scripture, we can concoct a biblical defense of almost anything—slavery, sexism, nationalism, war, etc. It's only when we measure such things against Jesus' life and teachings that we can confidently conclude they violate God's will. Thus, a biblical viewpoint isn't necessarily a *Christian* viewpoint, and biblical ethics don't always match *Christian* ethics.

This changes how we interpret the OT's portraits of God. It requires that we use Jesus to judge the accuracy of what they say about God, instead of using them to judge the accuracy of what Jesus says about God. McLaren explains:

> The doctrines of the incarnation and deity of Christ are meant to tell us that we cannot start with a predetermined, set-in-stone idea of God derived from the rest of the Bible and then extend that to Jesus. Jesus is not intended merely to fit into those predetermined categories; he is intended instead to explode them, transform them, alter them forever, and bring us to a new evolutionary level in our understanding of God.[38]

Just as the OT law was "only a shadow of the good things to come" and not a full picture of reality, the OT portraits of God were only a shadow of the things to come and not a full picture of reality (Heb. 10:1 NRSV). On both counts, "the reality … is found in Christ" (Col. 2:16-17). Or as John's gospel puts it, "For the law was given through Moses; grace and truth came through Jesus Christ" (John 1:17).

The early church called this way of interpreting the Bible "the rule of faith," as Green explains:

> The rule of faith is an early church premise that interprets the conceptual pictures of God through the lens of God's self-disclosure in Jesus Christ. When Christian readers come to difficult texts … they must always hearken back to the Christian conviction that the character and purpose of God is seen most clearly in the person of Jesus Christ. So how are Christians to understand election, holiness, and the use of violence? A

Christian investigation must take place both within both the social and historical context of the texts themselves and in light of the self-disclosure of God through the person of Jesus Christ.[39]

This doesn't mean that we dismiss all the OT's depictions of God as wholly inaccurate, but it does require that we dismiss as inaccurate all aspects that conflict with Jesus' superior revelation. Any OT depiction of God is accurate to the extent it reflects Jesus' character and inaccurate to the extent it doesn't. Jesus is the picture of God that trumps all other pictures, the one by which all others are measured.

By the way, this isn't only true for the OT conceptions of God. It's also true for all non-Jesus based conceptions of God, including philosophical and metaphysical ones. Any such human speculations or theories about God are wrong to the extent Jesus' life and teachings contradict them. We must not rely on our own knowledge, wisdom, and rationality to determine God's true character. We must not try to define God ourselves.

We also must not try to improve upon God's own self-definition. Jesus is his complete and perfect self-definition, one that cannot be outdone. We must not replace, add to, or subtract from what he reveals about God. Just as Moses commanded the Israelites to not add to or take anything away from God's commands[40] and just as Jesus warned the Pharisees not to alter Scripture with their own human traditions,[41] we must not modify what Jesus revealed about God with our own philosophical reasoning. Like Paul, we must resolve to know nothing "except Jesus Christ and him crucified" (1 Cor. 2:2). We must "take captive every thought to make it obedient to Christ" (2 Cor. 10:5), including our thoughts about God's character. To do otherwise is to remake God in our own image.

To state it another way, we must not start by rationalizing what God must be like and then try to fit Jesus into that rationalization. We must not begin with our own philosophical hypotheses and then interpret what Jesus reveals about God in light of them. We must not concoct our own picture of God, no matter how clever it might be, and then use it to assert that God can't be like Jesus in one way or another. When we start with our own ideas, we always get into trouble, as Boyd explains:

> When our picture of God is built on any foundation other than Jesus Christ—whether a foundation of experience, philosophy or Scripture interpreted apart from Christ—we will be vulnerable to believing a lie about God. We will be eating from our own knowledge of good and evil and constructing a false picture of God on the basis of our own fallible

judgments. We will embrace a god that is consistent with our jaded presuppositions and fallible expectations, which keep us in bondage to the serpent's lie.[42]

That's why the Bible tells us to do the exact opposite. That's why it tells us to start with what Jesus reveals about God and fit everything else into it, why it tells us to ground our understanding of God's character in Jesus, not in our own metaphysical conjectures, and why it tells us to make Jesus the starting and ending point for our conception of God.

Don't misunderstand me. I'm not saying things like philosophy, metaphysics, and experience have no role to play. I'm saying such things can only inform, never trump, Jesus' revelation. They can illuminate but not override. I'm not saying there's no general truth to be found outside of Jesus. I'm saying we must measure all truth claims against Jesus to determine if they are actually true.

To summarize, because Jesus is the fulfillment of all Scripture and the perfect picture of God, we must interpret all Scripture through him, including the OT's portraits of God. To interpret God's character through any other lens is to misinterpret it. It is to place our faith in something other than Jesus, usually some combination of our own philosophizing and the pre-Jesus, ANE-shaped perceptions of the OT authors. Consequently, any conception of God, including those put forth by the OT writers, is inaccurate to the extent it contradicts Jesus. And, if the NT's claims (1) that God kept his full wisdom hidden until the time was right, (2) that no one had ever truly seen God until he revealed himself in Jesus, (3) that Jesus is the exact representation of God, and (4) that the OT was only a shadow of the things to come are true, we should expect to discover such inaccuracies. We should expect to find that some of the OT's depictions of God, or at least some aspects of them, were wrong.

This conclusion should seem reasonable. We now have more information than the OT writers did. We now know things—big, essential, paradigm-shifting things—they didn't. This new and better information demands that we humans reanalyze what we thought we knew before we received it. Just like scientists who obtain more information about some natural phenomenon use it to reevaluate man's theories about that phenomenon, we must use the new information about God we obtained through Jesus to reevaluate man's OT theories about God. Or as Paul put it, "The person with the Spirit makes judgments about all things, but such a person is not subject to merely human judgments, for, 'Who has known the mind of the Lord so as to instruct him?' But we have the mind of Christ" (1 Cor. 2:15-16). In other words, to those who say we can't question the OT's violent depictions of God, Paul essentially says, "Yes we can! We have Jesus. They didn't."

This isn't a novel approach to interpreting Scripture. It's simply a more consistent application of the traditional approach. The church has always attempted to read the entire Bible through the lens of Jesus, but it is a collection of humans and therefore occasionally has blind spots. The OT's violent depictions of God is one example. Instead of reinterpreting them in light of Jesus, the church has essentially interpreted them as if Jesus never existed.[43]

So what does all of this mean for God's use of violence?

Jesus Revealed a Nonviolent God

Jesus was entirely nonviolent (he never used violence nor commanded it) and antiviolence (he explicitly opposed it). Of course, there's some debate about whether he was *entirely* those things, but no reasonable biblical interpreter claims he wasn't at least almost entirely so. I'm confidently in the "entirely" camp, but a detailed refutation of the few scattered passages the "almost entirely" camp holds dear must be saved for another day. For our purposes, we are only going to perform a big picture, commonsensical review of his entire life, one that accepts the plain meaning of his commands and actions.

Let's start with what Jesus said and taught. He never commanded anyone to use any type of violence for any reason. On the contrary, he (1) perfected the law by replacing an "eye for an eye" with "do not resist" and "turn the other cheek," (2) commanded people to refrain from many specific acts of violence (e.g. don't murder and don't steal), (3) instructed them to follow the golden rule, which leaves no room for violence because we don't want others using violence against us, and (4) ordered them to love even their enemies, which also excludes all violence because there's no one left to use violence against. In fact, when it came to murder, he instructed people to refrain from even thinking about committing it.[44] That's how far from violence he wanted his followers to be.

His conversations with his disciples and others bear this out. Whenever his followers used or discussed using violence, he rebuked them, even when they were simply trying to protect him from being unjustly arrested.[45] When Roman governor Pilate was questioning him about his movement, he declared that nonviolence was the distinguishing characteristic of his followers.[46] When he sent his disciples into the world, he told them he was sending them out "like sheep among wolves" (Matt.

10:16-18), i.e. as physically harmless and defenseless creatures in the midst of predators. When his disciples were quarreling about who would have the most power and prestige in his kingdom, he commanded them to not "lord it over" others like the rulers of the Gentiles but instead to become non-coercive servants like him.[47] Extrapolating on such instructions, Paul later ordered Christians to not even use justified legal force against each other (i.e. not sue each other), but instead allow themselves to be wronged.[48]

This is radical stuff. Jesus didn't teach his followers how to morally use violence. He didn't educate them on the difference between just and unjust violence. He didn't train them to use violence only when the just war criteria were met. Instead, he taught them to refrain from using violence. All violence. Always. Even against their enemies.

And that's not all. Jesus went further. He didn't just command them to refrain from using violence against their enemies. He commanded them to love them—to proactively and self-sacrificially do good to them.[49] In Paul's words, "Bless those who persecute you; bless and do not curse.... If your enemy is hungry, feed him; if he is thirsty, give him something to drink.... Do not be overcome by evil, but overcome evil with good" (Rom. 12:14, 20-21).

And here's the real kicker: Jesus told them to do such things *so they would be like God*.[50] Cowles explains:

> Over against a bloody history saturated with violence, believed to be divinely initiated and sanctioned, Jesus issued a new commandment that was as astonishing as it was radical: "But I tell you: Love your enemies and pray for those who persecute you" (Matt. 5:44). In this unprecedented pronouncement, Jesus said something that no prophet or priest ever uttered. His love ethic directly countermanded Moses' genocidal commands, predicated as they were on loathing the enemy.
>
> On what basis did Jesus make such a nonscriptural, impractical, and impossible command? His startling answer was "that you may be sons of your Father in heaven. He causes his sun to rise on the evil and the good, and sends rain on the righteous and the unrighteous—Be perfect [in love for enemies], therefore, as your heavenly Father is perfect [in love for enemies]" (Matt. 5:45–48). What Jesus introduced was an entirely new way of looking at God. God does not hate sinners or despise foreigners; much less does he desire their annihilation. He loves them with boundless and unconditional, self-giving love. He bestows his gracious "sun" of life and "rain" of favor on the just and the unjust, on those who love him and those who hate him. His love is "perfect": that is, it is all-encompassing, whole, complete, life-giving, life-sustaining, life-enhancing, and life-affirming for all humankind.[51]

Remember, Jesus commanded his followers (including us) to mimic him (not the God of the OT), to obey his commands (not God's OT commands), and to obey all of his commands (not just those that don't conflict with the OT). So did all the NT authors.

Then there's Jesus' actions. They perfectly embodied all of his nonviolent and antiviolence teachings. He never used violence. He could have chosen the path of the violent zealot or the path of a typical, violence-wielding, earthly king, but didn't. When an admiring crowd wanted to make him into such a king, he fled.[52] When Satan offered him all the political power in the world, he declined.[53] He could have used supernatural violence whenever he wanted, but never did. Although twelve legions of angels were standing at the ready, he refused to employ them, even when he was unjustly arrested and then tortured to death.[54] When violence and injustice were done to him, he could have responded with justified force, but refrained. "When they hurled their insults at him, he did not retaliate; when he suffered, he made no threats. Instead, he entrusted himself to him who judges justly" (1 Pet. 2:23). He demonstrated how to absorb violence, not how to use it justly. He never shed blood in the name of love or justice. In fact, the only bloodshed he was ever involved in was his own. He definitely never initiated force against anyone, and with one possible exception (the temple cleansing), he never even used *reactive* force.

Furthermore, as we mentioned earlier, he fulfilled all the nonviolent Messianic prophecies and none of the violent ones. As Isaiah predicted, he was "assigned a grave with the wicked ... *though he had done no violence*, nor was any deceit in his mouth" (Isa. 53:9). He eradicated all violence from the organizational structure of God's followers by denationalizing them, making the cross his banner instead of a national flag. He de-violenced Christian warfare by clarifying who the real enemy is (evil itself, not flesh and blood) and demonstrating it can only be defeated by the non-fleshy, nonviolent weapon of love. And remember, the primary reason God's use of violence in the OT is so problematic is because Jesus was the polar opposite, avoiding violence at all costs, even that of his own life.

Most revealingly, all of this—all of Jesus' words and deeds—culminate in the cross. The cross was his defining moment. It was the supreme expression of everything he was about, the ultimate goal of his earthly mission, the climax of his saving work, and the event around which his entire life revolved.

Just as Jesus' ministry is the focus of all Scripture, the cross is the focus of Jesus' ministry. The biblical story leads to Jesus and Jesus' story leads to the cross. The entire direction of the NT is towards the cross. The pre-Crucifixion narratives point forward to it and the post-Crucifixion ones point back to it.

Consequently, Boyd points out, "The cross is the absolute center of God's revelation to humanity and his purpose for creation."[55] To use N. T. Wright's words, "The cross stands at the center of the story of Jesus, Israel, the human race, the creator God, and his world. This is where the biblical narrative finds its heart."[56] "For the cross is at the center of the evangelical faith" and "lies at the center of the historic, biblical faith," writes John R. W. Stott.[57] Ultimately, the cross is the lens through which all Scripture must be interpreted and the key to properly understanding it all. Or as Martin Luther succinctly put it, "the cross alone is our theology." Moltmann hammers the point home:

> The death of Jesus on the cross is the center of all Christian theology. It is not the only theme of theology, but it is in effect the entry to its problems and answers on earth. All Christian statements about God, about creation, about sin and death have their focal point in the crucified Christ. All Christian statements about history, about the church, about faith and sanctification, about the future and about hope stem from the crucified Christ.[58]

Most importantly for our purposes, the cross is where Jesus' nonviolence is most clearly, fully, and powerfully displayed. First of all, it was an act of love. It was done *for our good*. The NT says the cross was the means by which God demonstrated his love for us, forgave our sins, atoned for our sins, redeemed us, reconciled us to himself and others, made us righteous, gave us eternal life, defeated evil, and freed us from slavery to sin.[59]

Second, the cross was an act of *self-sacrificial* love. It was done for us at Jesus' own expense. He didn't force someone else to pay the price. He paid it himself. And he did so voluntarily. He willingly gave himself over to the Romans to be tortured to death for our good. It was a freely chosen act of self-emptying love, not an accident or something he couldn't have avoided.

Third, the cross was the *ultimate* act of self-sacrificial love. By laying down his own innocent life for us, Jesus sacrificed as much as is humanly possible. He took his love to the farthest human extreme. "Greater love has no one than this: to lay down one's life for one's friends" (John 15:13). On the cross, Jesus demonstrated how far love goes to make loves point—all the way.

The same is true of God. He too paid the ultimate price. He sent his one and only perfectly righteous and blameless son as a living sacrifice for us.[60] Or to put it another way, he became a man, bore our sins, and allowed himself to be murdered on our behalf. Great sacrifice is a sign of great love, and the ultimate sacrifice is a sign of the ultimate love.

Fourth, not only was the cross the ultimate act of self-sacrificial love, it was endured on behalf of everyone, even Jesus' enemies. In Paul's words, Jesus "died for the ungodly" and the unrighteous (Rom. 5:6-7). He died for us "while we were still sinners" (Rom. 5:8). As he was being crucified, he even asked God to forgive his crucifiers.[61] On the cross, Jesus paid the supreme price for everyone, even those unbelievers who hated him enough to murder him.

In all four of these ways (as an *act of love*, an act of *self-sacrificial* love, an *ultimate* act of self-sacrificial love, and an ultimate act of self-sacrificial love *for everyone*, even enemies), the cross defines Christian love. "This is how we know what love is: Jesus Christ laid down his life for us" (1 John 3:16). "This is love: not that we loved God, but that he loved us and sent his Son as an atoning sacrifice for our sins" (1 John 4:10).

To put it another way, the cross defines how to behave Christianly (i.e. how to obey Jesus, love God and others, do God's will, advance his kingdom on earth, etc.). Jesus proclaimed, "Whoever wants to be my disciple must deny themselves and take up their cross and follow me. For whoever wants to save their life will lose it, but whoever loses their life for me will find it" (Matt. 16:24-25).[62] "Whoever does not take up their cross and follow me is not worthy of me" (Matt. 10:38). "And whoever does not carry their cross and follow me cannot be my disciple" (Luke 14:27). Notice Jesus didn't say "believe in" or "talk about" or "worship" the cross. He said "take up" and "carry" the cross.

Jesus' apostles taught the same lessons. "Jesus Christ laid down his life for us. And we ought to lay down our lives for our brothers and sisters" (1 John 3:16). "This is love: not that we loved God, but that he loved us and sent his Son as an atoning sacrifice for our sins. Dear friends, since God so loved us, we also ought to love one another" (1 John 4:10-11). "In your relationships with one another, have the same mindset as Christ Jesus ... who made himself nothing by taking the very nature of a servant ... and humbled himself by becoming obedient to death—even death on a cross!" (Phil. 2:5-8). "Follow God's example, therefore, as dearly loved children and walk in the way of love, just as Christ loved us and gave himself up for us as a fragrant offering and sacrifice to God" (Eph. 5:1-2). "To this you were called, because Christ suffered for you, leaving you an example that you should follow in his steps...." (1 Pet. 2:21). "Husbands, love your wives, just as Christ loved the church and gave himself up for her...." (Eph. 5:25). "I want to know Christ—yes, to know the power of his resurrection and participation in his sufferings, becoming like him in his death...." (Phil. 3:10). "Therefore, I urge you, brothers and sisters, in view of God's mercy, to offer your bodies as a living sacrifice, holy and pleasing to God—this is your true and proper worship" (Rom. 12:1). "Join with me in suffering, like a good soldier of Christ Jesus" (2 Tim. 2:3). "Follow my example, as I follow the example of Christ" (1 Cor. 11:1).[63]

Most theologians concur. According to Yoder, "Every strand of New Testament literature testifies to a direct relationship between the way Christ suffered on the cross and the way the Christian, as disciple, is called to suffer in the face of evil...."[64] Likewise, Sprinkle asserts that "the New Testament highlights Jesus' nonviolent response to violence as a pattern to follow *more than any other aspect of his ministry*."[65] In Professor Lee Camp's words, "The point of imitation of Jesus is found in the cross. It is the cross we are called to imitate, joyfully accepting suffering, joyfully bearing the injustices and oppression and rebellion of our world...."[66] Or as Hays puts it, "Jesus' death on a cross is the paradigm for faithfulness to God in this world."[67] It is "a paradigm for *ethics*" and "one of the features that most sharply differentiates the New Testament from the Old Testament."[68] Psychologist Richard Beck says the cross is what it looks like to put our identity in Christ because "when our identities are rooted in God, we cling to nothing and thus have the psychological capacity to make sacrifices for the sake of others."[69]

The cross wasn't just something Jesus did for us. It was an example he set for us. As the academics say, the cross is normative for us. That's why Dietrich Bonhoeffer declared, "When Christ calls a man he bids him come and die."[70]

Everything Jesus was about came together on the cross and expressed itself in the ultimate act of wholly nonviolent, other-oriented, enemy-embracing, self-sacrificial love. "As the gospel stories explain," writes John Dear, "Jesus embodies the covenant of nonviolence. He incarnates it, teaches it, practices it, suffers through it and remains obedient to the God of nonviolence even unto death."[71]

And remember, because Jesus is the perfect revelation of God's character and the cross is the culmination of everything he was about, the cross is also the perfect revelation of God's character, the point where the true Christian God is most clearly, fully, and accurately displayed. "Above all things," writes Zahnd, "the cross, as the definitive moment in Jesus's life, is the supreme revelation of the very nature of God."[72] Or as Boyd puts it, "the cross is the summation, culmination, and perfect expression of the central theme of Jesus's whole ministry, which is about putting on display ('glorifying') the loving character of God."[73] "For the revelation of the crucified God is primarily a revelation of God's moral character."[74]

As such, the cross reveals a wholly nonviolent God. It reveals a God who self-sacrificially suffers violence instead of inflicts it, a God who ends the cycle of violence by absorbing it instead of forcefully overpowering it, and a God who would rather allow violence to do its worst to him than use it himself, even to defend himself against murder. It reveals a God who fights violence with love instead of superior might, a God who defeats evil with good instead of stronger evil, and a God who dies for his enemies instead of destroys them. It reveals a God who accomplishes his objectives with wisdom instead of force, a God who respects free will instead of violently overriding it, and a God who wins hearts and minds through self-sacrifice instead of coercion. It reveals a God whose power lies in his limitless capacity to humbly serve others instead of forcefully control them, a God whose greatness is found in his ability to continue to love those who hate and mistreat him even when faced with death, and a God whose means of ruling is foolishness to fools but the epitome of wisdom to the wise.[75] It reveals a God who saves instead of kills, a God who goes to the furthest extremes possible to rescue us from sin instead of punish us for it, and a God whose idea of justice is restorative instead of retributive. It reveals a God whose character, power, beauty, and glory are all not only entirely nonviolent but also wholeheartedly antiviolence in every way, shape, and form.

I love how Zahnd describes it:

> In the defining moment of the cross Jesus defines what God is really like. God is love—co-suffering, all-forgiving, sin-absorbing, never-ending love. God is not like Caiaphas sacrificing a scapegoat. God is not like Pilate enacting justice by violence. God is like Jesus, absorbing and forgiving sin.

> At the cross a world of sin is absorbed by the love of God and recycled into grace and mercy. *This* is what the cross is about! This is what Christianity reveals.[76]

In fact, according to Jesus' death on the cross, God's very nature is nonviolent. Violence goes against God's very being. This is the point the author of 1 John made when he defined love by pointing to the cross and then declared that "God is love" (3:16; 4:8, 10, 16). In other words, God's nature is love and the cross is what his loving nature looks like.

Let that sink in for a moment. Could God or love be defined any more anti-violently? Is there any act more opposed to violence than self-sacrificially allowing your enemies to unjustly torture you to death? Isn't such an act precisely the opposite of violent?

The author of 1 John doesn't merely say that love is an attribute of God. He doesn't simply say God is loving. He says God *is* love. He says love is his essence. Philosophy professor Peter Kreeft explains the gravity of such a statement:

> Nowhere else does Scripture express God's essence in this way. Scripture says God is just and merciful, but it does not say that God is justice itself or mercy itself. It does say that God is love, not just a lover. Love is God's very essence. Everything else is a manifestation of this essence to us, a relationship between this essence and us. This is the absolute; everything else is relative to it.[77]

Or as Mildred Bangs Wynkoop put it, "Love *is* the gospel message. Christian love, revealed by God in Christ…. It stands against any human concept of love projected into a theory of God's nature and His way with man."[78]

Plus, everything else the NT says about God and love confirms both of these points—that God is love and that love is wholly nonviolent. First, the Bible stresses the inherent connection between God and love in a variety of ways, some explicit and some implicit. It says God is the source of love, we can't know God unless we love, we can't live in God or have God live in us unless we love, love is what identifies us as Christian, without love we are nothing and have nothing, love conquers all, love binds all the virtues together in perfect unity, love is greater than faith and hope, faith without love is dead, all of God's commands can be reduced to a command to love, to convince humans to love has been God's goal since the beginning, and to inherit eternal life we must love.[79]

Second, the Bible's definitions and descriptions of love also demonstrate its nonviolence. For example, the Bible's most famous, precise, and comprehensive definition of love describes it as patient, kind, non-envious, non-boastful, humble, honoring, selfless, not easily angered, forgiving, protecting, trusting, hopeful, persevering, and truthful.[80] Likewise, Paul's most detailed description of love in action says it is sincere, honors others above yourself, serves, is patient in affliction, shares with those in need, practices hospitality, blesses those who persecute you, lives in harmony with others, doesn't repay evil for evil, strives to live at peace with everyone, doesn't take revenge, provides care for enemies, and overcomes evil with good.[81] Furthermore, the Christian virtues, which love binds together in perfect unity, include faith, hope, charity, joy, peace, patience, kindness, generosity, faithfulness, gentleness, self-control, goodness, knowledge, perseverance, godliness, mutual affection, compassion, humility, and forgiveness.[82]

Obviously, none of those characteristics involves using any violence. Try to imagine being violently patient, violently forgiving, or violently selfless towards someone. Try to picture yourself violently practicing hospitality, violently blessing those who persecute you, or violently living in harmony with others. Absurd. Not only are those characteristics wholly nonviolent, they are essentially the exact opposite of violent.

On the other hand, however, the Christian vices (lust, gluttony, greed, sloth, wrath, envy, and pride and others like lying, devising wicked schemes, bearing false witness, rushing into evil, stirring up conflict, dissension, thievery, drunkenness, slander, jealousy, and selfish ambition)[83] are behaviors that are either violent themselves or frequently lead to violence. Ever been so envious, so angry, or so offended that you wanted to or did resort to violence? Me too.

In conclusion, Jesus' life and death crucified the notion of a violent God. "For when the sin of the world was nailed to the cross with Christ," writes Boyd, "the sinful conception of God as a violent warrior god was included."[84] By living a wholly nonviolent life and then becoming a victim of unjust violence without using violence even to defend himself, Jesus revealed the falsity of the OT's violent portraits of God.

The overall logic here is straightforward: Because Jesus is the full and perfect picture of God (according to Jesus himself and all the NT writers) and he was entirely nonviolent (according to the plain meaning of his words and actions, including those on the cross), we must conclude that God is entirely nonviolent. And because God is entirely nonviolent, we must also conclude that the violent OT portraits of him were wrong. Of course, this doesn't mean they were entirely wrong, just wrong to the extent they attributed violence to God.

Two quick caveats before we move on. First, with all of this talk about the cross, we must also give the resurrection its due. It too is essential. It proved that Jesus truly was God and consequently that God truly is the type of God revealed on the cross. It proved the wisdom and power of what the cross accomplished. It proved that love really does conquer all, even death. It proved that we can self-sacrificially love others without fearing death because it doesn't have the last word. In other words, the resurrection is indispensable, but it didn't change what was revealed on the cross or its centrality. Instead, it verified them. Stott provides some perspective:

> Of course, the cross, the incarnation, and the resurrection belong together. There could have been no atonement without the incarnation or without the resurrection. The incarnation prepares for the atonement and the resurrection endorses the atonement, so they belong always together. Yet the New Testament is very clear that the cross stands at the center.[85]

Second, Jesus' pervasive, straightforward, wholly nonviolent message and example is not diminished, let alone overridden, because (1) he once explained the divisive nature of his truth by metaphorically claiming he came to earth to bring a sword and not peace,[86] (2) he once warned his disciples to mentally prepare to be persecuted by metaphorically instructing them to buy (not use) a sword,[87] (3) he once conversed with a soldier *about non-soldiering things* without condemning his profession (or anything else, for that matter),[88] (4) he once, in an act of prophetic symbolism, justly cleared a temple of swindlers by using a homemade whip to drive their *animals* out of it,[89] and (5) on a handful of occasions he told *parables* that depicted God using violence at the final judgment to teach lessons not related to violence, let alone the *human* use of violence. Such sparse and tangential incidents don't trump the overwhelming amount of antiviolence evidence we just explored.

So if God is as nonviolent as Jesus demonstrates, what was going on in the OT?

---

[1] Bradley Jersak, *A More Christlike God: A More Beautiful Gospel* (CWR Press, 2015), 137, Kindle.

[2] Gen. 2-3.

[3] Boyd, *The Crucifixion of the Warrior God*, 22879.

[4] Ibid., 22866.

[5] Boyd, *Is God to Blame?*, 191.

[6] A. W. Tozer, *The Knowledge of the Holy* (New York: HarperCollins, 1978), 1.

[7] Ibid.

[8] See also Col. 1:19.

[9] See also 5:36.

[10] See also 14:24.

[11] Boyd, *Is God to Blame?*, 205.

[12] See also John 6:46.

[13] Eph. 1:8-10; 3:8-9; Col. 1:25-26; 1 Cor. 2:7; 2 Cor. 3:4-5, 12-18; 4:6.

[14] Jersak, *A More Christlike God*, 1214.

[15] Boyd, *The Crucifixion of the Warrior God*, 1724.

[16] John 5:18; 8:58; 10:30-33; 19:6-7; Matt. 26:64-66; Luke 5:21.

[17] John 20:28-29.

[18] John 1:1, 14.

[19] Boyd, *Is God to Blame?*, 246.

[20] Albert Mohler, *The Scriptures Testify about Me: Jesus and the Gospel in the Old Testament*, ed. D. A. Carson (Crossway, 2013), 205, Kindle.

[21] C. S. Cowles, *Show Them No Mercy: 4 Views on God and Canaanite Genocide* (Counterpoints: Bible and Theology) (Zondervan, 2010), 487, Kindle.

[22] Matt. 1:22; 2:5-6; 2:15, 17, 23; 3:3; 4:14; 5:17; 8:17; 12:17; 13:14-15; 13:35; 21:4; 26:54, 56; 27:9; Mark 14:49; Luke 4:21; 24:44.

[23] Matt. 28:18-20; John 15:27; Acts 1:8; 22:15.

[24] John 14:26; 15:26; 16:13-14; 1 Cor. 12:3; Acts 16:7; Rom. 8:9; Phil. 1:19; Gal. 4:6.

[25] Boyd, *The Crucifixion of the Warrior God*, 9923.

[26] Bill Johnson, *God is Good: He's Better Than You Think* (Destiny Image, 2016), 781, Kindle.

[27] Brian Zahnd, *Sinners in the Hands of a Loving God: The Scandalous Truth of the Very Good News* (New York: WaterBrook, 2017), 50.

[28] Jersak, *A More Christlike God*, 147.

[29] Conrad Mbewe, *The Scriptures Testify about Me: Jesus and the Gospel in the Old Testament*, ed. D. A. Carson (Crossway, 2013), 1338, Kindle.

[30] Heb. 3:1; 12:1-2; Col. 3:1; 2 Cor. 11:3-4

[31] Boyd, *Is God to Blame?*, 240.

[32] Boyd, *The Crucifixion of the Warrior God*, 1515.

[33] N.T. Wright, "Why Does God Command Violence in the Old Testament? Q&A With N.T. Wright" posted in 2014 at http://jeffandalyssa.com/why-does-god-command-violence-in-the-old-testament-qa-with-n-t-wright/.

[34] 2 Cor. 3:13-16; see also 4:4-6.

[35] Boyd, *The Crucifixion of the Warrior God*, 2653.

[36] Ibid., 2748.

[37] Ibid., 2911.

[38] McLaren, *A New Kind of Christianity*, 1955.

[39] Green, *Deuteronomy*, 108-09.

[40] Deut. 4:2; 12:32.

[41] Matt. 15:1-9; Mark 7:1-13.

[42] Boyd, *Is God to Blame?*, 247.

[43] Boyd, *The Crucifixion of the Warrior God*, 438.

[44] Matt. 5:21-22.

[45] Matt. 26:50-52; Luke 9:51-56.

[46] John 18:36.

[47] Matt. 20:25-28; Mark 10:35-45; Luke 22:24-30.

[48] 1 Cor. 6:1-7; see also Rom. 12:14-21.

[49] Matt. 5:38-48; Luke 6:27-36.

[50] Matt. 5:45, 48; Luke 6:35-36.

[51] Cowles, *Show Them No Mercy*, 420.

[52] John 6:1-15.

[53] Luke 4:5-8.

[54] Matt. 26:52-53.

[55] Boyd, *Is God to Blame?*, 307.

[56] N.T. Wright, *The Day the Revolution Began: Reconsidering the Meaning of Jesus's Crucifixion* (New York: HarperOne, 2016), 255.

[57] John R. W. Stott, *The Cross of Christ* (Downers Grove, IL: InterVarsity Press, 2006), 13.

[58] Moltmann, *The Crucified God*, 204.

[59] Rom. 3:24-25; 5:8-11, 15-19; 6:6-7; 8:1-3; John 1:29; 3:16; Eph. 1:7-8; 2:14-16; 5:1-2, 25; Gal. 2:20-21; 3:13-14; 6:14; Col 1:19-22; 2:13–15; 1 John 4:10; 1 Pet. 1:18-19; 2:24-25; 3:18; 1 Cor. 15:3; 2 Cor. 5:14-21; 13:4; Heb. 2:14-15; 9:28.

[60] John 3:16.

[61] Luke 23:34.

[62] See also Mark 8:34; Luke 9:23; 17:33.

[63] See also 1 John 4:10-11; 1 Pet. 4:1-2; 1 Cor. 4:8-16.

[64] Yoder, *The Original Revolution*, 765.

[65] Sprinkle, *Fight*, 2139.

[66] Lee C. Camp, *Mere Discipleship: Radical Christianity in a Rebellious World* Second Edition (Brazos Press, 2008), 1402, Kindle.

[67] Hays, *The Moral Vision of the New Testament*, 5457.

[68] Ibid., 8665.

[69] Richard Beck, *The Slavery of Death* (Cascade Book, 2013), 1565, Kindle.

[70] Dietrich Bonhoeffer, *The Cost of Discipleship* (Touchstone, 2012), 1138, Kindle.

[71] Dear, *The God of Peace*, 63.

[72] Zahnd, *Sinners in the Hands of a Loving God*, 82.

[73] Boyd, *The Crucifixion of the Warrior God*, 4742.

[74] Ibid., 445.

[75] 1 Cor. 1:18-25; 2:14; 3:19-20.

[76] Brian Zahnd, *Water to Wine: Some of My Story* (Spello Press, 2016), 315, Kindle.

[77] Peter Kreeft, *Knowing the Truth of God's Love: The One Thing We Can't Live Without* (Ann Arbor, MI: Servant Books, 1988), 91.

[78] Mildred Bangs Wynkoop, *A Theology of Love: The Dynamic of Wesleyanism* 2nd Edition (Kansas City, MO: Beacon Hill Press of Kansas City, 2015), 18.

[79] 1 John 3:10, 11, 14; 4:7, 8, 12, 16; 2 John 1:5; Matt. 7:12; 22:36-40; Mark 12:28-34; Luke 10:25-28; John 13:35; 15:17; 1 Cor. 13:1-3, 8, 13; 1 Pet. 4:8; Col. 3:14; Jas. 2:17; Gal. 5:6, 14; Rom. 13:8-10; Jas. 2:5, 8; Deut. 6:4-9; Lev. 19:18.

[80] 1 Cor. 13:4-7.

[81] Rom. 12:9-21.

[82] 1 Cor. 13:13; Gal. 5:22-23; 2 Pet. 1:5-7; Col. 3:12-14.

[83] Prov. 6:16-19; 1 Cor. 6:9-11; Gal. 5:19-21; Eph. 5:5.

[84] Boyd, *The Crucifixion of the Warrior God*, 504.

[85] Stott, "Between Two Worlds: An Interview with John R. W. Stott" posted August 8, 2011 at http://www.albertmohler.com/2011/08/08/between-two-worlds-an-interview-with-john-r-w-stott/.

[86] Matt. 10:34.
[87] Luke 22:36.
[88] Matt. 8:5-13.
[89] John 2:13-17.

11

INCREMENTAL CHARACTER REVELATION

Jesus' revelation of a wholly nonviolent God tells us that God used incremental revelation not only for his ethics but also for his character. Just as he incrementally revealed his ethical ideal, he also incrementally revealed his true character. Just as he unveiled his full plan for human behavior within a developing story, he also unveiled his full character within a developing story.

Just as God temporarily accommodated some unethical practices in the OT, he also temporarily accommodated some misperceptions of his character. Just as he allowed some improper habits he no longer tolerates, he also allowed some misunderstandings about his nature he no longer tolerates. Just as he put up with some less-than-ideal ANE behavioral customs, he also put up with some less-than-ideal ANE beliefs about gods. Just as he worked around humanity's moral immaturity, he also worked around its conceptual immaturity. Just as he judged it counterproductive to immediately correct all of Israel's immoral conduct, he also judged it counterproductive to immediately correct all of its false ideas about him.

Just as Jesus finalized God's ethical revelation, he also finalized God's character revelation. Just as Jesus came to complete the law, he also came to complete our picture of God. Just as he perfected the law, he also perfected our conception of God. Just as he fully revealed what God really wants from us, he also fully revealed what God is really like. Just as he came to demonstrate how to perfectly do God's will, he also came to perfectly demonstrate God's true nature. Just as God gave Jesus the final word on his ethics, he also gave Jesus the final word on his character.

Just as nonviolence is the perfection of the law, nonviolence is also the perfection of God's character. Just as Jesus removed all violence from the law, he also removed all violence from our conception of God. Just as he revealed God's ethical ideal to be wholly nonviolent, he also revealed God's nature to be wholly nonviolent. Just as he taught that the law requires we refrain from violence, he also taught that God refrains from violence.

Just as the OT was only the beginning of God's ethical revelation, it was also only the beginning of his character revelation. Just as the OT only gives us a partial glimpse of God's ethical ideal, it also only gives us a partial glimpse of his true character. Just as God wasn't teaching a course on specific moral behaviors in the OT but instead was laying the necessary groundwork for a future course on them, he also wasn't providing a full and perfect picture of himself but instead was laying the necessary groundwork for a future one. Just as the Bible has an ethical arc that clearly bends towards nonviolence, it also has a human-understanding-of-God's-character arc that clearly bends towards nonviolence.

Why should we expect any differently? Don't the same reasons for why God had to use incremental ethical revelation apply here too? If God had to bring humanity along gradually in that regard, why not also in this regard? If he had to take a pedagogical approach to teaching humans about ethics, wouldn't he have also had to take such an approach to teaching them about his nature? If he believed it was necessary to first introduce himself, establish a relationship, prove his existence, demonstrate his superiority, teach them the basics of obedience, and develop trust before revealing his ethical ideal, why wouldn't he have believed it necessary to do those things before revealing his full nature too? If he had to design his ethical revelation to account for human limitations, why wouldn't the same be true for his character revelation? If he had to adjust his ethical requirements to meet humanity where it was, why wouldn't he have also had to adjust his appearance to meet it where it was? If he had to initially teach them ethics in the language of violence, why wouldn't he have also had to initially teach them his character in the language of violence? If like a missionary in a foreign culture he had to initially refrain from condemning some of humanity's culturally entrenched unethical practices, why wouldn't he have also had to initially refrain from condemning some of its culturally entrenched illusions about what it means to be and act like a god? If he had to first establish his concern for justice in terms they understood (i.e. violent terms), wouldn't that have meant allowing himself to initially be perceived as a god who enforces justice through violence? Maybe what we thought was him getting his hands a little dirty was really him allowing his reputation to be sullied. If humanity wasn't ready for God's ideal ethics in the OT, what makes us think it was ready for God's true character? After all, even two thousand years *after* Jesus, many people, including many Christians, still can't handle the concept of an entirely nonviolent, loving, Jesus-like God.

From this perspective, God's use of incremental character revelation should already make a lot of sense. Nonetheless, let's look at some additional evidence that indicates he employed it and further explains why.

God Works Through Humans

Because God chooses to redeem the world through the very people who need redeeming, his communications pass through sinful beings who have their own flawed preconceptions, motives, desires, and agendas. The Bible itself is no exception. He used such human beings to write, transmit, preserve, and translate it.

Yes, God inspired the biblical authors, but he didn't totally control them. He didn't possess their bodies and direct their every thought or dictate their every written word. He took the initiative and influenced their hearts and minds, but he didn't completely override their free will or entirely neutralize their humanity. There's a reason it's called divine *inspiration* and not divine *control*. God is a loving God who doesn't coerce, not even those through whom he is trying to transmit a message.

To view it another way, the OT writers didn't become the incarnation of God when they sat down to write. They did not morph into an exact representation of God or his will. In all of history, there has only been one such incarnation and exact representation: Jesus.

Of course, there's no consensus among theologians as to exactly how much control God exercised over the Bible's authors. But almost none ascribe to the total control theory. Almost all believe he gave the writers at least some freedom. Here's Boyd:

> For example, no major Christian theologian has ever denied the obvious fact that God's "breathing" of Scripture involved God allowing the distinct personalities, education, experiences, abilities and idiosyncrasies of individual authors to act upon him, for their writings clearly reflect these things. If God's "breathing" of Scripture had been a truly unilateral activity, however, would not Scripture uniformly reflect God's perspective on all matters? And would not this perspective have been communicated with a uniformly perfect writing style as opposed to the widely diverse abilities of Mark and Luke, for example?[1]

Scripture has no such uniformity. Instead, it contains a diversity of styles and opinions, a few contradictions, some imperfections, and even the occasional error. Two quick examples. In one of his NT letters, Paul confessed that he couldn't remember who he baptized.[2] If God was in total control of him, does that mean God forgot too? Similarly, Matthew mistakenly referred to Zechariah as the son of Berekiah, instead of Jehoiada.[3] Somebody somewhere along the way made a mistake, and I'm guessing it wasn't God. Instead, it seems God respected the intellectual limitations of those he inspired.

Plus, the Bible is not simply a long monologue in which God speaks to man. Large chunks of it are written from the perspective of humans speaking to God—praising him, questioning him, complaining to him, and pleading with him. Just read the Psalms. Why would God need, or want, to dictate man's questions and complaints, particularly when they often make him look bad?

It's safe to assume that the humanity of the OT authors influenced their writings. To one degree or another, their worldviews, cultural experiences, human limitations, and sinful natures affected how they perceived God and interpreted his actions. To state it more bluntly, and more accurately, their humanity *obscured* their view of God. It caused them to misperceive, misunderstand, and misconstrue him, just like ours often still does. As C. S. Lewis put it, "The human qualities of the raw materials show through. Naivety, error, contradiction, even (as in the cursing Psalms) wickedness are not removed."[4]

To a large extent, the OT writers saw what they were psychologically, socially, and historically conditioned to see. They were not blank slates. They brought their own subjective perspectives to the writing table, including some deeply engrained beliefs about what it meant to be a god, act like a god, and please a god.

Therefore, we must interpret the Bible, particularly the OT, knowing it may sometimes reflect the humanity of the author as much as God's actual will or his true character. To that end, we must seek to understand the authors' two primary influences: their fallen human nature and ANE culture. We must seek to better understand how such factors informed, and even distorted, what the authors wrote about God. So let's take a look at one aspect of their fallen nature and then spend more time exploring some relevant aspects of ANE culture.

As fallen humans, the OT writers likely projected many of their own selfish desires and agendas onto God, just like we do. They likely rationalized their own detestable behavior by telling themselves it was God's will. They likely invoked God's name on behalf of their own selfish desires for control, safety, and comfort. They likely enlisted him in endeavors he wants nothing to do with, endeavors he actually detests. They likely remade him in their own violent image, much like we prosperous Americans are inclined to remake him in our own consumeristic image, painting him as a comfort-loving, self-help peddling, prosperity preaching, country club God. In fact, at one point, God told the Israelites that he had allowed them to do such a thing: "When you did these [sinful] things and I kept silent, you thought I was exactly like you" (Ps. 50:21).

Even with our fuller knowledge of God as revealed in Jesus, you and I engage in these types of God-distorting practices all the time. Why should we think the pre-Jesus Israelites would have been different? Pastor and author Adam Hamilton explains:

> But perhaps the most important reason for reading Joshua [i.e. Israel's conquest of Canaan] is to remind us of how easy it is for people of faith to invoke God's name in pursuit of violence, bloodshed, and war. The Crusaders marched into battle in Jerusalem in the name of Christ. Colonists from the Old World arrived in the New World, Bibles and weapons in hand, to claim America for Christ. Nazi belt buckles proclaimed, "Gott Mit Uns"—God is with us—as they sought the extermination of Jews and other "undesirables." "Christian" nations have often gone to war invoking God in their efforts. When America marches to war, patriotism and faith are quickly melded so that to be a good Christian is to support the war effort. At times those war efforts might have been morally justified (if one holds to the theory of just war), but at times they were "pre-emptive wars" that did not meet the criteria of the just war. Regardless of whether the war effort was morally justified or not, our troops marched off to battle to the tune of "God Bless America." If this is the case today, it should not surprise us that people who lived 3,500 years ago also invoked God as they marched off to war.[5]

In fact, besides being pre-Jesus, there are cultural reasons for believing that such projections would have been even more commonplace in the ANE than they are today. At that time, there was no such thing as the separation of church and state. And I don't just mean politically. In all areas of life, they believed not merely in the divine right of kings but in the actual divinity of kings. The king was seen as an extension of the national deity, and as such, his commands and actions were viewed as the national deity's commands and actions. Thus, in the eyes of ANE humans, for their king to command, commit, or condone violence was for their national god to command, commit, or condone violence.

Such a worldview would have inevitably caused the OT writers to attribute at least some violence to God's will that was in reality the will of Israel's human leaders. Of course, that assumes Israel followed the common practice of its day, but we have no reason to suspect it didn't.

And that's not the only cultural reason to believe the OT writers often misattributed violence to God. In many ways, the God of the OT looks suspiciously like all other ANE gods, particularly in regards to violence. As Seibert points out, "People in the ancient world believed the gods were intimately involved in their experience of war."[6] They "were convinced that God/the gods commissioned war, participated in it, and determined the outcome of it."[7] In fact, "divine involvement in war was a theological given in the ancient world.... It was so much a part of the air they breathed that it went unquestioned and unchallenged."[8] In other words, Israel's concept of holy war and its assumption that military victories reflected God's favor while military defeats reflected his disfavor were commonplace in the ANE.[9] According to theology professor Daniel L. Gard, even Israel's practice of *herem* was not unique within the ANE "insofar as others also engaged in the destruction and consecration of their enemies to their gods."[10]

Similarly, as Boyd explains, "The OT's warrior portraits of Yahweh bear a striking resemblance to the violent warrior deities of other ANE people. Indeed, we [find] that certain biblical authors were not above simply borrowing violent depictions of deities among their ANE neighbors and applying them to Yahweh with little modification."[11] For example, "Almost all of the imagery that OT authors employ in their warrior portraits of Yahweh, including their frequent depictions of him as a 'mountain deity' and a 'storm deity,' have close parallels in ANE literature, as numerous scholars have demonstrated."[12] "We find something similar" in Ezekiel 21:31 wherein God is "depicted as a ferocious fire-breathing dragon—a portrait that is, significantly enough, similar to the way deities were sometimes depicted in ANE literature (e.g., Job 41:19–21; cf. 2 Sam 22:9; Ps 18:8; Isa 30:33)."[13]

In one OT passage, God appears to look forward to the day when his followers would no longer view him like ANE peoples viewed their national gods: as slave masters. "In that day," declares the Lord, "you will call me 'my husband'; you will no longer call me 'my master'" (Hos. 2:16).

Furthermore, in the ANE, attributing violence to your god was a common means of glorifying him, as Boyd explains:

It is important to remember that the people of the ANE uniformly assumed that the primary way people exalt their national warrior deity was by crediting their nation's military victories to this god while exaggerating the ruthlessness of the bloodletting that led to these victories. The shared commonality of divine warrior imagery between OT authors and their surrounding neighbors makes it abundantly clear that OT authors generally shared this assumption.[14]

In fact, Boyd adds,

To not "credit" your national deity with the violence your nation's army carried out on their way to victory would have been considered sacrilege. And the more extreme the violence that was attributed to your god, the more his stature was glorified. Hence, it was common for ANE authors to grossly exaggerate the amount of violence as well as the macabre nature of the violence that their nation's army carried out in a battle and that they, of course, attributed to their national deity. In the context of the ANE, this was simply how you offered up praise to a god, which means that Peter Enns is likely not far off when he claims that ancient Israelites "had no choice" but to associate Yahweh with extreme violence. And so it is no surprise that OT authors sometimes resort to macabre hyperbole when they depict Yahweh as a victorious warrior. When these authors ascribe grisly, *Anat*-like violence to Yahweh, depicting his arrows and sword eating the flesh and drinking the blood of his foes, for example, they are, in their mind, simply offering up the praise they believe he is due.[15]

The OT's account of the conquest of Canaan is a great example of such "macabre hyperbole," and therefore a great example of how thoroughly ANE customs and beliefs influenced the OT writers' depictions of God. When God ordered Israel to conquer Canaan, he instructed them to "completely destroy" its cities and inhabitants, to "not leave alive anything that breathes," and to "show them no mercy" (Deut. 7:1-2, 16; 20:16-17). And according to the book of Joshua, that's exactly what Israel did. Repeatedly, it says Israel attacked a specific Canaanite city and "totally destroyed everyone in it," "put it to the sword," "left no survivors," exterminated "them without mercy," including "men and women, young and old," etc.[16] One verse even proclaims Israel annihilated the entire population of Canaan.[17] Another verse concludes, "As the Lord commanded his servant Moses, so Moses commanded Joshua, and Joshua did it; he left nothing undone of all that the Lord commanded Moses" (Josh. 11:15).[18] In short, a literal reading of the OT's account of the conquest indicates God ordered Israel to annihilate the Canaanites and Israel fully complied.

But on the other hand, the OT indicates that's not what happened at all. Here's the first verse in the later-written book of Judges: "After the death of Joshua, the Israelites asked the Lord, 'Who of us is to go up first to fight against the Canaanites?'" The rest of the first chapter and part of the second go on to describe multiple skirmishes with the Canaanites, the same people Israel had supposedly annihilated years before. For example, the book of Joshua says the Israelites exterminated everyone in Hebron, Debir, the hill country, the Negev, and the western foothills, but the book of Judges says they later fought the Canaanites who were still living in those places.[19] The end of the first chapter even explicitly admits that Israel "never drove them out completely" (v. 28).

Even the book of Joshua itself contains conflicting accounts. Joshua 11:21 says, "At that time Joshua went and destroyed the Anakites from the hill country: from Hebron, Debir and Anab, from all the hill country of Judah, and from all the hill country of Israel. Joshua totally destroyed them and their towns," but in Joshua 14:12, Caleb requests permission to drive out those same people from the same area.[20] Likewise, after Joshua 10:40 and 11:23 declare that Israel subdued all of Canaan and annihilated its entire population, Joshua 13:1 declares "there are still very large areas of land to be taken over."

Many other passages in Joshua and Judges tell us that Israel not only didn't kill all the Canaanites but also didn't fully drive them out of the Promised Land.[21] Later, the book of 1 Kings concurs: "There were still people left from the Amorites, Hittites, Perizzites, Hivites and Jebusites (these peoples were not Israelites). Solomon conscripted the descendants of all these peoples remaining in the land—whom the Israelites could not exterminate—to serve as slave labor, as it is to this day" (9:20-21).

Israel's apparent slaughter of the Amalekites provides another set of similar contradictions. According to 1 Samuel 15, God instructed the Israelites to "attack the Amalekites and totally destroy all that belongs to them. Do not spare them; put to death men and women, children and infants, cattle and sheep, camels and donkeys" (v. 13). Then Israel did exactly that. It "totally destroyed" all the Amalekites (v. 8).

But wait a minute. Later in the same book, it says, "David and his men went up and raided the Geshurites, the Girzites, and the Amalekites" and "did not leave a man or woman alive" (1 Sam. 27:8-9). And then a few chapters later, it says David encountered the Amalekites again and "fought them from dusk until the evening the next day" (1 Sam. 30:1-18). Then roughly 250 years later, the author of 1 Chronicles says the

Simeonites "killed the remaining Amalekites who had escaped" (1 Chron. 4:42-43).

The conclusion that the OT writers used hyperbole provides the best explanation for such contradictions. Their descriptions of total destruction, annihilation, and extermination were not attempts to record historical facts. As was customary, they were exaggerating for effect. They were saying more than they literally meant as a means of glorifying God. In Copan's words, they were "merely following the literary convention of the day."[22]

The historical record supports this conclusion. Numerous OT scholars and ANE historians have documented the widespread use of such hyperbole amongst Israel's neighbors, including the Egyptians, Assyrians, Hittites, and Moabites.[23] As Lamb puts it, "The major point of similarity between the biblical conquest narratives and those of their neighbors is the hyperbolic language."[24] Likewise, Sprinkle writes, "The point is well-known and thoroughly documented by historians: hyperbolic language about comprehensive defeat was typical war rhetoric and wasn't intended to be taken literally."[25] According to Christopher J. H. Wright, "the language of warfare had a conventional rhetoric that liked to make absolute and universal claims about total victory and completely wiping out the enemy" but "such rhetoric often exceeded reality on the ground."[26] Butler concurs: "The Old Testament makes clear it is using ancient trash talk, exaggerated war rhetoric. This way of speaking was common throughout the ancient Middle East; when you beat an enemy in battle and the adrenaline was rushing, you bragged. But no one expected to take you seriously."[27]

The historical record also indicates the OT writers were likely using hyperbole when they employed phrases like "all men, women, and children." According to Copan, such phrases were "merely stock ancient Near Eastern language that could be used even if women and young and old weren't living there."[28] Butler agrees: "Hebrew scholars note this was a stock phrase used to imply totality, and to Hebrew ears the use of this phrase does not require that women and children were *actually present* in the militarized outposts, only that the forts were totally depopulated in the aftermath of victory."[29] Therefore, writers used such phrases to indicate total victory through hyperbole, not to convey historical facts about the gender or age of those killed.

The discoveries of modern archeology also support this hyperbole theory. According to Copan, "all the archaeological evidence indicates that no civilian populations existed at Jericho, Ai, and other cities mentioned in Joshua."[30] "So when Israel 'utterly destroys' a city like Jericho or Ai," Butler concludes, "we should picture a military fort being taken over—not a civilian massacre."[31]

Others claim the archeological evidence indicates there wasn't even much of a military takeover. According to Douglas S. Earl, "A significant number of interpreters of the archaeological data gleaned from Palestine have concluded that there was no Israelite conquest of Canaan."[32] Seibert explains:

> The majority of biblical scholars no longer regard the conquest narrative as a historically reliable account of how Israel came to possess the land of Canaan.... One primary reason for this is the considerable amount of archaeological evidence that is impossible to correlate with the biblical description of the conquest recounted in the book of Joshua. Many cities that were reportedly destroyed by the Israelites show no evidence of destruction during the supposed conquest, whereas other cities that were destroyed during this time period are never mentioned in the book of Joshua. It is especially striking to note that both Jericho and Ai were uninhabited when the Israelites supposedly conquered them.[33]

Von Rad concurred, at least in regards to Ai: "Excavations have demonstrated with certainty that Ai was abandoned already in the Early Bronze Age and was first resettled only in the early Israelite era. Thus a military conquest by Israel could not have taken place here."[34]

Instead, the archeological evidence indicates Israel's "conquest" of Canaan was much more of a gradual infiltration than a swift, strategic, offensive campaign. In Copan's words, "archaeology has confirmed … that widespread destruction of cities didn't take place and that gradual assimilation did."[35] Or as Earl puts it, "some scholars have recently traced another portrait of the emergence of Israel in Canaan" as one "of gradual peaceful emergence that is possibly more fitting with the archaeological data."[36] Nugent agrees: "Archeological evidence is lacking for both the vast military incursion presupposed by the biblical narrative and for the occupation of key cities in the biblical account, including Jericho and Ai," and that has caused many OT scholars to replace "the conquest model of Joshua with other theories such as peaceful infiltration and/or peasant revolt."[37]

There's also scriptural evidence for such a view. For example, when describing Israel's conquest of Canaan, the OT writers use "driving out" or "dispossessing" language much more often than they use "total destruction" or "annihilation" language.[38] Such language implies something less than extermination or a Nazi-like blitzkrieg. It implies a forced relocation, not a massacre. Dispossessing isn't destroying. Driving out isn't wiping out. At least that's how the author of Genesis used the term when he noted that God "drove" Adam and Eve out of the Garden of Eden and "drove" Cain into the wilderness.[39]

Furthermore, before the conquest, God warned the Israelites that it would be a slow process: "But I will not drive them out in a single year.... Little by little I will drive them out before you, until you have increased enough to take possession of the land" (Exod. 23:29–30).[40] And after the conquest, the author of Judges confirmed that it occurred gradually: "The Lord had allowed those nations to remain; *he did not drive them out at once* by giving them into the hands of Joshua" (Judg. 2:23). Therefore, as Yoder concludes, "It seems more likely, according to the critical historical reconstruction, that the Israelites gradually infiltrated in the interstices between the Canaanite settlements, gradually becoming more settled and less nomadic...."[41]

In short, much cultural and historical evidence suggests the OT writers employed hyperbole, not recorded historical facts, when they described Israel engaging in extreme violence during its "conquest" of Canaan.

So here's the question: If we should view such depictions as hyperbolic, shouldn't we also view the depictions of God commanding, condoning, or participating in such violence as hyperbolic? Doesn't the same logic apply? After all, the same OT writer who described Israel's victories in extermination terms also concluded that those victories fulfilled God's original extermination commands.[42] In other words, if the descriptions of Israel's victories were hyperbolic and those victories fulfilled God's original commands, then those original commands must have also been hyperbolic.

For that matter, why couldn't we attribute all of God's supposed involvement in violence in the OT to ANE beliefs and customs? If the Israelites (1) were inherently predisposed to project their own selfish agendas onto God, like all fallen humans are, (2) believed that the will of its king was the will of its god, as was customary, and (3) believed that all gods were inherently violent, were deeply involved in national violence, and were glorified by being credited with violence like all other ANE peoples did, wouldn't they have been inclined to attribute heaps of violence to God that he never actually performed, commanded, or condoned? Wouldn't they have been predisposed to read their cultural beliefs into their perceptions of God? Couldn't their ANE ears and eyes have heard and seen things God didn't really say or do?

Regardless of how far you feel comfortable extending the reach of these cultural practices and beliefs, they illustrate that the OT writers' descriptions of God's violence were unquestionably influenced by ANE culture. To use Walter Wink's words, they reveal that the OT "violence is in part the residue of false ideas about God carried over from the general human past."[43] Or as Boyd puts it, they provide "further evidence that the OT's violent divine portraits reflect the culturally conditioned mindset of their authors more than they reflect authentic spiritual insights into the true character and will of God."[44] As such, they help explain why God's use of violence in the OT was so unlike Jesus' nonuse of violence in the NT.

On a side note, even if you don't buy the Bible's claim that God is most fully and perfectly revealed in Jesus, this cultural analysis still helps us understand the God of the OT by further establishing the justness of his violence. More specifically, it (particularly the hyperbole evidence) demonstrates that the God-sanctioned violence in the OT was even *more* limited, *less* aggressive, and *more* just than we concluded in Chapter 7.

All of that being said, I want to highlight one more informative ANE belief. It's one that would have not only motivated the Israelites to misattribute violence to God but would have *incentivized* God to allow them to do so. Polytheism. Or more specifically, Israel's historically unprecedented transition from polytheism to monotheism.

When God began interacting with OT Israel, the concept of monotheism didn't exist. Humans only knew polytheism and only knew an all-encompassing version of it. There was a god for every arena of life (e.g. health, fertility, war, weather, etc.) and each god directly controlled his respective arena. Everything that occurred was due to the conscious will of some god—good harvests and natural disasters, health and sickness, fertility and barrenness, victory and defeat, etc. All good flowed straight out of a pleased god and all evil out of an angry one. Seibert elaborates:

> In the ancient world, many things that happened were understood theologically. People perceived divine involvement and causality in events we would typically explain in other ways. Take, for example, natural disasters. Things like hailstorms, earthquakes, famines, and floods were thought to be caused by God and thus were fraught with theological significance. They were not viewed as mere "natural" disasters—and for good reason. People in the ancient world had no

scientific explanation for why these kinds of things occurred. Therefore, they explained them the only way they knew how: theologically.[45]

So when God showed up and proclaimed himself the one and only real God, the Israelites naturally applied the same perspective to him. They attributed everything that happened, whether good or bad, to his direct involvement. They had no concept of a God who might have intentionally created a world in which humans and spirits were free to defy his will. Such an idea would have violated their notion of what it meant to be a god, for to be a god meant to be a puppet master.

Apparently, God was okay with such misattribution, at least temporarily. He likely had to be. To convince the Israelites to discard the conventional wisdom that everything in the world was ruled by many conflicting gods and instead accept the notion of a world wherein everything is ruled by one creator god, he had to vigorously, consistently, and unequivocally emphasize his exclusive control over everything, particularly the types of things humans believed other gods directly controlled, like violence.

Before God could do anything of substance with or through the Israelites, he first had to prove he was in charge and other gods weren't. Before he could use them to carry out his world-saving plan, unveil his ethical ideal, or reveal the finer points of his true character, he first had to establish himself as the one and only true God. In a world that only knew polytheism that required *overemphasizing* himself as the ultimate source of everything that happened. He was pedagogically incentivized to temporarily allow the OT Israelites to believe he caused and controlled everything, including violence.

To explain it another way, God had to first transition the Israelites from believing in all-controlling polytheism to believing in all-controlling monotheism before he could transition them into believing in non-all-controlling monotheism. Correcting both misbeliefs (the polytheism belief and the all-controlling belief) at the same time would have likely been too much for them to handle and arguably too much for God to accomplish without resorting to coercion or trampling free will. Plus, trying to correct the polytheism belief before the all-controlling belief would have been counterproductive. God's primary goal was to establish himself as the one and only true God (which, by the way, was one of those fundamental principles he never compromised on). Defining precisely how much he directly causes or controls everything that happens to humans on earth was a far secondary concern at the time.

Again, even with our superior knowledge of God, many Christians still struggle with this issue today. Although we have both the Old and New Testaments and have lived in a monotheistic culture for hundreds of years, we still have a hard time conceiving of a God who is sovereign but doesn't cause or control everything, a God who is all powerful but chooses not to exercise all power. Why should we expect the early polytheistic Israelites to have been any different?

Given everything above, it shouldn't surprise us that the OT contains a palpable human struggle over what events and characteristics to attribute to God. Evidence of it is everywhere, particularly in its contradictory claims about him. The author of Jeremiah says God can change his mind while the author of 1 Samuel says he can't.[46] The author of Deuteronomy declares, "Just as it pleased the Lord to make you prosper and increase in number, so it will please him to ruin and destroy you" (28:63), but the prophet Ezekiel later writes, "As surely as I live, declares the Sovereign Lord, I take no pleasure in the death of the wicked, but rather that they turn from their ways and live" (33:11). Many passages describe and depict God as merciful while others describe and depict him as killing without mercy or ordering others to do so, and often it's the same OT author making both claims.[47] As theologian Derek Flood deduces, "we find within the Old Testament the direct words of God proclaimed by the prophets contradicted by the direct words of God proclaimed by other prophets...."[48]

Plus, such contradictions aren't found only in the OT. They exist between the Testaments too. Consider how each one views physical ailments. The OT writers often attributed them to God's direct punishment for sin,[49] but the NT provides a different view. For example, one day when the disciples came across a man who had been blind since birth, they asked Jesus, "Rabbi, who sinned, this man or his parents, that he was born blind?" "Neither," he responded (John 9:1-3). In other words, the disciples, taking their cue from the OT, assumed the man's blindness was direct punishment from God, but Jesus knew better.

In fact, every time Jesus encountered someone with a physical ailment, he always diagnosed it as something God did not will and often also directly attributed it to the work of Satan or his demons. For example, Luke 13 tells of Jesus healing a woman "who had been crippled by a spirit for eighteen years," and in the story, Jesus himself refers to her as someone "whom Satan has kept bound for eighteen long years" (13:11-16). Jesus spent much of his ministry healing such people, including a mute, a demon-possessed boy suffering from seizures, and "a demon-possessed man who was blind and mute."[50] He also gave his disciples the "authority to drive out impure spirits and to heal every disease and sickness," which they did (Matt. 10:1). Thus, in contrast to the OT writers, the NT writers never suggested that God causes physical ailments to punish people or teach them a lesson. Instead, they made the exact opposite claim.

Similarly, there are many other instances, both within the OT itself and between the Testaments, in which one biblical writer attributed something to God that another attributed to Satan. For example, the author of 2 Samuel says God incited David to perform a distrustful military census and then punished him for it, but when the writer of 1 Chronicles tells the same story later towards the end of the OT, he says Satan incited David to take the census.[51] Then, about a millennium later, the NT writer of James agreed with the chronicler's perspective: "When tempted, no one should say, 'God is tempting me.' For God cannot be tempted by evil, nor does he tempt anyone" (1:13). Likewise, when the writer of Exodus described the killing of Egypt's firstborn, he first said God would "strike down the Egyptians," then in the same verse he said "the destroyer" would do it, and finally a few verses later he claimed God had done it (12:23, 29). And a few hundred years later, the NT author of Hebrews asserted "the destroyer" had done it (11:28). In similar fashion, the OT writer of Numbers said God burned 250 men alive and sent a plague that killed 14,700 more, but in the NT Paul attributed those deaths to "the destroying angel" (1 Cor. 10:1-10). And in maybe the most telling example, the author of Job begins by informing the reader that Satan inflicted great pain and suffering on Job, but all the humans in the story, including Job, spend the entire book misattributing such pain and suffering to God.[52]

Notice the general biblical trend here. As the narrative progresses, the writers gradually move away from attributing things like suffering, destruction, and death to God and toward attributing them to Satan. "As God is increasingly unveiled as life-giver rather than death-dealer," Jersak writes, "the biblical authors reflect this perspective more and more, becoming ever more careful to assert that God is not to blame."[53]

We can trace this development through the text as the biblical writers gradually discover Satan's existence and influence. He is almost nonexistent in the early OT, gradually gains some visibility by the end of the OT, and ends up a relatively prominent character in the NT. As Thompson notes, "one of the great surprises in the actual reading of Scripture is the very poor publicity which the Adversary receives in the Old Testament."[54] In fact, "specific references to the demonic, to Satan, or the Devil are very sparse indeed."[55] Yet, "Traditional Christian theology assigns a fairly significant role to Satan, and he certainly is quite prominent in the New Testament."[56]

So if the NT and Christian tradition both claim Satan has been at work in the world sowing destruction since the beginning,[57] why is he almost totally absent in the OT? Maybe because God used incremental character revelation? Maybe because humanity's conception of God developed gradually over time as he progressively revealed more of himself and slowly broke through humanity's culturally conditioned misperceptions? This theory solves the problem quite well.

Recognizing God's need to transition Israel from polytheism to monotheism also helps explain why God was in no hurry to introduce humans to the concept of Satan. As Thompson observes, "Ancient Israel emerged from a thoroughly polytheistic society in Egypt. Had God chosen to highlight the role of a satanic figure, the condition of the people could have made dualism, if not polytheism, a likely threat to the purity of the faith that God was seeking to establish."[58] He elaborates:

> In a world permeated with polytheism, convincing Israel that there is one true God in heaven who is God over all was no easy task and the route may seem to us to have been circuitous. But as Israel grew towards the revelation of God in Jesus Christ, the principles of the great cosmic struggle [between God and Satan] began to emerge more clearly, until finally in the New Testament the issues and the key protagonists stood out in bold relief for all to see.[59]

Most importantly for our purposes, this is as true for violence as it is for anything. The biblical writers struggle over what violent events and characteristics to attribute to God. After all, some OT passages depict God as committing mass murder and causing parents to cannibalize their own children while the NT depicts him as self-sacrificially choosing to be tortured to death for a crime he didn't commit rather than use violence merely to defend himself. There's even much disagreement within the OT itself, as Seibert reminds us:

> First, it is important to keep in mind that the Old Testament does not speak with one voice on the issue of violence. Rather, the Old Testament contains enormous diversity.... The Old Testament says so many different things about violence that it is impossible to speak about "the Old Testament view on violence." There is no such thing. There are many Old Testament views and perspectives on violence, and some of these are diametrically opposed to each other.[60]

For example, according to Boyd, "many narratives containing violent depictions of God make it clear that the violence they ascribed to

God was actually carried out by other agents who were already 'intent on violence.'"[61] Citing the conflicting accounts in Jeremiah 13:13-14 and 21:7, he asserts that "Jeremiah frequently ascribes the same violent actions, and the same merciless attitude, to Yahweh and to Nebuchadnezzar, the king of Babylon."[62] Similarly, according to the author of 2 Kings, the prophet Elisha told Jehu God wanted him to destroy the house of Ahab and Jezebel, which he did, but later the prophet Hosea said God would punish Jehu for doing so.[63]

Furthermore, as the story progresses, the biblical writers gradually move away from attributing violence to God and toward attributing it to Satan. Initially, they attributed all violence to God because that's what they were accustomed to doing when they first met him, but then as they slowly received more information about his true character, they slowly attributed less violence to him. McLaren elaborates:

> If we were studying the Bible together over a period of time, we could trace the maturation process among biblical writers regarding *God's character*. In some passages, God appears violent, retaliatory, given to favoritism, and careless of human life. But over time, the image of God that predominates is gentle rather than cruel, compassionate rather than violent, fair to all rather than biased toward some, forgiving rather than retaliatory.[64]

Once again, the incremental character revelation theory nicely explains this pattern. The Bible's conflicting perspectives on violence and its trend toward nonviolence perfectly support such a theory, including its assertions that God's divine inspiration was something less than total control.

To summarize, there's much cultural, historical, pedagogical and biblical evidence to support the conclusion that God used incremental character revelation. Everything indicates he allowed the OT writers to be influenced and shaped by the social context that surrounded them and, in doing so, permitted them to (1) believe things about him that weren't true and (2) portray him in ways that weren't accurate. This is particularly true for violence. ANE culture provided the OT writers with lots of reasons to believe God used violence to advance his agenda. In fact, the ANE worldview powerfully incentivized them to credit him with violence, and not just common everyday violence but extreme, genocidal-type violence.

To state it another way, God allowed humanity's view of him to evolve as he gradually revealed more of himself and his will. To use Zahnd's words, "The Old Testament is the inspired telling of the story of

Israel coming to know their God. It's a process. God doesn't evolve, but Israel's understanding of God obviously does."[65]

And why not? If he allows our view of him to change as we mature from children to adolescents to adults, why wouldn't he allow humanity's view of him to undergo a similar transformation throughout its ethical maturation? Likewise, if we all accept certain conceptions of God that aren't expressed anywhere in the Bible and weren't officially adopted by the church until about 250 years after the last NT book was written (as is true of the doctrine of the Trinity and the canonization of Scripture itself), why should we hesitate to admit that some of the biblical writers' beliefs about God changed from the beginning of the OT to the end of the NT?

If you believe God used incremental ethical revelation, you already believe he allowed humans to temporarily believe things about him that weren't true. By permitting things like divorce, polygamy, and slavery without ever telling the Israelites his permission was only temporary, he allowed them to believe he was entirely okay with such behaviors. Only in hindsight do we know he wasn't.

Why couldn't God have done the same thing with violence? Why couldn't he have also allowed the OT Israelites to temporarily believe he was a God who engaged and gloried in violence, as was uniformly believed about gods throughout the ANE? If he judged it necessary to allow them to incorrectly believe it was okay to own slaves, why couldn't he have also judged it necessary to allow them to incorrectly believe he commanded and participated in violence? If he was willing to put up with some of the Israelites sins to cultivate a relationship with them, why wouldn't he have also been willing to put up with some of their misperceptions of him to achieve the same thing? If he allowed the ANE culture to dictate the Israelites' ethical code, why couldn't he have also allowed it to dictate their perception of him? Is there a better way to explain the Bible's conflicting portraits?

Maybe the violence in the OT says as much about humans as it does about God. Maybe it provides as much information about humanity's ethical evolution as it does about how God actually interacts with the world. Maybe it reveals as much about our fallen human nature as it does about God's divine nature. Maybe it's the story of humanity's moral development as much as it's the story of what God is really like. Maybe biblical scholar and anthropologist Ingrid E. Lilly is right and human "conceptions of God cannot be divorced from the cultures that produced them."[66] Maybe Jersak is right and "God didn't evolve; our conception of him did, in greatest part because Jesus came to show and tell us exactly who God is in ways *no* prophet had the capacity to anticipate—not Moses, David or even Isaiah."[67]

Here's the point: When analyzing the Bible, we must decipher God's true character the same way we decipher his true ethics. Just as we had to place his moral instructions within their cultural context to properly understand them, we have to place the OT writers' depictions of God within their cultural context. Just as we must evaluate God's OT actions from the perspective of the ancient Israelites instead of our modern, post-Jesus perspective, we must do the same with the OT's descriptions of God. Just as we must not read the Bible as a static, constitution-like list of eternally and universally applicable moral laws, we must not read it as an unchanging, encyclopedia-like list of facts about God's character. Just as we must read it as a narrative account of humanity's ethical development, we also must read it as a narrative account of humanity's evolving view of God. McLaren explains:

> Human beings can't do better than their very best at any given moment to communicate about God as they understand God.... Scripture faithfully reveals the evolution of our ancestors' best attempts to communicate their successive best understandings of God. As human capacity grows to conceive of a higher and wiser view of God, each new vision is faithfully preserved in Scripture like fossils in layers of sediment. If we read the Bible as a cultural library rather than as a constitution ... we are free to learn from that evolutionary process—and, we might even add, to participate in it.[68]

This profoundly impacts how we interpret the OT's violent portraits of God. Here's McLaren again:

> In light of this unfolding understanding of biblical revelation, when we ask why God appears so violent in some passages of the Bible, we can suggest this hypothesis: if the human beings who produced those passages were violent in their own development, they would naturally see God through the lens of their experience. The fact that those disturbing descriptions are found in the Bible doesn't mean that we are stuck with them, any more than we are stuck with "You cannot subtract a larger number from a smaller number" just because that statement still exists in our second-grade textbook. Remember, the Bible is not a constitution. It is like the library of math texts that shows the history of the development of mathematical reasoning among human beings.[69]

When reading the OT, we need to bear in mind that its authors were culturally conditioned to view God as violent and culturally incentivized to credit him with violence, extreme violence.

In fact, we should disagree with some of the OT writers' portrayals of God because we have much more (and much more accurate) information than they did. We have Jesus and the NT. They didn't. For that matter, they didn't even have the OT. They were living it.

Plus, as we've previously discussed, Jesus didn't merely provide us with a *little* more or *slightly* better information about God. He provided us with a *full* and *perfect* picture of him. He provided us with the *key* to understanding the OT portraits of God and differentiating between which aspects of them were influenced by the authors' humanity and which ones were divinely inspired. In Boyd's words, "God's definitive self-revelation on the cross gives us a perspective that can discern a dimension of truth in OT passages, and especially in its violent depictions of God, that the authors of these passages could not have discerned."[70]

If we don't use God's self-revelation in Jesus to inform our understanding of the OT's human portraits of him, what does it mean to profess that all Scripture ultimately testifies about, points to, and should be interpreted through Jesus? What does it mean to declare that Jesus is the "exact representation" of God and "the word of God in its fullness?" What does it mean to proclaim that to know Jesus is to know God? What does it mean to assert that no one had ever seen God before Jesus made him known? What does it mean to contend that the OT law was "only a shadow of the good things" to come but "the reality ... is found in Christ"?

We must not read the OT as if Jesus never existed or the NT was never written. We must not read it as if God's revelation ceased at the end of the OT. We must not adopt a pre-Christian view of God.

We also must not turn the Bible into a false idol. We must not commit bibliolatry. The Bible is not God. It points to and witnesses to God, but it isn't God. Only Jesus is. "Jesus is greater than the Bible," writes Zahnd.[71] "The Bible is sent by God and inspired by God, but the Bible is not God. The Holy Trinity is Father, Son, and Holy Spirit—not Father, Son, and Holy *Bible*."[72] He elaborates:

> The Bible is not the perfect revelation of God; Jesus is. Jesus is the only perfect theology. Perfect theology is not a system of theology; perfect theology is a person. Perfect theology is not found in abstract thought; perfect theology is found in the Incarnation. Perfect theology is not a book; perfect theology is the life that Jesus lived. What the Bible does infallibly and inerrantly is point us to Jesus....[73]

Let's not be misled by the OT writers' depictions of God. Let's not mistakenly grant them the same status as Jesus' depiction of him. Let's not subordinate God's own claims to our non-biblically based notions of divine inspiration and scriptural inerrancy. God has blessed us with superior information about his character. Let's make use of it. Let's not revert back to the relative ignorance of the OT writers. They played an indispensable role in the conceptual education of humankind, but it was a temporary role that merely laid the groundwork for the additional knowledge we now possess.

This claim to greater knowledge shouldn't offend you or strike you as arrogant. It is a natural product of how God intervened into human history and how the Bible records that intervention. To recognize that the Bible is a narrative in which God incrementally revealed himself and his will is to recognize that the early biblical writers had much less information about him than the later ones, with the earliest writers having almost none. Not coincidentally, the earliest writers were the ones who depicted him most violently.

Divine Inspiration

A lengthy caveat is in order. To conclude that the OT's violent portraits of God were inaccurate is not to conclude they weren't divinely inspired. It's to assert that their divinely inspired meaning is something other than their surface-level meaning. It's to recognize that we have to dig deeper to find their true, God-breathed meaning. In other words, it doesn't change the fact that God inspired them. It simply changes what God inspired them to say.

To state it another way, the divinely inspired meaning of a passage can be different than its literal meaning. No rational biblical interpreter believes everything in the Bible should be taken literally, not even everything Jesus said. For example, no one believes Jesus is actually a gate even though he proclaimed, "I am the gate" (John 10:9). Likewise, no one believes Jesus was speaking literally when he instructed his listeners to gouge out their eye if it caused them to sin.[74] Instead, everyone recognizes Jesus was employing two common literary techniques: metaphor and hyperbole. Such techniques are employed throughout the Bible. Thus, not only *can* the divinely inspired meaning of a passage differ from its literally meaning, it often *must* differ.

Similarly, the divinely inspired meaning of a passage can also be different than the author's originally intended meaning. Just as God is fully capable of using people's actions to accomplish objectives other than what those people intended their actions to accomplish (as is evidenced by his use of one nation's imperialistic violence to punish another nation's injustices), he is also fully capable of inspiring authors to write words that communicate information other than what those authors intended their words to communicate.

At least the NT authors themselves often interpreted the OT authors in such a way.[75] Why should we stick to the biblical writers' originally intended meanings when the biblical writers themselves didn't always do so? And why can't a Scripture passage have multiple legitimate meanings? Why must it have only one and why must that one be what the less-informed author intended? Plus, given that the Bible is a narrative, why can't a passage's meaning evolve alongside its bigger, unfolding narrative? Is God not powerful enough to inspire Scripture in such ways?

Furthermore, a Scripture passage doesn't have to be historically accurate to be divinely inspired. The Bible contains multiple literary genres—chronicles, legal codes, poetry, wisdom literature, prophecies, gospels, letters, and apocalyptic writings—and not all of them aim to record historical facts. In fact, about half of the books in the OT fall into one of the less-historically factual genres. And even those within the more-historically factual genres don't always try to be 100% historically accurate. They vary in their form and function and in the degree to which they employ various literary techniques, like allegory. Some might even be labeled historical fiction.

It's important to note that none of this affects any passage's ability to be "useful for teaching, rebuking, correcting and training in righteousness" (2 Tim. 3:16-17), as Paul declared all Scripture is. A statement doesn't have to be historically accurate (or literally true) to teach us something. God is fully capable of using fiction to convey meaning and truth. After all, Jesus did when he spoke in parables.

Consider Genesis's seven-day creation story. Its primary message is that God created the universe, created a good universe, and created humans in his image. Nothing about that message depends upon the historical accuracy (or scientific plausibility) of creation being completed in seven literal days, instead of seven allegorical days. In other words, whether God literally created the world in seven days is irrelevant to the theological claims made in the Bible's creation story. Maybe he did it in seven days. Maybe he didn't. Maybe he used hundreds of millions of years of evolution. Theologically, it doesn't matter.

I struggle to understand why so many Christians insist on interpreting such biblical stories literally. Why tie the Bible's status as God's divinely inspired word to the historical or scientific accuracy of such extraneous and ultimately irrelevant issues? To do so is to place your faith on shaky ground, as Boyd explains:

> I'd like to suggest that the truly dangerous view is one that believes that the Bible must be 100% accurate to be God's inspired Word. This view means that your confidence in Scripture depends on your ability to resolve every one of the contradictions, scientific errors, and historical problems associated with it, and … most who explore these issues in a thorough and an intellectually honest way eventually come to the conclusion that it can't be done.[76]

Simply put, the Bible is not merely a historical or scientific document. It is much more than that.

That being said, there are a few aspects of the Bible that must be historically accurate for Christianity to be true (e.g. Jesus' life, death, and resurrection), but the OT's violent portraits of God isn't one of them. In fact, the historical accuracy of such portraits has little impact on the general problem they present. Whether or not God engaged in such violence, he still allowed the OT writers to portray him doing so. Either way, the presence of such portraits within the Bible demands explanation.

Don't misunderstand me. I'm not saying that interpreting Scripture literally is bad. It isn't. In fact, it should probably be our default method of interpretation, one that we set aside only when context requires it. I'm also not saying we shouldn't try to discern each author's originally intended meaning. We should. Doing so always teaches us something. Nor am I saying we shouldn't read Scripture in a historically critical way. We should. And we must. Intelligent interpretation demands it.

I'm saying the divinely inspired status and meaning of a passage doesn't depend upon the results of such things. I'm saying a passage's God-breathed meaning can be different than its literal meaning and the meaning its human author intended. I'm saying a passage's status as the inspired Word of God does not depend upon its historical factuality. Ultimately, I'm saying the incremental character revelation theory (and its claim that the OT's violent portraits of God are inaccurate) does not conflict with the belief that all Scripture is divinely inspired.

Note that all of us are forced to interpret Scripture in these ways. We are forced to decide what it does and doesn't mean. That's how reading works. Everything has a context and everything's meaning is dependent upon its context. Every word, sentence, paragraph, chapter, and book in the Bible has a literary context (i.e. a genre and a type of speech), a historical context (i.e. a location within humanity's ethical and conceptual development), a cultural context (i.e. a location within the prevailing beliefs and assumptions of the time), and a biblical context (i.e. a location within the biblical narrative), and it is only within all of those contexts that each passage's true meaning can be found.

Borrowing an example from Kit Barker, Boyd illustrates how the meaning of even a relatively simple and straightforward statement like "It's after nine o'clock" is entirely dependent upon the context in which it is communicated:

> Depending on the context, this locutionary act could be intended as an assertion in response to a question (e.g., someone asking, "What time is it?"); it could itself be intended as a question (e.g., a way for a mother to ask her teenage son over the phone, "Where are you?"); it could be intended to be a request (e.g., a way for someone to ask, "Could I please have decaf rather than regular coffee?"); it could be intended as a command (e.g., an angry conference organizer telling a speaker to end their speech); it could be intended as an expression of grief (e.g., of a person who was promised a call by 9:00 p.m. if they got the job they applied for); or it could even be intended to be a petitionary prayer (e.g., made by this anxious person to God to miraculously get them this job even though it is past the time their potential employer promised to call).... It all depends on the context in which a communicative act is performed and received.[77]

Therefore, Boyd concludes,

> As much as we might wish it were otherwise, I'm afraid that we flawed human beings are already the "arbiters of truth." For example, you, as a flawed human, had to decide to accept the Bible as the Word of God rather than the Koran, the Book of Mormon, the Bhagavad Gita, or any other book. Even after deciding to believe the Bible, you, as a flawed human, have to decide what you were going to do with (say) its pre-scientific view of the earth and sky resting on pillars; its view of the sky as a rock-solid dome that holds up water with windows that get opened when it rains; and its view that the earth was created in six days, with light being created three days before the sun, moon, and stars. And, finally, you as a flawed human have to decide what parts of the Bible you think are still relevant for today, and which aren't. For example, you must decide whether you think God still wants people to stone children to death if they sass back to their parents ... or whether God still forbids women to speak in church and to wear braided hair and jewelry. So I'm afraid we have no choice but to decide matters of truth.[78]

Seibert also explains it well:

> It helps to recognize that everyone who reads the Bible engages in an ethical critique of it to some degree, whether they realize it or not.... Even though the Old Testament approves of slavery, we do not. To take such a position is to engage in an ethical critique of the Old Testament. Recognizing that we already evaluate and critique the Old Testament in

some ways, and seeing this as both legitimate and beneficial, should free us to do so in other ways as well.[79]

Yes, it should. And one other aspect of the OT we should feel free to evaluate and critique is its violent depictions of God.

We already contextualize everything else in the OT (including its ethical demands), so why not also contextualize its violent depictions of God? We all understand we aren't required to offer regular animal sacrifices to God, avoid eating "unclean" foods, follow the ritualistic temple practices, or put to death those who commit adultery (and are actually required to not do some of those things) because we interpret them within their proper location in the biblical narrative. Shouldn't we treat the OT's violent depictions of God the same way? Shouldn't we properly contextualize them as pre-Jesus understandings of God that are also no longer applicable? If we interpret God's OT commands in light of the additional information provided by the NT, shouldn't we do the same with the OT's violent depictions of God? If we already allow Jesus to redefine so many other things in the OT, like God's ethical requirements, why shouldn't we also allow him to redefine our perception of God's character? If we let Jesus convince us that God doesn't approve of polygamy or slavery or animal sacrifice, why don't we also let him convince us that God doesn't use or condone violence? If we believe everything else the NT writers assert about Jesus (e.g. that he was God, was sinless, died on the cross for us, rose from the dead, etc.), why don't we also believe their assertion that God is exactly like him?

Not only does context force these types of decisions on us, the claims of Jesus and the NT writers do too. They claimed Jesus was the exact representation of God, a full and picture portrayal of him, the portrayal that trumps all others, and the only way to truly know his character. They claimed what God revealed in Jesus was superior to what he revealed through the OT writers. And by doing so, they force us to choose whether we will believe the NT's claims and give it greater authority than the OT or disbelieve its claims and attempt to find some other way to rectify their inconsistencies.

By the way, the NT is the only Testament that claims superior authority. The OT never does. On the contrary, it frequently points to a future messiah who would be more authoritative than anyone or anything that had come before him. In other words, according to Scripture itself, not all Scripture is equally authoritative.

Furthermore, the Bible's internal contradictions also force interpretive decisions on us. The OT allows some ethical practices the NT prohibits. One OT passage claims a group was totally annihilated while another demonstrates it wasn't. One OT author says God did something while another says Satan did it. The OT portrays God causing parents to cannibalize their own children while Jesus portrays him as self-sacrificially choosing to be tortured to death for a crime he didn't commit rather than use violence merely to defend himself.

These conflicts, which occur not only between the Testaments but also within the OT itself, force us to choose between them. They force us to label some Scripture passages as more accurate than others. They force us to interpret some nonliterally and non-historically. By definition, contradicting statements can't be equally authoritative. Thus, under its own terms, the Bible forces us to give some passages greater weight than others. And anyone who looks to the Bible to determine how they should act or what God is like *must* do so.

Here's the core logic: Because (1) every Scripture has a context whose meaning is dependent upon that context, (2) Jesus claimed his revelation trumps the OT's revelation, and (3) the Bible contains contradictions that prevent us from believing everything it says, we are forced to analyze, critique, and question Scripture. Thus, the question isn't *whether* you interpret Scripture. The question is *how* you interpret it, i.e. what you base your interpretation decisions on.

We should base them on what the Bible itself says we should: Jesus. We should interpret the Bible in its ultimate context: the context of Jesus. That's the only objective way to do it. That's the only way to make the Bible itself the final arbiter of truth. Traditionally, the church has done this with most of the OT, including its ethical requirements. But unfortunately, it has largely failed to apply the same approach to its violent depictions of God.

How we interpret the OT's violent depictions of God is not a matter of having faith or not having faith. It is a matter of who or what we place our faith in. Concluding that God *didn't* commit the violence the OT attributes to him requires having faith in the NT's claim that Jesus was the perfect and full picture of God. In contrast, concluding that God *did* commit the violence the OT attributes to him requires having faith that the NT's claims about Jesus were wrong. Either way, we are placing your faith in someone, either the OT writers or the NT ones.

In addition to everything we've already discussed, I see at least three more reasons why we should place our faith in the NT writers rather than the OT ones. First, unlike the OT writers, the NT writers were recording the words and actions of a real, live human being, not a spiritual deity they usually couldn't even see. Second, unlike the corrupted human subjects the OT writers were working with, the NT writers were working with a perfect vessel for God's message: sinless Jesus. Third, we have more non-biblical reasons for trusting the accuracy of the NT than we have for trusting the OT, such as its greater historical, philosophical, and experiential reliability.

One quick philosophical/experiential example: Ask yourself which Testament's depictions of God more closely resemble typical human impulses and views. Which ones look more like a deity whom we have remade in our own image? The answer is obvious and adds credibility to the NT.

The Deeper Meaning

Although we are forced to prioritize some passages over others, we can't simply dismiss those we deem less authoritative or less accurate. We can't just flush whatever doesn't comply with God's revelation in Jesus. Because "All Scripture is God-breathed and is useful for teaching, rebuking, correcting and training in righteousness" (2 Tim. 3:16), we must go deeper to find the true, God-intended meaning of such passages. We must determine why God inspired humans to write them and then allowed them into the Bible. Most importantly, we must determine how they bear witness to Jesus.

We already do this for many passages and events in the Bible. Consider the Crucifixion. If you are a Christian, you look past the surface-level description to discern its true meaning. You look past its mere facts (a convicted criminal was cruelly put to death) to see what was really going on (God was conquering evil and graciously offering salvation to all humankind). We should do the same with the OT's violent portraits of God. We should look past their surface level descriptions, their mere facts, to discern their true meaning and see what God was really doing.

To put it another way, we must interpret the OT's violent portraits of God with the same faith we interpret the Crucifixion and the Bible itself. We must trust God that more is going on than meets the eye. After all, without faith, the cross is just another state-sponsored murder of an innocent man and the Bible is just another collection of ancient human writings. Likewise, without faith, the God of the OT is just another violent deity. Thus, we should expect that the true meaning of many biblical passages, just like the true meaning of the cross and Bible itself, will be located beneath the surface and will require faith to discern.

So what is the deeper meaning of the OT's erroneously violent depictions of God? What was God doing in and through them and why? And how does it point to and testify about Jesus?

The answer has been right in front of us this whole time. He was doing the same thing he was doing when he employed incremental ethical revelation. He was humbly and mercifully lowering himself to accommodate and work with humans where he found them so that he could patiently and gradually help them to a better place.

But here's the real question: Why? Why would God choose to help inferior, ungrateful, spoiled, immature, selfish, unjust, rebellious beings to a better place? And why would he do so via such humble, patient, service-oriented means?

Because he is love! And that's what love does! It always seeks what is best *for others* and does so *nonviolently*. It respects free will, doesn't coerce, and influences through persuasion and self-sacrifice, not violence. Instead of forcing others into behaving or believing correctly, it self-sacrificially bears with their misbehaviors and misperceptions while it attempts to persuade them to change via selfless acts of love.

In other words, God's use of incremental revelation is evidence of his love and his nonviolence. If he doesn't love us, why did he expend the effort to reveal anything to us? And if he isn't wholly nonviolent, why did he employ such a wholly nonviolent means of revelation? Simply put, God's use of incremental revelation reveals a lot about his character: that it is wholly loving and wholly nonviolent.

Therefore, instead of proving God is violent, the OT's violent depictions of him actually prove how nonviolent he is. They demonstrate he is so nonviolent he would rather sacrifice his own reputation than use force to protect it. He would rather allow humans to misperceive him than coerce them. He would rather they sully his perfect and holy good name than forcefully override their free will. He would rather humbly and patiently put up with such insults until he can more clearly reveal himself in a non-coercive way than violently correct them and risk destroying the possibility of true relationship. He would rather allow humans to smear his character than jeopardize his plan to rescue them by forcing information upon them they aren't ready to handle. He so badly wants to save us (i.e. to reestablish right relationship with us) he is willing to tarnish his own sacrosanct reputation to do so.

In fact, the OT's violent depictions themselves demonstrate that even God's divine inspiration is nonviolent, as Boyd explains:

> Even in "breathing" his written witness, God refuses to undermine the personhood and freedom of people by lobotomizing them so that they perfectly conform to his will. Even in "breathing" through people, God respects the integrity of a mutually impacting relationship, which is what a relationship of love requires.[80]

That's why there are conflicting accounts of God's use of violence within the OT itself. Sometimes God's non-coercive inspiration broke through the human author's misperceptions and sometimes it didn't, as Boyd again explains:

> Unlike Jesus, the authors of the OT had fallen and culturally conditioned aspects of their hardened hearts and minds that "got in the way" of the Spirit's revelatory activity, to one degree or another. And it is precisely because God refused to coercively remove these obstacles that certain portraits of God in the inspired written witness to his faithful covenantal activity reflect, to one degree or another, the fallen and culturally conditioned way his ancient people conceived of him.[81]

To explain it another way, God was doing the same things in the OT that he did on the cross. Just as he allowed his own son to be murdered rather than protect him, he allowed his reputation to be defiled rather than protect it. Just as he allowed violence to temporarily have its way with his son but then later redeemed him by raising him from the dead, he allowed violence to temporarily have its way with his reputation but then later redeemed it by sending Jesus to reveal his true character. Just as he stooped on the cross to bear humanity's misperception of him as a criminal traitor, he stooped in the OT to bear its misperception of him as a violent deity. Just as he self-sacrificially took on the appearance of a sinful, guilty criminal on the cross, he self-sacrificially took on the appearance of a violent warrior god in the OT. Just as he bore the sins of the world on the cross, he bore the world's sinful misperceptions of him in the OT.

Furthermore, just as God did those things on the cross to save us, he also did those similar things in the OT to save us. Just as he willingly sacrificed his son on the cross for our good, he willingly sacrificed his reputation in the OT for our good. Likewise, just as he was innocent of the crimes attributed to him in the NT, he was innocent of the violence attributed to him in the OT. Therefore, just as he wasn't trying to tell us he had actually sinned when he willingly suffered the consequences of sin (i.e. death) on the cross, he wasn't trying to tell us he actually uses violence when he willingly allowed the OT writers to depict him doing so. Instead, in both instances, he was trying to show us how he interacts with and saves humans: self-sacrificially and nonviolently.

Because we know God operated in such a loving, self-sacrificial, nonviolent way on the cross (which was where God's character is most perfectly and fully revealed), we can reasonably deduce he operated in a similar way in the OT. We can safely assume what was going on behind the scenes during the Crucifixion was similar to what was going on behind the scenes in the OT. If you can stomach the former, you can stomach the latter.

After all, if God was willing to bear *all* of humanity's sins on the cross (and suffer the consequences of those sins), why couldn't he have also been willing to bear a *few* of humanity's sins in the OT, like its sinful ethical practices (e.g. polygamy, slavery, divorce on demand, etc.) and sinful misperceptions of him (e.g. that he commits violence)? In this regard, Boyd goes so far as to assert that interpreting the OT's violent portraits of God as accurate depictions of his character actually indicates a lack of faith in Jesus and dishonors what he did on the cross.[82]

This how the OT's violent depictions of God point to and testify about Jesus. They are a foretaste and microcosm of his work on the cross. They foreshadow the loving and nonviolent means he employed on the cross to conquer evil and save the human race. And, like the cross, they exemplify how he is able to use human evil for good.[83]

Notice the only way to see this deeper meaning is to (1) believe Jesus was the full and perfect revelation of God, (2) acknowledge that the OT's violent depictions of God contradict Jesus' depiction of him, and (3) then push beyond the literal, surface-level descriptions of those OT depictions. That's the only way to see how they testify to the fullness and beauty of God's love, the only way to see how truly nonviolent God really is, and the only way to see how brilliant God's wisdom is, so brilliant that even grossly inaccurate and repulsive portrayals of him eventually proclaim his goodness. And, that's how one of the ugliest parts of the Bible becomes one of the most beautiful.

To summarize, the deeper meaning behind the OT's conflicting portraits of God is the same deeper meaning behind the OT's conflicting ethical practices and Jesus' death on the cross. In each case, God was self-sacrificially lowering himself to accommodate and work with humans where he found them so that he could patiently and gradually help them to a better place because he is love and that's what love does. Furthermore, the only way to see that meaning in each of those instances is to look beyond their literal, surface-level descriptions and analyze them within their proper literary, historical, cultural, and biblical contexts. Most importantly, such an approach allows us to conclude that God didn't commit the violent atrocities the OT says he did while also (1) fully respecting the God-inspired nature of all Scripture and (2) explaining how such erroneous depictions of God bear witness to Jesus.

There are lessons to be learned about God's character from the OT's violent depictions of him, but that he uses violence is not one of them. Precisely the opposite.

Conclusion

In this chapter and the last, we have explored some of the scriptural, theological, historical, cultural, literary, and philosophical evidence that suggests God did not actually commit the violence the OT says he did (i.e., some of the evidence that suggests he is not only opposed to violence but also wholly nonviolent himself). Maybe you have been persuaded by it or maybe you haven't. Maybe you now believe God is exactly like Jesus or maybe you don't. Maybe you buy into some of it but not all of it. Maybe you aren't convinced God never uses violence but are convinced his use of violence in the OT was much less extensive than it first appears. Or maybe you believe none of it. Maybe you think this chapter is wrong on every point.

For the two primary points of this book, it doesn't matter. First, it doesn't matter for God's goodness. As the first nine chapters of this book demonstrate, he is still a good and loving God even if he employed the violence the OT attributes to him. (Plus, a God who at the end of the day commands his followers to mimic and obey Jesus—and Jesus alone—can't be too bad of a fella, right?)

Second, it doesn't matter for our use of violence. As the first nine chapters of this book also demonstrate, God is opposed to all human violence even if he sometimes uses violence himself. Although the Bible isn't entirely clear on God's moral standard, it is clear that ours is the nonviolent Jesus. Although the Bible may not be entirely clear on whether God sometimes used violence, it is clear that we humans never should.

To state it another way, believing that God is wholly nonviolent himself is not a prerequisite to believing in a wholly nonviolent Christian ethic. You don't have to believe God is a pure pacifist to believe he hates all human violence. It's reasonable to believe that a divine being who possesses infinite knowledge and unlimited power is capable of using violence justly while inferior beings who lack such knowledge and power aren't. But it's not reasonable to conclude that such a God's occasional use of violence justifies our use of it.

Although we have covered a lot of ground in this chapter, we've barely scratched the surface of the theory that God never uses violence. If you would like to explore it further, I highly recommend Boyd's magnum opus *The Crucifixion of the Warrior God: Interpreting the Old Testament's Violent Portraits of God in Light of the Cross*, which addresses many of the other theological questions I haven't: How does this theory fit into the doctrine of the Trinity? How does it affect the penal substitutionary theory of the atonement? How does it affect our interpretation of the book of Revelation? What does it mean for how God's judgement and punishment operate? Etc.

Frankly, I am still working through many of those issues myself. But if we are going to take seriously the Bible's own claims about Jesus, it makes sense to structure our answers around Jesus' revelation instead of our own philosophical and metaphysical musings. It also makes sense to (1) place our faith in the accuracy of the later more-informed biblical writers rather than the earlier less-informed ones, (2) to defer to God's own self-revelation, (3) to give Jesus' depiction of God the benefit of the doubt whenever it conflicts with the OT's depictions, and (4) to conclude that the OT writers were sometimes mistaken rather than to conclude Jesus was. After all, apart from Jesus, we can concoct a biblical defense of almost anything—slavery, sexism, nationalism, war, etc.

On the other hand, what makes less sense is concluding that the OT's violent portraits of God must be deemed accurate to avoid denigrating Scripture but Jesus' conflicting nonviolent portrait of God need not be. What makes less sense is insisting that the OT's violent portraits of God must be interpreted literally but Jesus' straightforward antiviolence commands (e.g. turn the other cheek and love your enemies) need not be (or even *must* not be). What makes less sense is an ability to stomach the notion of a barbaric ANE-like God but not the notion of a pacifistic Jesus-like God. What makes less sense is insisting that orthodoxy requires believing God sometimes uses violence while believing he never does is heresy. You can believe either and still be Christian.

One final clarification. Notice that nothing in this chapter contradicts any of the fundamental lessons we learned about God in previous chapters. Even if we conclude he didn't use *any* violence in the OT, that doesn't mean he wasn't still involved in humanity's violence in a way that communicated real truths about his character and ethics. It simply means he used the *appearance* of his involvement in violence, instead of *actual* violence, to do so. In other words, even if he didn't actually use violence to do things like establish his sovereignty, build trust, demonstrate a hatred of injustice, and condemn militarism, he still could have used the Israelites' misperceptions of him doing so to accomplish such things. Such a move would have been just one more example of how he brilliantly uses everything for good, even mankind's erroneous beliefs.

---

[1] Boyd, *The Crucifixion of the Warrior God*, 11212.

[2] 1 Cor. 1:16.

[3] Matt. 23:35; 2 Chron. 24:20.

[4] C. S. Lewis, *Reflections on the Psalms* (Orlando, FL: Houghton Mifflin Harcourt, 1958), 111.

[5] Adam Hamilton, "God's Violence in the Old Testament, Part 3: Possible Solutions" posted on August 15, 2014 at http://www.adamhamilton.org/blog/gods-violence-in-the-old-testament-part-3-possible-solutions/#.WGui3PkrKUk.

[6] Seibert, *The Violence of Scripture*, 2512.

[7] Ibid.

[8] Ibid.

[9] Boyd, *The Crucifixion of the Warrior God*, chap. 14.

[10] Daniel L. Gard, *Show Them No Mercy: 4 Views on God and Canaanite Genocide* (Counterpoints: Bible and Theology) (Zondervan, 2010), 1894, Kindle.

[11] Boyd, *The Crucifixion of the Warrior God*, 26902.

[12] Ibid., 16398.

[13] Ibid., 19195.

[14] Ibid., 26904.

[15] Ibid., 16537.

[16] Josh. 6:21; 8:26; 10:28-43; 11:10-23; Judg. 1:17; Deut. 2:32-35; 3:3-6; Num. 21:1-3.

[17] Josh. 10:40.

[18] See also 10:40; 11:12, 20, 23.

[19] Josh. 10:36-40; Judg. 1:9-11.

[20] See also 15:13-19.

[21] Josh. 13:1-6, 13; 15:63; 16:10; 17:12-13; 23:12-13; Judg. 1:19-34; 2:20-21.

[22] Copan, *Is God a Moral Monster?*, 3935.

[23] K.A. Kitchen, *On the Reliability of the Old Testament* (Grand Rapids: Eerdmans, 2003), 173-74; K. Lawson Younger, Jr., *Ancient Conquest Accounts: A Study in Ancient Near Eastern and Biblical History Writing* (Sheffield, UK: Sheffield Academic, 1990), 227-28, 245; Lori L. Rowlett, *Joshua and the Rhetoric of Violence: A New Historicist Analysis* (NY: Continuum, 1996), 197-237.

[24] Lamb, *God Behaving Badly*, 737.

[25] Sprinkle, *Fight*, 1133.

[26] Wright, *The God I Don't Understand*, 1513.

[27] Butler, *The Skeletons in God's Closet*, 3975.

[28] Copan, *Is God a Moral Monster?*, 3768.

[29] Butler, *The Skeletons in God's Closet*, 3959.

[30] Copan, *Is God a Moral Monster?*, 3776.

[31] Butler, *The Skeletons in God's Closet*, 3945.

[32] Douglas S. Earl, *Holy War in the Bible*, ed. Heath A. Thomas, Jeremy Evans, and Paul Copan (InterVarsity Press, 2014), 2484, Kindle.

[33] Seibert, *The Violence of Scripture*, 2090.

[34] von Rad, *Holy War in Ancient Israel*, 53.

[35] Copan, *Is God a Moral Monster?*, 3939.

[36] Earl, *Holy War in the Bible*, 2632.

[37] Nugent, *The Politics of Yahweh*, 2705.

[38] Josh. 3:10; 13:1-7; 14:12; 16:10; 17:18; 23:5, 9; Deut. 4:37-38; 7:1; 9:1; 11:22-23; 18:14; 19:1-2; Exod. 23:27-30; 34:11, 24; Num. 21:32; 32:20-21; 33:51-55; Lev. 18:24; 20:23.

[39] Gen. 3:24; 4:13-14.

[40] See also Deut. 7:22.

[41] Yoder, *The Original Revolution*, 1324.

[42] Josh. 10:40; 11:12, 15, 20, 23.

[43] Wink, *The Powers That Be*, 84.

[44] Boyd, *The Crucifixion of the Warrior God*, 15764.

[45] Seibert, *The Violence of Scripture*, 2502.

[46] Jer. 18:7-10; 1 Sam. 15:29.

[47] Deut. 4:31; 7:1-2; 20:16-17; Ps. 86:15; Exod. 34:6; Jon. 3:10; 1 Sam. 15:2-3; Gen. 7:21-23.

[48] Derek Flood, *Disarming Scripture: Cherry-Picking Liberals, Violence-Loving Conservatives, and Why We All Need to Learn to Read the Bible Like Jesus Did* (Metanoia Books, 2014), 1366, Kindle.

[49] Exod. 4:11; Deut. 28:21-22; 2 Kings 15:5.

[50] Matt. 9:32-33; 12:22; 15:21-28; 17:14-18; Luke 4:38-41; 7:21; 8:2; 11:14; Mark 9:25; Acts 10:38.

[51] 2 Sam. 24:1-16; 1 Chron. 21:1-17

[52] See 2:6-7, 10:8-9, and 42:11-12.

[53] Jersak, *A More Christlike God*, 2707.

[54] Thompson, *Who's Afraid of the Old Testament God?*, 612.

[55] Ibid., 614.

[56] Ibid., 616.

[57] 1 John 3:8.

[58] Thompson, *Who's Afraid of the Old Testament God?*, 652.

[59] Ibid., 973.

[60] Seibert, *The Violence of Scripture*, 215.

[61] Boyd, *The Crucifixion of the Warrior God*, 18557.

[62] Ibid., 19152.

[63] 2 Kings 9:6-10; Hos. 1:4.

[64] McLaren, *A New Kind of Christianity*, 1762.

[65] Zahnd, *Sinners in the Hands of a Loving God*, 30.

[66] Lilly, *A Faith Not Worth Fighting For*, 2703.

[67] Jersak, *A More Christlike God*, 1139.

[68] McLaren, *A New Kind of Christianity*, 1791.

[69] Ibid., 1834.

[70] Boyd, *The Crucifixion of the Warrior God*, 10400.

[71] Zahnd, *Sinners in the Hands of a Loving God*, 57.

[72] Ibid., 29.

[73] Ibid., 31.

[74] Matt. 5:29.

[75] Boyd, *The Crucifixion of the Warrior God*, 12103.

[76] Greg Boyd, "Answering an Objection to a Cross-Centered Approach to Scripture" posted in May, 2012 at http://reknew.org/2012/05/answering-an-objection-to-a-cross-centered-approach-to-scripture-qa/.

[77] Boyd, *The Crucifixion of the Warrior God*, 12120.

[78] Boyd, "Answering an Objection to a Cross-Centered Approach to Scripture."

[79] Seibert, *The Violence of Scripture*, 1512.

[80] Boyd, *The Crucifixion of the Warrior God*, 11320.

[81] Ibid., 11358.

[82] Ibid., 30417.

[83] Rom. 8:28.

12

CONCLUSION

Context is Key

As we have seen throughout this book, the key to understanding the violence in the OT (and to properly interpreting everything in the Bible, for that matter) can be summed up in a single word: context. Nothing in the Bible was written in a vacuum nor intended to be interpreted in one. The true meaning of every word, sentence, paragraph, chapter, and book can only be found by analyzing them within their biblical, literary, historical, and cultural contexts. Therefore, the problem of violence in the Bible is ultimately a problem of interpretation: ignorance of (or indifference to) context.

In this regard, I want to highlight two more context-related points before we conclude. First, the Bible doesn't condone everything it describes. (It's unfortunate I need to make this point, but I do.) Just because it's in the Bible doesn't mean God approves of it. There's a difference between reporting something and endorsing it. The OT writers often documented Israel's actions without ever explicitly or implicitly indicating that God ordered them, partook in them, or approved of them.

Likewise, the Bible doesn't condone every bad act it doesn't explicitly condemn. We can't assume God approved of everything he could have denounced but didn't. The OT writers often didn't comment on the morality of Israel's actions, either positively or negatively. To infer that God approved of everything he didn't specifically condemn is to make a fallacious argument from silence. In fact, as we saw earlier, the OT actors and writers wouldn't have even noticed many of the same ethical issues that concern us today, let alone known enough about God's will to have condemned them. Remember, there was no universal standard yet by which to denounce much of Israel's behavior. God hadn't yet sent Jesus to reveal it.

Furthermore, as we learned in the previous chapter, God didn't even approve of everything the OT writers approved of. They had their own human perspectives, which didn't always match God's and which God didn't always correct. At least to some degree, he allowed their cultural influences and fallen natures to distort their view of him and his will.

Thus, even when the OT portrays something in a positive light, that doesn't necessarily mean God himself viewed it positively.

Respecting the immediate literary context surrounding each violent OT passage is actually relatively easy. We simply need to ask ourselves a few basic questions: What is the genre in which the violence occurs—narrative, poetic, prophetic, apocalyptic, etc.? Who is using violence—God, one of God's followers, or someone else? Does the passage merely describe what occurred or does it indicate God actually ordered it or otherwise approved of it? What do other passages say about it? Do they say it was praiseworthy or condemnable? What is the purpose of the violence? Is it offensive or defensive? Is it perpetuating or combatting injustice? Who is harmed by it and who benefits from it? Were the recipients of the violence warned and given time to repent? Is there some other non-violence related lesson clearly being taught?

If we answer these simple, introductory questions, we will notice that most of the violence in the OT is described but not condoned and the violence that is condoned is almost always aimed at an obvious injustice. In other words, we don't even have to know anything about the extra-biblical historical or cultural contexts to see that most of the violence in the OT is not presented in a favorable light. We simply have to read it carefully enough to avoid jumping to scripturally unsupported conclusions.

Second, and along similar lines, the OT largely portrays life on earth as it is, not as it should be. It gives us a raw, unembellished, gritty, and realistic picture of the human experience. As Craigie notes, "It does not draw a false and romantic picture of the reality of the human situation, and consequently it forces us to face up to the reality of our own world."[1] It makes no attempt to present its human characters as perfect role models or ethical ideals. Instead, it portrays them as quintessentially human: morally complicated, morally conflicted, and morally flawed. It is essentially the early history of humanity's ethical journey, a journey that did not unfold along a clean, succinct, and straight line but instead traversed a wild, previously untraveled, meandering, often confusing, and occasionally backsliding path.

There's a reason for this. There's a reason why the OT spends so much time describing what "is" instead of what "ought to be." Through it, God identified and described the human problem. He demonstrated that we are sinful and broken, the extent to which we are, and the pain and suffering it produces. He demonstrated the existence and reality of our fallen condition. This is another reason why the OT law seems so harsh and its demands so unrealistic—because our current fallen state is so far from the state of wholeness God originally created.

God also demonstrated that we can't solve our own problem. We can't fix our own brokenness or cure our own fallen condition. We can't save ourselves. Even when given specific instructions on exactly how to do so by God himself, we are incapable of carrying them out. As such, God demonstrated humanity's need for a savior, for his son Jesus. As Johnson puts it, "The Old Testament was to prepare humanity for a savior—not just to prepare them to receive one, but to prepare them to ask for one."[2]

This is what Paul believed was the purpose of the OT law. He viewed it as serving the good and necessary but temporary purpose of demonstrating that (1) we are severely broken, (2) we are unable to fix our brokenness, and (3) therefore we need a savior who can.[3] The law was never intended to be the solution. It was never intended to make humans right with God. It was intended to demonstrate humanity's inability to become right with God through its own efforts.

Had God not demonstrated all these things in the OT, humans would likely not have been receptive to the NT message. Had he not clearly identified and diagnosed the problem, ignorant humans would not have woken up to the fact they had one. Had he not allowed them to fully indulge their fallen desires and reap the consequences, shortsighted humans would not have seen the severity of the problem. Had he not given them instructions on how to fix the problem themselves and stood by while they repeatedly failed to follow them, arrogant humans would not have believed they needed rescuing. They would not have seen their need for a savior. Had he not shown them what the solution was *not*, stubborn humans would not have been receptive to the actual solution.

This is why the OT is so full of wickedness and injustice, why it spends so much time describing life as it is, and why it's not until the NT that life as it ought to be is described. In fact, that's one oversimplified way to distinguish between the two Testaments: The OT describes the problem and the NT describes the solution. We must not mistake the descriptions of the problem for the solution. We must not let the overwhelming amount of descriptions of life as it is subtly convince us that is how life should be.

In this regard, much (if not most) of the OT is a negative object lesson. It demonstrates what *not* to do. In other words, not only does the Bible not condone all the behavior it describes, but much of the behavior it describes is intended to show us how not to act. It's intended to warn against, not promote, such behavior. It's intended to teach us about what isn't helpful, what doesn't work, and what won't fix our problems. Just as historical descriptions of the Holocaust serve not as an example to be followed but as a reminder of the dangers of things like racism, nationalism, and centralized power, much of the behavior described in the OT serves not as a positive example but as a reminder of the dangers of things like sin and violence.

Paul made this point in his NT letter to the Corinthian church:

> Nevertheless, God was not pleased with most of them, and they were struck down in the wilderness.

> Now these things occurred as examples for us, so that we might not desire evil as they did. Do not become idolaters as some of them did; as it is written, "The people sat down to eat and drink, and they rose up to play." We must not indulge in sexual immorality as some of them did, and twenty-three thousand fell in a single day. We must not put Christ to the test, as some of them did, and were destroyed by serpents. And do not complain as some of them did, and were destroyed by the destroyer. These things happened to them to serve as an example, and they were written down to instruct us, on whom the ends of the ages have come. (1 Cor. 10:5-11 NRSV)

Similarly, when the NT does praise OT actors, as in Hebrews' Faith Hall of Fame (Chapter 11), it commends their faith and trust in God, not the general integrity of their overall character or the exemplary way in which they embodied God's ethical ideals. Again, God hadn't yet given them any such ideals. In fact, it's only because of Jesus that we know the OT is largely a negative object lesson. Without his perfect example and teachings, we would still view many of its behaviors as God's will.

To explain the issue in terms of violence, God used the OT to demonstrate that (1) humans have a problem, (2) violence is a large part of it, (3) more or better violence isn't the solution, and (4) only God can fix it. Had God not demonstrated all of these realities in the OT, humanity would not have been receptive to the NT's message of nonviolent, self-sacrificial love. Had he not stood by while humanity unsuccessfully tried to solve its problem through violence, had he not allowed humanity to fruitlessly put its trust in violence, it would never have been open to trusting in nonviolence. This is why there is so much violence in the OT, why it spends so much time describing human violence as it is, and why it's not until the NT that human violence is described as it ought to be—nonexistent.

Thus, the violence in the OT serves as a negative object lesson. It serves as a warning against the human use of violence. It demonstrates the destructiveness, futility, and counter-productivity of human violence. It shows that humans aren't capable of using violence morally, justly, or productively, even when under God's personal direction. It teaches that human violence can't advance God's kingdom on earth, not even when God provides it with precise instructions on exactly how to do so.

All of this is equally true for governmental power. The OT indicates that nationalism isn't the answer, not even theocratic nationalism, as Craigie explains:

> First, the history of the old covenant, of the nation state of Israel, provides an insight into the nature of political man. Even the Hebrews, with their high and special calling from God, failed in their attempt to maintain a state. The Kingdom of God in the form of a political state was not viable because of the violence, a part of the order of necessity, in the nature of man and of society. The Hebrew people, in their failure, are not portrayed in the Old Testament to be criticized; they simply demonstrate the failure of all men, the fundamental nature of us all. Thus the history of the nation of Israel functions as a parable of warning: political institutions may be essential to the existence of human society, but they cannot be equated with the Kingdom of God.[4]

Again, in this regard, the OT reveals as much about human nature, the human condition, and how humans develop as it does about God's ideal ethics and true character.

Revisiting the Biblical Narrative

If you take nothing else from this book, take this: The Bible is a narrative. It's a story, not a list of facts or rules. Most importantly, it's a narrative with a trajectory, a clear one. It starts in one place and goes to another. It has a beginning and an end and progression in between. And we must read it as such. We must not read it like an encyclopedia or constitution. We must not get hung up on the isolated, literal meaning of any single word, verse, paragraph, chapter, or book. We must interpret everything within the larger biblical narrative. We must follow the story, which goes like this:

God created an entirely nonviolent world (one in which there was no violence between God and man, between man and man, between man and beast, or between beast and beast) in a uniquely nonviolent manner (he spoke it into being), humans introduced violence into it, God was immediately saddened by such violence, condemned it, and tried to restrain it, but then humans proceeded to spread violence over the entire earth until things got so bad God had to intervene in a more direct manner. He did so by forming OT Israel into his redeeming nation, and right away, he made ethical improvements in every area of its life, improvements that immediately dialed back its violence, pointed it in the right moral direction, and started humanity down the path to his ethical ideal of nonviolent, self-sacrificial love. Although those improvements were incomplete, imperfect, fell far short of creation ideals, and left much to be desired by today's standards, they were notably more progressive and civilized than anything the world had ever seen. In fact, they were likely as progressive and civilized as the historical circumstances allowed. Furthermore, they sowed seeds that would eventually produce much greater nonviolent fruit as they gradually took root and blossomed in man's conscience—seeds like the dignity and equality of all humans and the subordination of human government to a higher moral authority.

Unfortunately, the Israelites had a hard time following God's instructions. They backslid into militarism, becoming like all the other ANE nations, particularly in their use of violence for nationalistic purposes. (And remember, most of the violence in the OT occurred within that rebellious period.) So God sent in the prophets to keep his antiviolence message alive, to give Israel a vision of a future entirely free of violence, and to complete preparations for Jesus' arrival. That's how the OT ends, with a yearning for peace, a hunger for an end to all war and violence, and a hope for a Messiah who would accomplish it all.

Then in the NT, God sent such a Messiah: Jesus. In him, he finalized his ethical revelation by revealing his perfect, eternal, and universally applicable moral code. He did so by taking fundamental components of the OT law and expanding them. For example, he took the limited retaliation of an eye for an eye and expanded it into complete non-retaliation by commanding us to turn the other cheek. He took the notion of loving your neighbor and expanded it into loving everyone, even your enemy. He took the exclusivity of nationalism and expanded it into complete inclusivity by reorganizing God's followers into a transnational church. Simply put, he gave Jesus the final word on Christian ethics and that final word was love.

To state it in terms of violence, God sent Jesus to remove all remaining violence from his ethical instructions. Jesus lived and taught complete nonviolence. Instead of teaching us how to morally or justly use violence, he taught us to not use it, even against our enemies. His (1) commands to turn the other cheek and follow the golden rule, (2) his denationalization of God's followers, and (3) his restructuring of

Christian warfare from physical fighting to spiritual fighting, left no room for human violence of any kind.

In fact, Jesus went beyond advocating mere nonviolence. He promoted antiviolence. Not only did he command us to refrain from violence, he commanded us to oppose it and overcome it. Not only did he instruct us to not do evil, he instructed us to repay it with good. Not only did he teach us to never use violence against others, he taught us to love them, to proactively and self-sacrificially serve them. He taught us to go so far as to die on a cross for them if necessary. In short, Jesus taught us to love all others and then defined love as the precise opposite of violence.

What the Narrative Tells Us About Violence

This narrative contains a distinct, explicit ethical trajectory toward nonviolence. From the moment humans introduced violence into the world, God has worked to return them to his originally created state of complete nonviolence. Yes, early in the process (i.e. in the OT) he may have temporarily used limited violence to advance his antiviolence agenda, but his use of such violence was always good and just. It was always patient, calculated, controlled, focused, and short-lived, never arbitrary, selfish, bloodthirsty, indiscriminate, or open-ended. It was always aimed at freeing the oppressed and punishing their oppressors (as the conquest of Canaan demonstrates). It was always reactive. It was always a compassionate, loving, and just response to human wickedness and violence, never aggressive, imperialistic, or domineering. It was always done on behalf of the poor, weak, and vulnerable, never the rich, powerful, or comfortable (regardless of whether or not they were God's followers). It was always just in its ends and its means. It was always God-centered and God-led, never humanistic. It was always aimed at convincing humans to trust in God, never their own violence. It was always aimed at ending violence. It was always done to further God's plan to save the entire world (not just Israel) from violence. It was always antiviolence.

The narrative also reveals that our current marching orders are completely nonviolent. On every level, it indicates that we are to mimic and obey the nonviolent Jesus, not the God of the OT, not Moses, and not the OT Israelites. We are to embody God's new, universal, perfect ethical ideal, not his old, Israel-specific, sin-accommodating, less-than-ideal moral code. We are to follow the ethical guidelines God has given us as part of his covenant with us, not those he gave to the OT Israelites as part of his covenant with them, guidelines which no longer even apply to them. We are to bear witness to God's eternal, fully revealed, Jesus-centered NT kingdom, not his temporary, partially revealed, human-centered OT kingdom. We are to be a transnational, interethnic, nongovernmental, geographically dispersed people that refuses to use violence for any purpose, not a theocratic nation that sometimes uses violence for specific and limited purposes. We are to be set apart by our complete refusal to use violence, not by our slightly less-unjust use of violence. We are to be distinguishable by our self-sacrificial love for others, not by our superior ability to forcefully make the world safer and more comfortable. We are to be recognizable by our reliance on God to control history, not by our greater ability to do so ourselves. Post Jesus, this is how we are to participate in God's ongoing, world-saving plan. This is how we are to do his will.

Despite all the essential good the OT accomplishes, it does not provide us with a moral standard. For that, God sent Jesus. He, and he alone, is our ethical ideal, our moral compass, our one and only standard of conduct. The cross, not the conquest, defines how to behave Christianly.

To put it another way, nothing in the OT justifies our use of violence today. The God-sanctioned violence in the OT was tied to a specific set of commands given to a specific group of people under specific circumstances at a specific point in history for a specific and temporary purpose, none of which still exist or even applied to you and I in the first place. In other words, God only ever sanctioned human violence for a few generations of people from one nation at one time in history in one geographic location for one divine purpose, and we aren't those people, don't live at that time or in that location, and don't share their purpose. Simply put, we aren't OT Israel.

Even if we were, the OT's violence still doesn't justify the types of militarism we usually want it to. God made it abundantly clear to the Israelites that he didn't want them relying on, getting used to, training for, or trusting in violence. He didn't even let them maintain a standing army or adopt the superior weaponry of their defeated foes, let alone use such things in selfish ways that prioritized their own safety, comfort, and control above that of others. Instead, he commanded them to completely rely on him for such things and usually sent them into battle greatly outmatched to prove they could. He only sanctioned wars wherein *he* was the cause of victory, not human military might.

To conclude that the OT justifies violence, we essentially have to read it as if Jesus never existed, the NT was never written, and God's revelation ceased at the end of the OT. We have to ignore the entire second half of the Bible. We have to adopt an unbiblical, pre-Christian view of ethics. For as Zahnd explains, "To set aside what Jesus taught about nonviolence in favor of what we can dig up in the violent conquest narratives of the Old Testament is to turn away from the light of salvation and rush headlong back into the darkness."[5]

To conclude that the OT justifies violence, we also have to ignore its literary, historical, cultural, biblical, and theological contexts. We have to employ a shallow, uninformed, and intellectually lazy analysis, an analysis that is so bad it hardly qualifies as analysis. We have to leap to all sorts of unsupported conclusions and approach biblical interpretation in a way that no intellectually serious person would approach any other book.

With such poor logic, the Bible can be used to justify anything, including polygamy, slavery, and mass murder. The only way to disarm the Bible of such behaviors is to read it in its proper contexts. That bears repeating: Context disarms the Bible, particularly the OT. That's one of the beautiful things about its context. Here's another: Once you've seen it, you can't unsee it.

In this sense, the larger biblical narrative also reveals that the OT's purpose had little to do with teaching eternally and universally applicable ethical lessons. Its purpose was to lay the groundwork for such things, to build the foundation upon which they could eventually be received, understood, and accepted. God was meeting humans for the first time and introducing himself. He was establishing his existence, proving his supremacy, forming a relationship, and demonstrating the fundamentals of his character, things like his love for and commitment to humanity, his concern for universal justice, and his desire for complete obedience and trust. These are the introductory and rudimentary ethical lessons the Israelites would have seen. They would not have even thought of most of the more advanced moral questions we ask today, questions that only make sense to us *because* of the ethical groundwork God laid in the OT.

To state it another way, the OT's purpose was never to show us precisely how to combat evil and injustice. God was teaching us more basic lessons, things like the difference between good and evil, the reality of his goodness, and that he is doing something about the problem of evil—fighting it.[6] He was teaching us that we need to faithfully, humbly, and completely obey him if we want to help him fight evil. Lessons on precisely what to obey, i.e. lessons on exactly how to behave to help him conquer evil, would come later in the life and teachings of Jesus, who would teach us to use the only effective means possible: nonviolent, self-sacrificial love.

Simply put, the violence-related commands and examples in the OT were never intended to be normative for us. They were never intended to be demonstrations of the proper and moral way to use violence. Instead, they were intended to teach us other normative ethical lessons. Primarily, they were intended to teach us to trust God to take care of what we think we need to use violence to accomplish. They were intended to teach us to leave things like vengeance and justice to him. That is the eternally and universally applicable violence-related ethical lesson of the OT, not that violence is justified when used to advance God's kingdom on earth or when used to enforce what we think constitutes justice.

From this perspective, the biblical narrative reveals yet another interesting conclusion: What the OT and NT each say about violence doesn't conflict. The biblical case for nonviolence begins not in the NT but in the OT—at creation, in fact. The NT's antiviolence grows out of the OT's antiviolence. It takes the OT's relatively implicit case against violence and makes it explicit. It builds upon, fulfills, and perfects it. It is the climax of the OT's violence storyline. Thus, both Testament's general postures towards violence compliment, not contradict, each other. They share the same vision of, and hope for, a world without violence.

At least this is how Jesus saw things. He saw his ethical instructions as a continuation and perfection of the OT's ethical guidelines.[7] Remember, the OT was his Bible and he knew it well, frequently quoting from it to support his teachings. Yet he didn't read and interpret it as advocating for or justifying human violence. Nor was he embarrassed by it. He never tried to explain away its violence. Instead, he understood it as laying the foundation for, and pointing to, the nonviolence he taught and embodied.

So did all the apostles, the NT writers, and the early church. They adopted Jesus' view of the OT. Arguably, they were all pacifists even though their Bible was the OT. That alone should caution us against citing it to justify violence.

To state the point another way, the God-sanctioned violence in the OT doesn't contradict God's more obvious antiviolence message in the NT. Instead, it reinforces it. In the OT, God was employing violence against violence. He was waging war on war. He was using violence to combat, suppress, and end violence. He was using violence to lay a foundation upon which complete nonviolence could be built. Such a use of violence is consistent with the NT's antiviolence agenda.

God hasn't changed. We have. His ethical ideal hasn't changed. Our capacity to handle it has. His truth hasn't changed. Our ability to receive it has.

As we have seen throughout this book, not only does the biblical narrative tell us a lot about the ethics of violence, it also tells us a lot about God's character. It reveals a good, just, and loving God, one who is relational, faithful, merciful, patient, slow to anger, and not legalistic. It reveals a God who (1) chose to intervene into human history to rescue inferior, ungrateful, spoiled, immature, selfish, unjust, rebellious beings and (2) chose to enact such a rescue through humble, patient, non-coercive, free-will-respecting, self-sacrificial means because he is love and that's what love does. It reveals a God whose intervention into human history and whose use of incremental revelation both testify to his boundless love for all humans. It reveals a God who employs the tactics of a good and caring teacher, not the tactics of a domineering prison warden. It reveals a God who instead of forcing others into behaving or believing correctly chooses to selflessly bear with their misbehaviors and misperceptions while he attempts to persuade them to change via self-sacrificial acts of love. It reveals a God who is willing to stoop to meet humans where they are, establishes common ground with them, and communicates to them in their own language, even when doing so requires that he dirty his own pure hands and sully his own holy reputation. It reveals a God who doesn't start, celebrate, or even condone violence, but who does self-sacrificially get involved in it to save us from it. It reveals a God who is willing to be a selfless missionary to the human race. It reveals a God who not only doesn't enjoy using violence to make us suffer but who hates violence precisely because it causes us to suffer and thwarts the flourishing he so strongly desires for us. It reveals a God who is not only not bloodthirsty but one who is wholly opposed to bloodshed. It reveals a God who is not only not a bigot, racist, or misogynist but one who is precisely the opposite, a God who introduced the world to radically progressive ideas regarding women's rights, slavery, oppression of the poor, and treatment of foreigners. It reveals a God who is not only not a moral monster but who is positively good and praiseworthy.

Furthermore, many of our conclusions about the OT's descriptions of violence also apply to the OT's descriptions of God's character. Just as the broader biblical narrative is the proper framework within which all the OT's violence must be interpreted, it is also the proper framework within which all the OT's depictions of God must be interpreted. Just as the OT was never intended to teach us eternally and universally applicable ethical lessons, it was never intended to provide us with a full and perfect picture of God. Just as the OT reveals a lot about the ethics of violence but not that it is sometimes justified, it also reveals a lot about God's character but not that he has an inherent propensity for violence. Precisely the opposite. Just as what the OT and NT each say about violence doesn't conflict, the God of the OT and the God of the NT don't conflict. Just as the biblical narrative reveals God's ethical ideal hasn't changed but instead our capacity to receive it has, it reveals God's character hasn't changed but instead our ability to understand it has. The good, just, and loving God described in the NT is also present in the OT. We simply need to read it a little more carefully.

On the other hand, to conclude that the God of the OT is a moral monster, we have to make some serious interpretive mistakes. For example, instead of comparing his actions and instructions to what came before them and what existed at the time, we have to compare them to today's moral standards, standards which only exist *because* of his OT actions and instructions. Ironically, we have to use the moral principles that he introduced into the world as the standard by which we condemn the actions he employed to introduce them. We also have to get dangerously close to an entirely subjective and selective view of the God of the Bible. We essentially have to conclude that every negative thing the Bible says about him is true and every positive thing false.

Such a narrow, shallow, non-contextual reading can produce whatever type of God we want it to, including a sexist, racist, bloodthirsty, pro-slavery, mass-murdering one. But once again, context disarms him. As Zahnd concludes, "God is not a monster. There are monster-god theologies, but they are mistaken theologies."[8]

Lastly, note that all of this is true even if God actually committed the violence the OT says he did. The Bible still contains a clear antiviolence storyline. It still displays a good, just, and loving God. It still exhibits a God who is antiviolence, one whose violence was always aimed at ending violence and who opposes all human violence. It still says we are called to be entirely nonviolent. It still claims Jesus is our moral standard. It still forces us to conclude the OT doesn't justify our use of violence today. It still reveals we aren't OT Israel. It still indicates the OT's purpose had nothing to do with teaching us how to morally and properly use violence. You don't have to believe God has never used violence to see these things.

You don't have to believe he is wholly nonviolent himself to believe in a wholly nonviolent Christian ethic.

The evidence that suggests God may not have committed some or even all the violence the OT attributes to him is simply icing on the nonviolence cake. The OT's case for nonviolence is not based on such evidence. It is simply strengthened by it.

Not only does the OT not advocate violence, it advocates the precise opposite: nonviolence. It isn't indifferent about violence. It is antiviolence. And here's the best part: The Bible's case for nonviolence merely gets warmed up in the OT. It really takes off in the NT. But that's another book.

Final Thoughts

Recall the issues we identified at the conclusion of Chapter 1. We have addressed all of them: Can the OT's violence be reconciled with the NT's nonviolence? Who are we to imitate and obey? What is God really like?

Furthermore, we have addressed these issues by attacking them head on. We have avoided the easy excuses. We haven't dismissed or ignored the most troubling texts. We have tackled all of them. We haven't written the disturbing passages off as something less than God-breathed. We have respected their divine inspiration. We haven't assumed the violence they describe never actually happened, that it was all just allegorical, symbolic, metaphorical, or mythological. We have taken it at face value. We have assumed what was described is what happened. We also haven't proof-texted. We haven't built our case for nonviolence on a few isolated verses or examples that we pulled out of context. We have built it on the overarching narrative and its historical, cultural, and literary contexts.

Of course, we haven't covered everything. We haven't thoroughly analyzed every violent incident in the OT. We haven't gone verse by verse through the entire OT to prove that all of our conclusions are 100% accurate. That would take a lifetime and fill a library wing.

But we have done as much as possible in a book of this length. We have explored enough of the OT, its prominent themes, and its relevant contexts to give us the information we need to understand its violence and its God—to understand them as good, just, loving, and antiviolence. We now know God had many good reasons for everything he did in the OT, reasons based on self-sacrificial love for all of humankind. Hopefully, we now possess all the information we need to remove the OT as a stumbling block to a nonviolent Christian ethic, a beautiful picture of God, and maybe even faith itself.

But please don't take my word for any of it. Test it yourself. Get yourself a chronologically ordered Bible and study it. I have quoted, cited, and referenced a multitude of Scripture passages, theologians, and other books. Look them up. Read them.

If you do, please look at the preponderance of the evidence. Don't let one or two outliers drive your entire conclusion. Don't let a couple of incidents you can't fully explain override the mountain of evidence you can. Don't make the exception the rule. And don't get distracted by an inability to fully remove every doubt or definitively answer every question. No one's burden of proof should be to prove something beyond *all* doubt. No one on either side of any debate can establish their case to such a degree.

In fact, there's a sense in which some doubt is a good thing, even necessary. If God were to definitively prove his existence and goodness to us, we would no longer possess free will, which in turn means we would no longer be capable of relationship or love. We would be robots. God doesn't want robots. He wants relationship and love. And for those things, he needs people of faith, which means there must be room for doubt.

The ball is now in your court. You now have some choices to make. You can choose to see or to ignore the narrative and its antiviolence trajectory. You can choose to see or to ignore the historical and cultural contexts. You can choose to see or to ignore God's good intentions and actions. You can choose to read the OT however you like, as promoting good or harm. It's up to you. God's non-coercive, nonviolent, relationship-seeking love gives you that freedom.

---

[1] Craigie, *The Problem of War in the Old Testament*, 100.

[2] Johnson, *God is Good*, 2271.

[3] Gal. 3; Rom. 5:13.

[4] Craigie, *The Problem of War in the Old Testament*, 81.

[5] Zahnd, *Sinners in the Hands of a Loving God*, 68.

[6] The real irony here is that the story written to tell us what God is doing about the problem of evil (including violence) ends up being used to condemn him as evil (and violent).

[7] Matt. 5:17-19.

[8] Zahnd, *Sinners in the Hands of a Loving God*, 97.

A Message from the Author

First, thank you for reading my book! I hope you enjoyed it and have been blessed by it.

Second, a little bit about me. I'm a reader, writer, and attorney with a passion for exploring God's beauty and brilliance. I live in Oklahoma City with my amazing bride and three spectacular children. If you'd like to learn more or sign up to be notified of future books, new blog posts, and other goodies, please visit www.matthewcurtisfleischer.com. You can also find me on Facebook or on Twitter at @MatthewCurtisF.

Lastly, if you would like to help this book reach a wider audience, please consider (1) leaving a review on Amazon, Goodreads, or anywhere else readers visit and (2) mentioning it on social media. I'd be honored to have your help. Thank you!

Sincerely,

Matthew

MatthewCurtisFleischer@gmail.com

Special thanks to my bride, Nicole, whose love, support, and encouragement made this book possible.